IMPOSSIBILITY FICTION

Rodopi Perspectives on Modern Literature

17

Edited by
David Bevan

IMPOSSIBILITY FICTION

ALTERNATIVITY — EXTRAPOLATION — SPECULATION

Edited by

Derek Littlewood
Peter Stockwell

Amsterdam - Atlanta, GA 1996

♾ The paper on which this book is printed meets the requirements of "ISO 9706:1994, Information and documentation - Paper for documents - Requirements for permanence".

ISBN: 90-420-0032-5 (bound)
ISBN: 90-420-0025-2 (paper)
©Editions Rodopi B.V., Amsterdam - Atlanta, GA 1996
Printed in The Netherlands

CONTENTS

Introduction   3

I. Alternativity

1. Mankind Vs. Machines: The Technological Dystopia in Kurt Vonnegut's *Player Piano* (David Seed)   11

2. T.H. White, Arnold Bax, and the Alternative History of Britain (Andrew Blake)   25

3. Re-theorising Textual Space: Feminist Science Fiction (And Some Critical Limitations) (Lucie Armitt)   37

4. Science Fiction as Postmodernism: The Case of Philip K. Dick (Andrew Butler)   45

II. Extrapolation

5. Utopias and Heterotopias: The 'Culture' of Iain M. Banks (Carolyn Brown)   57

6. Silence and Awkwardness in Representations of the Jewish Holocaust, The Bombing of Hiroshima and Nagasaki, and a Projected Nuclear Holocaust (Antony Rowland)   75

7. George S. Schuyler and the Fate of Early African-American Science Fiction (Ben Lawson)   87

8. On the Subversion of Character in the Literature of Identity Anxiety (Victoria Maule)   107

III. Speculation

9. J.G. Ballard: Neurographer (Mark Jones)   127

10. Lost in Space? Exploring Impossible Geographies (James
    Kneale)   147

11. Mary Shelley's *The Last Man* (The End of the World as We
    Know It) (Michael Bradshaw)   163

12. *Jurassic Park* and the Generic Paradox in Science Fiction
    Film (Dave Hinton)   177

13. Uneasy Readings/Unspeakable Dialogics (Derek Littlewood)   191

Index   208

ACKNOWLEDGEMENTS

The editors would like to thank Amanda Franklin for invaluable help in preparing the manuscript for this volume; and Andy Sawyer at the Science Fiction Foundation archive, Liverpool University, for his good-natured assistance with alien referencing systems.

INTRODUCTION

'Imagine, in your head, that two armies are facing each other across a vast battlefield. You look down on them from a great height, and there on one side are a mere handful of red soldiers, drawn up against millions of white troops. You see thousands of horses, cannons and flags, and the plateau stretches as far as the curved horizon, beneath unfamiliar stars inside your head. And every night when you sleep, you must dream that the red soldiers defeat the white army, and each night the victory is greater than the last, until the white generals come to realise that they can never win this battle in your head'.

This is an impossible story, a surreal fantasy. But it is a fiction which does things. Imagine this: a nine-year old girl in a hospital in the north of England, a few years ago, receiving chemotherapy for leukaemia. The treatment was not very successful, and she was becoming weaker and weaker. Then one of the medical staff told her every night to dream the battle, and concentrate on thinking it into her head as she went to sleep. Within a few weeks the leukaemia went into remission, with no medical explanation. This sounds an impossibility. It seems to be a wishful fantasy. But it is a true story.

Imagine this. In 1616, William Harvey stood before assembled expert medical opinion, in front of all the doctors and physicians of a learned society, and told them of his discovery of the circulation of blood in the human body. This fantastic new speculation was greeted with due scepticism. These rational minds required empirical proof. So Harvey invited them to provide their own evidence. Telling the men to place their hands in the mid-left of their chests, he directed them to feel the pump of their own heartbeats. They tried it, but not a single one of the eminent doctors and physicians could feel the blood pumping through their own hearts. Can this be true? It sounds incredible to us. But, in 1616, the idea of circulating blood was an impossibility, and therefore the possibility of a chest-pump was an absurdity.

Can a new idea really change so fundamentally the way the world is perceived? To a rational mind it sounds like a fantastic fiction. But both of these stories are true. There are, in reality, impossible stories that can do things in this world.

Impossibility is not a stable concept. It is dependent on perception and interpretation, on a human judgement of how the universe is and what its currently understood physical or social rules will allow. The reality out there might be stable, for all we humans know, but our idea of the reality is continually being revised or overthrown by religion, political ideology, science, and philosophy. Since our perception is the only access we have to that reality, we might as well live and engage with the fictions that we think ourselves into. The fictions themselves may seem, at the moment, literally impossible, but the metaphorical uses we make of them can be real enough.

The types of impossibilities explored here are threaded onto our apparent reality in a variety of ways. *Alternativity* is a fundamental comparative strategy used to perceive and make sense of the sensory world around. From cognitive science comes the idea of different orders of alternativity that need to be assimilated to the individual's worldview. 'Making sense' of phenomena is a primary function of intelligence: humans are not very good at accepting contradictory information without explanation or reconciliation. A tree with two trunks is an interesting but possible anomaly. A tree with no trunk at all, branches suspended in mid-air, polychromatic metallic leaves and an advanced competence in telepathy is a serious challenge to the integrity of most of our worldviews, I imagine. Such a tree would need to be 'downgraded' as an impossible phenomenon. One very strong downgrading strategy throughout human history has been to re-assign the category of the perceived phenomenon so that the features are acceptable within a reframed context: the tree is in a surreal painting; the tree is part of a psychotic illusion of some sort; or the tree is an element in a fantastic story. Anomalous phenomena which resist such downgrading will eventually cue a paradigm-shift in the entire categorisation system.

Of course, this perspective is the reader's strategy as interpreter of alternativity. Why should writers choose to create such alternativity in the first place? Might it be a desire to represent the entirety of the dialogic and dialectic pathways of which our own reality is merely one possible outcome among many?

If every cusp of determination in the process of the universe produces a massive set of possible outcomes, then only a sense of alternativity can create a true historical perspective on our own accumulated reality. The alternativity of impossibility fiction is the genuine comparative method in philosophical exploration. These texts represent a holistic approach to the exploration of ideas.

Alternativity is a metaphorical strategy whereby elements and processes from our apparent reality are worked out in another domain, as they might have been (perhaps as they *are* being) worked out, elsewhere. The working out is the discourse of the fantastic text, but writers sometimes provide textual clues to link the comparative domain back to our default reality. Otherwise, it is up to the reader to interpret the connection and see the alternation. Readers who fail to do this remain of the view that all they can see is disconnected escapism, not an alternating reality at all, but mere insignificance.

Where alternativity might then be seen as metaphorical in essence, the strategy of *extrapolation* is based on the metonymical extension of the ends of reality. Here is distortion rather than difference. Extrapolative texts are typically satirical, political, wearing their critiques of our apparent reality explicitly. The impossible reality represented is often a significant caricature of our own society or mind-set.

There are a variety of dimensions available for potential extrapolation. Science fiction has often taken the historical dimension to extrapolate from current realities into the future. Here the base is recognisable, and so the text-world is, if not literally yet possible, at least a potential that cannot be discounted in advance. The realism of many represented science fictional text-worlds is the tactic by which this potential is presented to the reader as a possibility. The paraphernalia of authoritative explanation, justification, and the accumulation of plausible detail contribute to this sense on a textual level.

Other dimensions include extrapolations of one significant technological development, or of a social factor such as the attitude to reproduction, gender relations, the psychology of crime and punishment. The other end of history can be extrapolated to produce a re-vision of the distant past, to provide a new explanation for the accumulation of history to the present. Conversely, extrapolation can take the form of 'intrapolation': the exploration, through a fictional reality, of potentials in the unknown processing capabilities of the human mind. Here the fantasy/SF distinction becomes indistinct and irrelevant.

Finally, *speculation* might be seen as the most literal strategy of threading realities together. Speculative fiction is most closely tied to the present apparent reality. This is the world as it is, or as it was, or as it will be, if only the perceiver could see it like this. The visual metaphor underlying 'speculation' is enormously strong and wide-ranging in our language system. Speculations are concerned with the material reality of visualisation, manifest in film or other graphic form. These forms are a very rich seam in fantastic narratives, with modern popular culture borrowing heavily from images of ancient art and mythology. 'Seeing' is also the way we conventionally figure conceptualisation, through the mind's eye. Speculation is imaginative figuring of reality, as well as understanding and empathising with elements of that figured world.

Above all, speculation in the process of impossibility fiction is imagination cast in a set of present beliefs. The coalescing of text out of this conceptual process might be seen as an exercise in practical imagination, one in which the reader is invited to participate. The distance travelled by speculation can be very far from the base reality, to the extent that the end-world can seem so divorced from it, so incredible and fantastic as to appear disconnected from any current concerns. However, the mass-cultural roots of the genre ensure that the impossible abstraction finds expression in readable fiction. Even the most experimental, most 'difficult' of impossibility fiction can accrue this sense of accessibility by association. It is one of the strongest reasons for the enduring appeal of these texts, and their current interest as areas of study.

So here is a book about impossibility fiction. This phrase is not an ontological commitment; it simply gestures towards an area that is as yet unformed, and inherently paradoxical. These articles are explorations that help to chart the boundaries of this fictional landscape. Impossibility fiction is a working name for those virtual regions where fantasy, science fiction, utopia, mythology, extrapolative, speculative and alternative worlds overlap. The writers here are explorers not empire builders, and many of them point out that the fictions they discuss figure an alternativity that is all too possible. Antony Rowland in particular explores the two major preoccupations of our century, now nearly ended, holocausts both already realised and designedly imminent for much of the post-war era.

We are not dealing here with something new-fangled or simply the literary response to the industrial revolution and its aftermath. Michael Bradshaw charts a landmark of proto-science fiction from the beginning of the new period of technologised life, but such stories have been around for much longer than recent history. Impossibility fictions form the ancient myths and legends of all societies, where they are used as a foundation and structure for present realities. They allow a readership to think about aspects relevant to themselves, as Ben Lawson explains in his article on early African-American science fiction. Western culture in particular has its Mediterranean mythologies, Central European legends and Northern sagas, where the boundaries of reality are bent but unbroken, surely for entertainment and escapism, and for other serious reasons too.

Here are transformations and metamorphoses. Dream visions and travellers' tales. The Medieval romance of green knights, invincible swords, pentangles and magic, all fictions set in another reality which is recognisable but not quite possible. It is a tradition that persists throughout the ages, though often repressed by Church and State. Impossible speculations were written by politician theologians like Thomas More, clerics like Bishop Godwin, scientists like Johannes Kepler, soldier-scholars like Cyrano de Bergerac. The dominance of Romanticism finally trivialised the tradition, devaluing allegory and symbolic character for psychology and lyricism. The old texts were seen as lacking in characterisation, the new touchstone of literary value. Vicky Maule here examines the nature of character within the genre. The tyranny of the literally real became the mainstream, and its values still persist as the sanctioned patterns, to the extent that some writers, such as Kurt Vonnegut (discussed by David Seed), have declared that they no longer want to be perceived as belonging to this older, recently devalued form.

There has always been an alternative, however, like another thread running through. Before 'science fiction' was coined, H.G. Wells called his fictions 'scientific romances'. And it is no coincidence that many academics writing now about impossibility fiction are also medievalists. The twentieth century has seen the old literature once more become important, and the interest of academics and critics turn once again to that other thread. Andrew Blake here untangles one such strand, in following one particular intergeneric thread through history.

But we have been somewhere else in the intervening centuries, before the current reinstatement of the old literature. Because of this, almost all of our analytical skills and reading tools have been generated by our education, both formal and personal, in mainstream canonical literature. The institutions of reading and discussion of which we are a part have cornered us into brilliant readings of increasingly minority fiction, so that the space between the university and the general population of our fellow humans can now only be perceived as a vast gulf. The two sides regard each other through a telescopic glass, dimly, and the space between encourages the cloistered life on one side and anti-intellectualism on the other. One of the most hopeful forces in the opposite direction is the re-evaluation that feminist readings offer, theorised here by Lucie Armitt's paper and placed into the newly-perceived tradition by Carolyn Brown.

At the same time, verbal art has moved from being imprisoned on paper to encompass a multitude of media. Impossibility fiction is truly the original and vibrant multi-media mode, now in literature, radio, television, performance, pseudo-science, psychoanalysis, dream, electronic cyberspace, virtuality, graphic art, music, computer games, video and film. Dave Hinton locates the latter in his chapter on one of the most successfully popular pieces of impossibility fiction of the last twenty years. As Andrew Butler points out, the boundaries between genres and media are increasingly and post-modernly blurred, and the intergenre of impossibility fiction seems to be the resort of increasingly large numbers of popular and influential writers and directors.

It is an area of human creativity that brings boundaries and categories into question by its very existence, as well as by its form and content. The ideas expressed by this area encompass some of the most profound literature of our culture, as well as much of the wonderful worst of pulp writing. It crosses traditional disciplines, exemplified here by James Kneale's geographical view, and draws in the natural sciences and hard technology. The fusion then with social and psychological issues, both individual and communal, provides an expression of imaginative life that is genuinely holistic. Mark Jones discusses the literature of Ballard's psychic geography in this spirit. Impossibility fiction is the art of science in its original meaning of 'knowledge' (*scientia*).

It also serves practical purposes. Writers can destroy the world, create universes, re-shape and extend society, remould the human shape and explore the workings of the human mind without recourse to racial experimentation or actual social engineering. Writing a holocaust is not the same as executing one in reality. This is social empiricism, or what Einstein called a 'thought experiment'. The realised world can contain all the controls and independent variables that allow an issue to be explored in its entire speculated environment.

Impossibility texts can thus use the alternative arena to explore moral understanding ahead of the enabling technology. Only the genres within impossibility fiction can link the valuable escapism of popular writing with the largest philosophical questions. The method is inherently always comparative in the fundamental sense of alternativity. Defamiliarisation of the world by the alteration of its natural or social laws provides another paradox in commenting on current issues in a distorting mirror. We are able to understand symbolic meanings through this most metaphorical of writing, in a way that the mainstream, post-Romantic realist tradition can only struggle towards.

However, our institutional reading practices are becoming increasingly partial. Readers don't know how to discuss and analyse impossibility fictions, because the academy outlaws them in advance and doesn't, in any case, provide a relevant and appropriate reading strategy to cope with them. The articles in this book, and especially Derek Littlewood's final piece, make the moves towards establishing appropriate readings for this intergenre that allow us to negotiate unreality. It is a skill that the end of the twentieth century is making increasingly necessary. Coping with ideas in fiction that are both impossible and realistically constructed and presented is the ultimate contemporary challenge. Our society and scientific understanding is not so much meaningless any longer as having an apparent infinity of chaotic and complex meanings. Impossibility fiction is a means of negotiating and gaining some sort of control over the infinite and contradictory complexity that the information explosion is creating around us. We are already inhabitants of spaces that are newly existent: inside networks of information, inside new understandings of the universe, encompassing new perceptions of inner space. Only the fictions of the really impossible can deal directly with these issues. They alone will enable us to read the time after the coming millennium. This is a book which begins to chart the shifting stars and perceptions of dynamic, converging and re-forming conceptual galaxies. It is a task that in itself is impossible and endless.

Peter Stockwell

I. ALTERNATIVITY

1.

MANKIND VS. MACHINES: THE TECHNOLOGICAL DYSTOPIA IN KURT VONNEGUT'S *PLAYER PIANO*

When during his 1973 *Playboy* interview Vonnegut was asked about his attitude to religion, he pointed to a felt need in American society: 'It's the longing for community. This is a lonesome society that's been fragmented by the factory system'.[1] Vonnegut's first novel *Player Piano* (1952) describes an America of the near future where this factory system has taken on extreme dimensions and he uses a method of virtual caricature to highlight the dangers perceived in contemporary commercial developments. 'Fragmented' was a carefully chosen term in Vonnegut's response since it reflects an emphasis within the novel on the separation of class from class and the masses from the processes of production. Above all Vonnegut was writing in opposition to the ethic of the factory system founded by Frederick Winslow Taylor which its historian Bernard Doray has summarized in these words: 'Taylorism is imbued with a utilitarian and instrumental vision of human labour which denies the existence of the worker's subjectivity'.[2] This system, as parodied in *Brave New World*, exerted a major influence on Vonnegut's and other postwar American dystopias, and is rendered in *Player Piano* as organized mystification and repression.

Every utopian novel faces a problem of how to describe its new world without lapsing into static exposition but in *Player Piano* Vonnegut side-steps the difficulty by positioning his opening paragraph in relation to two classical narratives - the Trojan War ('the topless towers of Ilium') and the Gallic Wars. Ilium, like Caesar's Gaul, is divided into three parts occupied respectively by the managerial elite, the machines, and 'almost all the people'. Caesar initially stresses the hostility between tribes and divides the inhabitants of Gaul into two classes. Of the larger he writes: 'the common people are treated almost as slaves, never venture to act on their own initiative, and are not consulted on any subject'.[3] They are subject to a ruling elite of druids and knights. In Vonnegut's novel Paul Proteus gradually comes to recognize a love for the 'common people' (although the phrase suggests his continuing assumption of superiority) who are explicitly and implicitly depicted as slaves. A barber helps to fill out the parallel by remarking that doctors and lawyers used to be 'sort of priests' before their offices were taken over by machines. Although Vonnegut purports to be giving us a neutral description the intertextual ironies proleptically undermine the cherished values of Ilium. Where togetherness and unity are stressed by the latter's ideologues the topography suggests separation and the allusions to Caesar lead us to expect conflict and suppression. As in the fiction of Frederik Pohl, Vonnegut sees commercial expansion as an imperialistic process. So a checkers-playing machine is boosted at one point as 'looking for new planets to conquer'. In anticipation state benevolence is questioned and with it a faith in progress: any resemblance at all between Ilium and primitive tribes carries its own irony.

Clearly then the bridge over the river separating the two social areas carries a symbolism of potential contact which the novel indicates (and questions) repeatedly and the fact that it traverses a river named after an Amerindian tribe (the Iroquois) raises the broadest irony of the novel's opening: that supposed peace and plenty have been achieved only after a series of wars and conquests. Ilium is explicitly described as the site of different historical battles and it is essential to recognize that the novel repeatedly refers to war as an agent for accelerating social change. Thus it was World War III which ensured a triumph of technological 'know-how', the gradual replacement of workers and secretaries by machines, and the confirmation of managers in their new role. The exact nature of this war is never specified beyond the fact that it was worldwide. When soldiers reminisce about their experiences in action the medley of place-names prevents the reader from identifying any clear enemy and their memories revolve symptomatically around military technology: electric fences, robot soldiers, and so on. As often happens in postwar dystopias - in *Nineteen Eighty-Four* and *Fahrenheit 451*, for example - the notion of an external military threat is transposed on to the internal social scene where opposition is classified as treasonable. Hence the Ilium works is surrounded by an electrified fence and guarded by armoured cars. When, early in *Player Piano*, a cat hurls itself against the fence its grisly fate alerts the reader to the symbolic opposition between inside and outside which the novel then goes on to develop.

Ilium functions as a metonym of the United States as a whole. It is not at all convincing for David Y. Hughes to exclude the novel from the dystopian tradition because the 'topography of Ilium relates to no rational social world'.[4] On the contrary, its layout renders schematically separations between the human and the mechanical, between the managers and an increasingly obsolete work force. The culminating sign that human activities have been taken over by machines is the fact that criteria of social efficiency and consumption levels are now determined by EPICAC XIV, a super-computer which characteristically was developed during the war.[5] Vonnegut does not pursue the implications of this computer beyond contrasting its power with the political diminution of the American president. One of his aides irreverently reduces the president even further to a set of physical functions: '...all the gorgeous dummy had to do was read whatever was handed to him on state occasions; to be suitably awed and reverent, ...to run wisdom from somewhere else through that resonant voicebox and between those even, pearly choppers'.[6] While the president casts himself as a man of the people, the observer dehumanizes him into a mechanism channelling thoughts originating from invisible agencies. Through this figure emerges yet another separation, this time of government from politics. One thrust of the narrative is to multiply the examples of such separation and to enact the gradual estrangement of its protagonist from the industrial establishment.

For his diagnosis of social change Vonnegut may well have been drawing on James Burnham's *The Managerial Revolution* (1941) which argued that the industrial world was moving out of a capitalist or bourgeois state into a new regime where power was in the hands of those 'managing the instruments of production'. He elaborates on the visible concentration of power in corporations and notes, under the accelerating effect of World War II, that society is gradually polarizing between a managerial elite and the masses. The locus of political sovereignty will shift accordingly from parliaments or congresses to 'administrative bureaus'.[7] While there is nothing to compare stylistically in *Player Piano* with Burnham's obsessive neutrality and professed intent of only tracing out the workings of historical and economic laws, we can see essentially the same structure in Vonnegut's Ilium where the character Kroner performs two simultaneous functions as the administrator of the Eastern Division and as district industrial security officer. Commercial, political, and legal spheres telescope together in the individual who stands near the head of the administrative hierarchy. Just as Burnham suggests that dominant groups retain and extend power for its own sake so Vonnegut uses the machine as an emblem of the efficient, self-justifying operation of that society.

Player Piano belongs with *Erewhon* and *Brave New World* in that line of dystopian fiction which expresses anxiety about the development of technology and Vonnegut introduces the machine into his novel both as a metaphor of social functioning and as a relation. When Paul Proteus, the manager of the Ilium works, is listening to the sounds in one of the buildings he fancifully orchestrates them as a chorus between tenors (the lathes), baritones (welders), and basses (punch presses). The analogy rehumanizes the machines briefly for, as we shall see in a moment, Vonnegut is alert to the human cost of automation.[8] The comparison also invites the reader to relate two kinds of operation - the aesthetic and the technological. It is an important detail that a character has a book rejected for publication because it is longer than the statistical mean and higher than the desirable 'readability quotient'. Such criteria are laid down by EPICAC which leaves only a minor area of mass production available for the arts. *Player Piano* in that respect predicts a world where the novel itself could not exist, and it also predicts a world where not only the means of production are streamlined but levels of consumption are determined at the centre. Vonnegut's subtitle, *America in the Coming Age of Electronics*, makes clear this predictive function and the novel gives several examples of the general process whereby human operatives become superseded. To take one such case, the movements of a master machinist are recorded on a computerized tape (a kind of 'memory') which is made into a loop and which then functions indefinitely, cutting out the original worker. As the machines gain sophistication they ceaselessly monitor themselves for efficiency and, as in Zamiatin's *We* and Mordecai Roshwald's *Level 7*, classify people numerically according to their function or social use.

There is a constant dialectic between past and present in *Player Piano* where Vonnegut exploits the reader's recognition of historical facts or recent industrial developments in order to substantiate his predictions. The vast Ilium works, for instance, incorporates an original machine shop as used by Edison. It is relevant to remember that this industrial complex is loosely based on General Electric at Schenectady where Vonnegut himself worked between 1947 and 1950, since one of the novel's captains of industry had speculated, expanded, diversified and finally become a director of that corporation; but only after following a varied career which the present system has made impossible. The museum within the Ilium works forces its human traces (photographs, graffiti, etc.) on Proteus' attention and significantly develops the theme of opposition between humanity and the machine. This opposition is dramatized when Proteus is challenged to play a machine (Checker Charley) at checkers. His first reaction is anger and frustration ('I can't win against the damn thing. It can't make a mistake') but the machine actually burns itself out during the game, thereby making a divergence from the general superiority of technology to the human in the novel.

Vonnegut draws on Norbert Wiener's *Cybernetics* (1949) to situate the technological developments historically. Wiener made a distinction between two kinds of industrial change: 'the first industrial revolution, the revolution of the dark satanic mills, was the devaluation of the human arm by the competition of machinery... The modern industrial revolution is similarly bound to devalue the human brain, at least in its simpler and more routine decisions'.[9] This proposition is incorporated into discussions of progress in chapters 1 and 5 of the novel, and is woven into the latter's symbolism in the novel's concentration on the hand as the organ of human skill. A former machinist identifies himself to Proteus simply by showing him his hands, toughened as they are by toil. Proteus' own hands, by contrast, have a softness which embarrassingly reminds him of their limited range of use - not much beyond smoking and writing. Competence in *Player Piano* is repeatedly evoked as a masculine quality signalled as often as not by the strength or size of the hand and Proteus' rejection by his wife in favour of a business rival suggests clear sexual undertones to this motif. Wiener proved useful to Vonnegut in helping to locate the human cost of industrial change. For every development in technology humans' commercial value falls: 'taking the second revolution as accomplished, the average human being of mediocre attainments or less has nothing to sell that is worth anyone's money to buy'.[10] Wiener spoke out against this commodification of human beings which had been accelerated by the massive changes in the factory system since World War II and Vonnegut makes a similar point in suggesting that vast numbers of workers have been incorporated either into a huge standing army or a semi-welfare organization called the Reconstruction and Reclamation Corps ('Reeks and Wrecks'), which loosely recalls the Works Progress Administration (WPA) of the 1930s, thereby juxtaposing economic depression with apparent prosperity. Vonnegut refers repeatedly to the Depression in interviews as a period which had a profound impact on his family and on his own political beliefs; in 1957 he even started a novel set in this period to be called *Upstairs and Downstairs* but subsequently abandoned the project.[11]

The novel's title clearly foregrounds the issue of the machine but conceals the fact that within the narrative the player piano is set against a more modern machine - television. The bar which Proteus visits in the Homestead district is an anachronism built in the Victorian style, but a commercial success nonetheless. Near it a 'fully mechanized saloon' had been designed which turned out to be a complete failure. Vonnegut contrasts two historical periods as a local preamble to showing the player piano itself which is built on virtually the same principle of automation outlined above, namely of copying human actions in such a way that they can be repeated indefinitely. Chapter 3 of the novel concludes with a former machinist telling Proteus: 'Makes you feel kind of creepy, don't it, Doctor, watching them keys go up and down? You can almost see a ghost sitting there playing his heart out' (p.35).[12] The ghost in this particular machine is an absence, its elided original human operative. On Proteus' second visit to the same bar he concentrates on a phenomenon of the second industrial revolution - television - and is drawn into a competition with a man who claims to be able to identify musical pieces visually if the sound is turned off. Instead of yielding passively to the new medium as do other Homesteaders (the nature and problems of leisure are repeatedly raised in dystopian fiction), the man responds to the television as a challenge to new kinds of perception. Ironically his skill has no commercial value and therefore remains basically a party trick.

The proliferation of labour-saving devices which Vonnegut evokes undermines any separation between home and work-place, and suggests even that the machine has supplied a model of social behaviour. Again and again in *Player Piano* members of the managerial elite reinforce their perception of power by acting out social rituals. Here repetition and correct responses to cues take precedence over all other farms of expression. The automatic exchange of phrases between Proteus and his wife ('I love you, Paul' / 'I love *you*, Anita') serves as reassuring couplet to conclude all of their dialogues. Such repetitions enact an individual's acquiescence to organizational structure. Thus Paul and Anita constitute in themselves a flawed family group (flawed because they do not possess the 'normal' children), but are recast as children within the larger quasi-familial group of the company presided over by Kroner, a substitute father, and his wife who is known generally as 'Mom'.

In his 1937 study *The Folklore of Capitalism* Thurman Arnold identifies a number of organizational criteria which bear directly on key scenes in *Player Piano*. He specifies the following:

> 1. A creed or a set of commonly accepted rituals, verbal or ceremonial, which has the effect of making each individual feel an integral part of the group...
> 2. A set of attitudes which makes the creed effective by giving the individual prestige...
> 3. A set of institutional habits by means of which men are automatically able to work together...
> 4. The mythological or historical tradition which proves that an institutional creed has been ordained by more than human forces.[13]

Point for point these general principles are realized in the bonding patterns between Proteus and his colleagues, as shown in two group scenes: dinner at a director's and the annual gathering at the Meadows (an island) designed to celebrate company solidarity. Both gatherings follow a familiar pattern with its own decorum. For instance at the dinner it is considered bad manners to make other than superficial comments on the food. Colleagues' dress must be identical (*Player Piano* appeared only a few years before Sloan Wilson popularized the gray flannel suit as a business 'uniform'). Participants structure their behaviour according to games where there is a tension between competition and team solidarity. What operates as an analogy in their business world becomes enacted ritualistically at the Meadows where teams are set against each other. Within this large group hierarchical distinctions operate according to status and age so that selection as team leader is tantamount to promotion. To promote what William H. Whyte calls 'togetherness' the Meadows enforce a buddy system and an obligation to socialize constantly. The keynote speeches at the dinner and the Meadows stress the role of progress and reassure participants that they are riding the crest of a historical wave. Addressing the assembled throng at the Meadows Kroner reinforces the symbolism of the oak tree: 'It is our custom, ...it is the custom here at the Meadows - our custom, our meadows - to meet here and under our tree, our symbol of strong roots, trunk, and branches, our symbol of courage, integrity, perseverance, beauty. It is our custom to meet here to remember our departed friends and co-workers' (p.171). Repetition functions as a bonding device to strengthen a collectivity reflected in the tree's physical unity. The key phrase 'it is our/the custom' places the present instance in relation to a mythical past of undefined extent which mystifies the historical development of the company and casts a magical light on the proceedings.[14]

Every group's solidarity, however, must be defined in opposition to non-members and this is where one of the novel's totem words (Thurman Arnold calls them 'magic words') comes in - the term 'saboteur'. This abusive label carries connotations far beyond its literal signification: 'Somehow the idea of a wrecker of machines had become the smallest part of the word, like the crown of an iceberg. The greatest part of its mass, the part that called forth such poisonous emotions, was undefined: an amalgam of perversions, filth, disease, a galaxy of traits, any one of which would make a man a despicable outcast. The saboteur wasn't a wrecker of machines but an image every man prided himself on being unlike' (pp.199-200). The characteristic dialogues between the managers consist of ones for agreement or expressions of conformity. Virtually every aspect of their behaviour is designed to reinforce their sense of being inside their group and spatial areas in the novel (clubhouse, island, northwest Ilium, etc.) articulate their bonding. 'Saboteur' is carefully glossed because it connotes all the opposing qualities which the bonding suppresses: dissidence, the alien, the sense of being outside.

It is significant that this term of abuse is applied to the novel's protagonist Paul Proteus and a signal of how far he has moved along a narrative trajectory taking him outside his social group. Named after the prophet who would change shape when seized, Proteus does not actually possess a prophesying function (this is taken over by a parson, of whom more in a moment) and gradually finds himself caught in a dilemma which, Irving Howe argues, is central to dystopian novelists:

'that what men do and what they are become unrelated; that a world is appearing in which technique and value have been split apart...'[15] Under the catalytic effect of contact with his former friend Finnerty, a social misfit, Proteus registers horror at being 'so well-integrated into the machinery of society and history as to be able to move in only one plane, and along one line' (p.38). Proteus' narrative charts a progression from latent to overt dissatisfaction and to a gradual exclusion from his managerial group. Signs of dissatisfaction occur very early in the novel: 'Objectively, Paul tried to tell himself, things really were better than ever' (p.13). Proteus later engages in an internal dialogue but, because he cannot articulate a counter-voice, opposition to the official view of history which he is quoting here can only show itself as a reluctance, a drag against private utterance. We have already seen that the opening paragraph of *Player Piano* ironically undermines the creed of commercial progress through intertextual and narrative implication. Vonnegut's novel, like *Fahrenheit 451*, narrates a progression within the protagonist towards manifest dissatisfaction with the prevailing regime, but Proteus' ambivalence towards figures of authority, his friend Finnerty, and above all towards business disqualify him from taking on a role of heroic defiance. In that respect Stanley Schatt is misleading when he suggests that 'Vonnegut's novel is really the story of Paul's movement toward freedom'.[16]

At every critical point in the action Proteus is moved by others - manoeuvred into withdrawing from the company so that his gesture of refusal ('I quit') collapses into theatre, rejected by his wife, drugged and taken to the meeting of a subversive society, and so on. Vonnegut repeatedly designates the protagonist by his official label ('Doctor Paul Proteus') long after it has ceased to refer to a social context. Proteus himself experiences a dissociation from his own experience as if he is 'disembodied', and a loss of social location (he becomes 'unclassified' - a calculated pun). He attempts a withdrawal into a neo-Victorian fantasy by acquiring a farmhouse preserved in its nineteenth-century state, and by so doing appears to confirm Eugen Weber's assertion that 'insofar as the anti-utopian allows us a glimmer of hope, it lies in the instincts, in fantasy, in the irrational, in the peculiarly individualistic and egotistic characteristics most likely to shatter any system or order...'[17] But Proteus is not about to shatter anything. He will not even make the symbolic gesture of David Potter in 'Deer in the Works' (1955) who opens the gate to the Ilium works and follows a freed deer into the woods.[18] Proteus' temporary fascination with the old house is as much triggered by the term 'farming' itself as anything; and it is not free from the nostalgia which informs the decor of Kroner's Victorian mansion. Nor does his fantasy involve a group withdrawal into an agrarian past like that which concludes *Fahrenheit 451*. It rather suggests that Proteus is no more than toying with an anachronistic role for himself. The paradox within the opposition noted by Howe above is that, although Proteus gradually recoils from the thought of being a component in a larger structure, his self has been shaped according to that structure and he can only escape into an existential void of non-definition.

One reason why Proteus can never engage in active opposition is that all the major scenes where he appears are scripted by others. The rituals of conformity at the club house and the Meadows, as we have seen, revolve around clearly defined sequences of cues and responses. The address which Proteus delivers at the former straddles commercial and ritualistic significance; it is at once a 'progress report' and a 'reaffirmation of faith' (p.52). Once Proteus joins the Ghost Shirt Society the distance between self and utterance widens. During his trial Proteus is confronted with a seditious letter in his name. Asked if they are his words, he replies: 'They were written by someone else, but I'm in sympathy with them' (p.262). The trial - a cross between legal interrogation and psychoanalysis - actually reveals Proteus' doubts about his own motives, so that even on what he assumes to be the most authentically chosen level of commitment, his actions, are determined by a psychic 'script' of oedipal hatred for his father. Proteus' name then ultimately signifies 'no shape', paradoxically since he is introduced as one of the most powerful men in Ilium.

It is Proteus' disenchantment which puts him in a position to recognize the contradictions in his colleagues' ideology and thereby facilitate the novel's satirical purposes. Kroner's declaration that it takes 'strength and faith and determination' to succeed and the story of Doctor Gelhorne's career (Gelhorne is another director) hark back respectively to the muscular vocabulary and the agile opportunism of the preceding century rather than the contemporary era of economic centralism. William H. Whyte's classic study of the structure of American business life *The Organization Man* (1956) demonstrates a shift away from the Protestant Ethic towards corporate ethics which are premised on the 'utopian faith... that there need be no conflict between the individual's aspirations and the community's wishes, because it is the natural order of things that the two be synonymous'.[19] Logically then Proteus should be an impossibility and Vonnegut delights in accumulating examples of frustrated desires and bureaucratic reversals because they contradict the utopian claim that the present is a Golden Age. The novel thus progresses, as Chad Walsh has noted, from an initial superficial impression of peaceful ordered prosperity to internal division and frustration.[20] Proteus is used in this process as a means of giving the reader critical eyes. Hence when he joins the Ghost Shirt Society (significantly underground) he feels as if a surface patina has been removed revealing the 'termite metropolis' beneath, a crucial passing reference to the classic Science Fiction novel and movie of industrial suppression.

Proteus' disenchantment helps to reinforce the various external perspectives which Vonnegut establishes on the novel's action and the means he uses derive partly from his studies in anthropology at the University of Chicago from 1945 to 1947. Here Vonnegut was taught by Robert Redfield ('the most satisfying teacher in my life') whose 1947 paper 'The Folk Society' was based on the following premise: 'understanding of society in general and of our own modern urbanized society in particular can be gained through consideration of the societies least like our own: the primitive, or folk, societies'.[21] Vonnegut's thesis adviser was J.S. Slotkin whose *Social Anthropology* (1950) similarly juxtaposes exemplary data from primitive societies and from contemporary America. Vonnegut was never awarded his thesis which in one draft discussed the American Indian Ghost Dance movement.[22] This background information helps to explain why an amateur anthropologist is introduced into *Player Piano* who explicitly models a dissident movement on the Ghost Dance movement, the latter being in effect a last-ditch attempt to restore the fast-disappearing values of the Indian tribes. Historical hindsight on the futility of this movement suggests that analogically the Ghost Shirt organization will also fail to make anything beyond a token protest against the status quo.

The impact of anthropology on *Player Piano*, however, is broader than this specific comparison. Science Fiction and dystopian novels regularly combine the familiar with the speculative in such a way that the latter estranges the reader from the former. Vonnegut establishes an external uncommitted narrative voice observing the Iliumites as if from an anthropological viewpoint and then writes this perspective into the action by introducing the Shah of Bratpuhr as a visiting potentate who tours various parts of the United States. As in Goldsmith's *Citizen of the World* an outsider sets up an even more estranged perspective on the action and Vonnegut uses the Shah's incomprehension as a means of commenting on automated society and of questioning some of its most cherished values. So when he sees members of the 'Reeks and Wrecks' he assumes immediately that they are slaves and asks who owns them; when he visits a middle-class house equipped with labour-saving devices he asks what time is being saved for; and when he sees the computer EPICAC to everyone's astonishment he gets down on his knees to pray. Of course the whole point of such episodes, which are dismissed as ignorant or mistaken by his guides, is that they offer an unflattering alternative to the official view of reality. The Shah is too inarticulate to create a true dialogue on what he sees; Vonnegut leaves the reader to draw his or her inferences. But one characteristic which distinguishes *Player Piano* from the other dystopias of the 1950s is the sheer diversity of voices raised against this new society. Vonnegut has declared: 'I like Utopian talk, speculation about what our planet should be, anger about what our planet is'; and *Player Piano* assembles a collage of critical statements which build up a context hospitable to the ironies exposed by the Shah's visit.[23] One critic has complained that *Player Piano* is a 'fragmented work' because of its different plots but in fact the broad alternation between the Shah's and Proteus' sections gives a counterpoint between the perspectives of an outsider and of an insider.[24] And the other sub-plots similarly offer variations on the dissatisfaction dramatised in Proteus.

The last section of *Player Piano* describes an armed insurrection which attempts to restore the humane values denied by the regime. In keeping with other dystopias of this period the question is not how to improve on the present, but how to recover a lost set of values and social circumstances which have been erased. The rebels attack the power centres of that regime and their machine-smashing sets up echoes of the past, within the novel's chronology of postwar riots, within history of the Luddites. Thomas Pynchon has located a 'Luddite impulse to deny the machine' in the Science Fiction of the fifties and, although he names no names, he must have had *Player Piano* in mind among other works.[25] For the uprising, the 'conspiracy' as the court calls it in anticipation, is directed specifically against industrial plants and achieves a surreal transformation of Ilium. The rising sun reveals the following spectacle; 'In the early light, the town seemed an enormous jewel box, lined with the black and grey velvet of fly-ash, and filled with millions of twinkling treasures: bits of air conditioners, amplidynes, analyzers, arc welders, batteries...' (p.281). The factories have been dismantled into their component parts, but Vonnegut does not allow the image to generate any hope on the reader's past since it is only at this point in the novel that he introduces the term 'utopia'. The leaders of the uprising plan a return to a society which would dominate the machine instead of being dominated by it. Here again, however, the ironies multiply. Rebels begin collecting components as if to start the process of technological expansion all over again and the majority have anyway by this time deserted the leaders, so that the uprising as a whole is doomed to failure.

Vonnegut's novel uses narrative for a quasi-expository purpose. As in the first half of Pohl and Kornbluth's *The Space Merchants* (1953), we are shown life from the top, from the perspective of the managerial elite; then from the bottom so that we register the system's casualties and internal contradictions. By the time we have seen *through* this system the time is ripe for its destruction through rebellion, but Vonnegut allows the power structure to remain intact. *Player Piano* concludes with the formulation and then suppression of the utopian slogan 'to a better world'. It goes unspoken because the whole novel demonstrates a scepticism towards the possibility of planned social improvement. The retitling of the 1954 Bantam reprint of the novel as *Utopia-14* perhaps tried to underline that pessimism, conflating social idealism with the number of the government computer. In a long essay on Burnham's *Managerial Revolution* George Orwell pointed out that the former's interpretation of political change was intrinsically anti-utopian because Burnham sees all political activity as a search for power for its own sake.[26] A similar pessimism informs Vonnegut's novel where the onward flow of evolutionary time seems irresistible. If anything his gloom deepened further in his 1965 parody of American utopian ideals *God Bless You, Mr. Rosewater* where the dream of a perfect society becomes reduced to a logo for a beer company: 'On the label of each can of beer was a picture of the heaven on earth that the New Ambrosians had meant to build'. In case any reader misses the point Vonnegut has an apologist for commerce declare roundly that 'money is dehydrated Utopia', but it is exactly this commodification of ideals which Vonnegut attacks throughout *Player Piano*.[27]

David Seed

NOTES

1. Kurt Vonnegut, *Wampeters, Foma and Granfalloons*, London: Jonathan Cape, 1975, p. 269.
2. Bernard Doray, *From Taylorism to Fordism* (trans. David Macey), London: Free Association Books, 1988, p.84.
3. Julius Caesar, *The Conquest of Gaul*, (trans. S.A. Handford), Harmondsworth: Penguin, 1958, p.31. This parallel is noted but not discussed in Stanley Schatt, *Kurt Vonnegut, Jr.*, Boston: Twayne, 1976: p.17.
4. David Y. Hughes, 'The Ghost in the Machine: The Theme of *Player Piano*', in Kenneth M. Roemer (ed), *America as Utopia*, New York: Burt Franklin, 1981, p.109.
5. This same computer figures in the 1950 story 'Epicac'. Though designed for military purposes the computer falls in love with a technician and burns itself out protesting 'I don't want to be a machine, and I don't want to think about war' (*Welcome to the Monkey House*, St. Albans: Triad/Panther, 1979, p.263).
6. Kurt Vonnegut, *Player Piano*, St. Albans: Granada, 1977, p.107. Subsequent references to this edition are in the text.
7. James Burnham, *The Managerial Revolution. What is Happening in the World*, Westport CT: Greenwood Press, 1972, pp.77, 89, 147.
8. Cf. James M. Mellard's remark that *Player Piano* 'humanizes machines and mechanizes humans' ('The Modes of Vonnegut's Fiction', in Jerome Klinkowitz and John Somers (eds), *The Vonnegut Statement*, St. Albans: Granada, 1975, p.178).

9. Norbert Wiener, *Cybernetics, or Control and Communication in the Animal and the Machine*. Boston: Technology Press, 1949, p.37. Wiener's research suggested to him that the 'automatic factory, the assembly line without human agents' was imminent. This development, he continues, 'makes the metaphorical dominance of the machines, as imagined by Samuel Butler, a most immediate and non-metaphorical problem. It gives the human race a new and most effective collection of mechanical slaves to perform its labor' (*ibid.*). The question of who is enslaved is taken up explicitly in *Player Piano*.

10. *Ibid.*, pp.37-8.

11. Vonnegut made three false starts on the novel and then abandoned it. The subject concerned a family who had lost their money in the Depression. (Letter from Jerome Klinkowitz, September 18, 1991).

12. The phrase 'the ghost in the machine' was coined by Gilbert Ryle in *The Concept of Mind* (1949) as a parody of the Cartesian mind/body split. Vonnegut carefully signposts his allusions to it: Proteus' wife, for instance, exclaims after this episode 'Darling, you look as though you've seen a ghost'. In the context of the novel, however, 'ghost' carries connotations of the erasure of human operatives, the trace of a lost function.

13. Thurman Arnold, *The Folklore of Capitalism*, New Haven: Yale University Press, 1960, p.25.

14. James Burnham makes related points about the new managerial ideology: 'In place of the "individual", the stress turns to the "state", the people, the folk, the race... In place of private enterprise, "socialism" or "collectivism"... Less talk about "rights" and "natural rights"; more about "duties" and "order" and "discipline"' (*The Managerial Revolution*, pp. 190-1).

15. Irving Howe, 'The Fiction of Antiutopia', *The Decline of the New*, London: Victor Gollancz, 1971, p.69.

16. Schatt, *op.cit.*, p.18.

17. Eugen Weber, 'The Anti-Utopia of the Twentieth Century,' *South Atlantic Quarterly* 58 (1959), p.446.

18. Collected in *Welcome to the Monkey House*. As the story's title suggests, the action revolves around a contrast between the Ilium system, and explicit and implicit misfits - the deer and the protagonist respectively.

19. William H. Whyte, *The Organization Man*, Harmondsworth: Penguin, 1960, p.12.

20. Chad Walsh, *From Utopia to Nightmare*, London: Geoffrey Bles, 1962, pp.86-7.

21. Robert Redfield, 'The Folk Society', *American Journal of Sociology* 52 (1947), p.293. Vonnegut pays tribute to Redfield and this particular essay in *Wampeters*, pp.204-5.

22. Jerome Klinkowitz, *Kurt Vonnegut*, London and New York: Methuen, 1982, p.31.

23. William Rodney Allen (ed), *Conversations with Kurt Vonnegut*, Jackson: University Press of Mississippi, p.166.

24. Howard P. Segal, 'Vonnegut's *Player Piano*: An Ambiguous Technological Dystopia,' *Studies in the Literary Imagination* 6 (1973), p.168.

25. Thomas Pynchon, 'Is it O.K. to Be a Luddite?', *New York Times Book Review* (October 28, 1984), p.41.

26. George Orwell, 'James Burnham and the Managerial Revolution', in *The Collected Essays, Journalism and Letters of George Orwell. Volume IV: In Front of your Nose 1949-1950*, (ed. by Sonia Orwell and Ian Angus), London: Secker & Warburg, 1968, p.161. Orwell aligns Burnham's predictions with those of such dystopian novelists as Wells, Zamiatin and Huxley.

27. Kurt Vonnegut, *God Bless You, Mr. Rosewater*, St. Albans: Granada.

T.H. WHITE, ARNOLD BAX, AND THE ALTERNATIVE HISTORY OF BRITAIN

This chapter is in two parts. Firstly I make a number of general points about the production of twentieth century British culture, and the place of fantasy literature and the equivalent musical form, the symphony, within that cultural set. I argue that one way of seeing this work is through its relation to a revival of a specifically north European culture which occurred during the nineteenth century. I then illustrate some of those points in a brief discussion of the work of the writer T.H. White and the writer and composer Sir Arnold Bax.

1. Seeing the Fantastic

The general points should be prefaced with an expression of the reasons why they have begun to surface in my set of research interests - which cover the cultural histories of music and literature. Thinking about the rather under-celebrated centenary of Tolkien's birth (in 1992), I became convinced of the need to study 'sword and sorcery' or 'quest' fantasy as an aspect of popular culture. Its commercial importance in our culture is undeniable: there are shelves in bookshops groaning with paperbacks, usually next to the science fiction, which tell of quests for magic powers sought and or wielded by the Good, which will put this or other worlds, currently under the influence of the Bad, to rights. Some of them are new versions of, or are based on aspects of, the Arthurian stories. But the Arthurian cycle is not their principal cultural authority. All of these have been written in the last twenty years or so, and all are derived from the work of a group of inter-war and post-war British writers, including Tolkien (the major authority whose success has validated all subsequent quest fantasy literature), C.S. Lewis, T.H. White, Charles Williams, and E.R. Eddison.[1] There are enough of these massive manichean tomes for one author (Terry Pratchett) to make a living by writing parodies of them.

There are worlds here beyond the text. There are the television cartoons for children such as *Dungeons and Dragons* and *Masters of the Universe*, often sponsored by toy manufacturers. There are dozens of interactive computer games, in which the player(s) take on roles as wizards, warriors and so on, and then chase the computer program's goals round a number of levels, again looking for magical solutions to problems usually presented as Good versus Evil (one of the first and most successful of these was based on Tolkien's story *The Hobbit*). Similarly there are many role-playing societies, in which people dress for the weekend as wizards or goblins and rush around the countryside waving various allegedly magic swords at each other.[2]

So there is an important cultural phenomenon here, whatever we think of its literary value, or its implicit or explicit political content; I would argue that it is as worthy of study as any popular cultural form. But it hasn't been studied enough, and not at all (as far as I am aware) as a whole, intertextual and intergeneric set. There is quite a lot of mainly American work on Tolkien, and a still small but growing amount of work on other aspects of fantasy literature, and there has been some work on video games; little or nothing which attempts to see across the forms and their connections.[3] What has been done doesn't seem to me either to ask or attempt to answer the important questions about cultural history that I am going to pose in this chapter.

The main critical tendency in regard to fantasy fiction, within British criticism, has been to ignore it. For anyone brought up within the post-Leavisite construction of English Literature, it fails to engage with life's truths: it is neither legitimately realist nor legitimately modernist. For anyone more concerned with structuralist reading, it is too realist in mode, insufficiently self-analytic, insufficiently textual to be of interest. For critics on the left, quest fantasy is politically reactionary, portraying neo-feudal values of heroic nobility and mass passivity. Rosemary Jackson, for example, in her influential psychoanalytic reading, *Fantasy* dismisses quest fantasy as a politically incorrect mode of what *could* be a subversive form; in her view, quest fantasy is an imaginary resolution of social tensions which reinscribes the reader within both patriarchal and feudal relations.[4] At least she talks about it; most academic critics do not; publishers, in my experience, are polite but uninterested. Despite the serious treatment accorded to many popular forms, including soap opera and (Mills and Boon) romantic fiction, quest fantasy remains largely beyond the academic pale.[5]

2. The Invention of (Fantasy) Tradition

This continued exclusion is particularly unfortunate for a form which I believe to be a crucial part of the cultural formation of twentieth century Europe. The provenance of these texts seems to be in that extraordinary and most fertile time of 'the invention of traditions', to use the title of the well-known book edited by Hobsbawm and Ranger.[6] The late nineteenth century saw the revival and reworking of ceremonies, literatures and languages as new European nations asserted themselves in the face of the long decline of the Austro-Hungarian and Turkish empires: this affected the new Germany and much of Eastern Europe. But the invention of tradition was pursued enthusiastically even in the comparatively stable regime of Britain. Hobsbawm and Ranger's book provides a fascinating array of examples, but no convincing overall framework within which they can be read. I suggest that a reading of current debates about postcoloniality and hybridity could illuminate the 'invention of tradition': what was being invented was a set of unstable if powerful identities which worked against an existing set of political and cultural structures. Even in Britain, gradually moving towards political democracy and troubled by the struggle for Irish independence, the rise of the labour party and the campaign for women's suffrage, the invention of tradition was an important part of the making of the modern state.

But the process is not reducible to the question of nationality. The 'invention of tradition' is part of a long process I call the counter-Renaissance; a postcolonial discourse which attempted with partial, very imperfect success, to distance itself from the long hegemony of dynastic rule and classical culture, and to re-imagine Europe as a number of 'imagined communities' based around notions of language and nation - thus necessitating the invention of history/myth as a constituent of the various proposed national identities.[7] More collective identities were also proposed. In order to combat the pervasive aesthetic, political and religious influence of the Meditteranean, one crucial aspect of the invention of tradition was the reinvention of the North. From the deliberate manufacture of the work of 'Ossian' in the late eighteenth century through the compilation by the scholar Elias Lonnröt of the Finnish national epic, the *Kalevala*, in the middle of the nineteenth century, the culture of northern Europe was disinterred, reworked and where necessary invented from scratch; one aspect of this process being the setting up of the Oxford English syllabus in the early twentieth century.[8]

This is only a part of a long story, some of whose aspects are well known. The hegemony within Europe of Rome, which was reinscribed by the Church in the early Middle Ages, was constantly challenged through the crusades, the Avignon papacy, various locally-based heresies, and the Reformation. There was during the High Middle Ages (c.1100-1500) a specific north European architectural form, Gothic, and a specific north European literary form, the chivalric romance, both of which stand for the cultural independence of northern Europe.

Despite the success of the Reformation, however, this cultural independence was then powerfully countered by a secularized counter-reformation, the Renaissance, which relocated the heart of Europe in its Greek and Roman past. For three hundred years thereafter Classical education remained the norm for the North European elite; but during the eighteenth century a counter to this norm emerged. This can be seen in emergent forms of cultural production such as the novel, the symphony, new forms of landscape painting and other so-called realist art, and in the long Gothic revival in architecture, which started at a very fanciful level in the late eighteenth century and became increasingly scholarly through the nineteenth. During this time the novel, in the hands of Scott (*Ivanhoe*, 1825), Bulwer Lytton (*Harold, Last of the Saxons*, 1843), and Charles Kingsley (*Hereward the Wake*, 1866), becomes one important site through which English (and in Scott's case also Scottish) history can be rewritten as fantasy; an imagined national past can be projected through the use of this fictional form.

In the similar revival and rewriting of folk tales, there is an almost immediate spinoff into opera, especially in Germany, where folk stories are increasingly used at the expense of the classical stories which were used as the norm in *opera seria*, (literally the serious form, unlike the comic opera in which contemporary local cultures could be explored). Weber's *Der Freischütz* (1821) and Marschner's *Der Vampyr* (1827), then, pave the way textually as well as musically for Richard Wagner's use of the Norse/Germanic Nibelung saga and Arthurian legend in his operas *The Ring* (written from 1848 on, first performed 1876), *Tristan Und Isolde* (1857), and *Parsifal* (1882). By the second half of the nineteenth century, it is seen as normal for musicians to portray their countries' cultures through the use of local folk legend and music. What is at issue in all this, as much as the nationalisms themselves, is the revaluation of a specifically North European culture, as a genuine rival for the hegemony of Rome for the first time since the high middle ages, the time of Gothic architecture and the Romance.

One other very important tradition was being invented at this time - the late nineteenth century also sees the rise of the academic profession, and in particular the study of the humanities subjects, which quickly oriented themselves away from the classical or indeed any other category than the national. The work that has been done on the growth of English studies emphasises this relationship. History, likewise, was about the rise of great nations, and in the case of Britain the story of a move from the Anglo-Saxon roots of democracy towards its flowering; literature was the literature of great nations, and in the case of Britain the story of a dominant language and a literature able to express fundamental truths about life. The study of English at Oxford University happily combined these interpretations into a long narrative of the emergence and consolidation of a language and literature, from Beowulf onwards; the place of the study of Early English at Oxford remains a matter of debate in the late twentieth century. Whatever the makeup of the syllabus, one problem was identified by those who taught it as it consolidated in the early twentieth century. There was no originary myth: no equivalent to the *Kalevala*, the *Eddas*, the *Odyssey*, the *Bahagavad Gita*. They therefore tried to provide one. Tolkien's work with Anglo-Saxon, Norse, and Celtic languages and legends, and the literature of Christianity, was as he himself said intended to produce 'a mythology for England'; the best known part of this, *The Lord of the Rings*, is only a snippet, a fragment of the massive amount of work he did on this project, much of which has been posthumously published.[9]

Tolkien was not alone in this project. His Oxford contemporary C.S. Lewis' efforts also remain well known - the Narnia stories, and the three science fiction novels, especially in this context the last one, *That Hideous Strength* (1945); the novelist John Cowper Powys and the poet Charles Williams also have their followers. All three used the Arthurian myth, trying to rework it to provide contemporary significance in much the same way as Tennyson had done for his society in the *Idylls of the King* (1859-1884). The Arthurian cycle is convenient in that in some senses it is local, and that in the Glastonbury legend it provides a counter to the claimed authority of the Roman church (the claim is that the British church was founded independently by Joseph of Arimethea, who landed at Glastonbury and planted the famous winter-flowering Glastonbury Thorn). But as these scholars all knew, the Arthurian myth underlines the impossibility of this particular fiction of a national literature: by origin and by subject matter it is Celtic; it therefore has to do with Brittany as well as the British Isles; and the relationship between England and the internal colonies remains, of course, highly problematic. There is no unitary discourse available within which to write this mythology for England; in that one powerful source of mythological story is Ireland, there is clearly a huge problem for anyone who wishes to construct such a mythology and to claim it for England. Thus Tolkien's invention of a new mythology. For the remainder of this chapter I turn to two people for whom this particular problem was acute both personally and artistically; and for whom it was, artistically at least, fruitful.

3. T.H. White

To start with the younger of these, T.H. White, because as a reworker of the Arthurian myth he is closest to the immediate line of argument I have been proposing. Despite the continuing popularity of some of his work, which has never been out of print, White has received very little critical treatment. Apart from the biography by Sylvia Townsend Warner, there is to my knowledge only one full-length monograph, by Martin Kellman.[10] The biographical details, in brief, are as follows: White was born in Bombay in 1906, educated at Cheltenham and Cambridge, taught at Stowe school for a few years, wrote pulp novels whose success encouraged him to leave school teaching and live as a writer, often in poverty and squalor and only finally achieving financial success late in life when in 1959 Lerner and Lowe based their musical *Camelot* on *The Once and Future King*, and Disney capitalised on the show's success by making *The Sword in the Stone* as a cartoon feature. White died, a tax exile resident in Alderney, in 1964.

White's texts deal with his own life (*England Have My Bones*, 1936), with memory, life story and history (*Farewell Victoria*, 1933; *The Age of Scandal*, 1950), with literary history (*Mistress Masham's Repose*, 1946) and with natural history (*The Goshawk*, 1952). His life's work centred around the text of which *The Sword in the Stone* is the first part: the Arthurian tetralogy *The Once and Future King*. Here autobiography, history, literary history and natural history become intertwined as White reworks Malory's text of the fourteenth century, usually known as the *Morte d'Arthur*. He sets it against the 'real' history of the fourteenth century - the wars against France, and Edward III's own, lived Arthurian fantasy, in which he constructed the huge round table now on view in Winchester castle - and insisting that what he and Malory provided is the real history, not the pallid story of the victories and death of Edward the Black Prince. White's natural history is used in the training of Arthur, as he is transformed by Merlin into various animals, in order to learn patterns of social interaction. Animals continue to comment on Arthur's (in)abilities throughout the text; in one draft of the end of the tetralogy, the animals gather round the dying King and give very pessimistic views of mankind's future.

As Kellman points out, one force for unity in this very multi-faceted text is the use of this recurrent commentary, quite consciously a *leitmotif* technique borrowed from another of the recreators of the North, Wagner.[11] In its way White's tetralogy is as complex an undertaking as Wagner's *Ring* cycle. *The Once and Future King* reinscribes the boundaries between mythology and history. Through the (semi-autobiographical) character of Merlyn, White provides a commentary on the present, the past, the self, and the status of fiction and history: 'I am looking through 1939 at 1489 itself looking backwards'.[12] Interacting with White's knowledge of the actual fourteenth century past, the troubled present of Nazism and the second world war, and with his knowledges of Malory's work and other Arthurian romances, classical culture, and nature, are the contradictory drives and desires of the author's psychic makeup: his almost manic-depressive mood swings, his alcoholism, his painful liaisons with boys and young women, his homoerotic sadomasochism. From this heady but almost intolerable mixture White produced a narrative of imagined fact whose status is precisely that of history; of a credible story of the past, complete with factual, moral and theological 'truths':

Merlin was indignant.

'The link between Norman warfare and Victorian fox-hunting is perfect. Leave your father and King Lot outside the question for the moment, and look at literature. Look at the Norman myths about legendary figures like the Angevin kings. From William the Conqueror to Henry the Third, they indulged in warfare seasonally. The season came round, and off they went to the meet in splendid armour which reduced the risk of injury to a foxhunter's minimum. Look at the decisive battle of Breneville in which a field of nine hundred knights took part, and only three were killed. Look at Henry the Second borrowing money from Stephen, to pay his own troops in fighting Stephen. Look at the sporting etiquette, according to which Henry had to withdraw from a siege as soon as his enemy Louis joined the defenders inside the town, because Louis was his feudal overlord... That is the inheritance to which you have succeeded, Arthur. You have become the king of a domain in which the popular agitators hate each other for racial reasons, while the nobility fight each other for fun, and neither the racial maniac nor the overlord stops to consider the lot of the common soldier, who is the one person who gets hurt'.[13]

White's chronicle of an idealised high middle ages, like his two-volume account of eighteenth century England, *The Age of Scandal* (1950) and *The Scandalmonger* (1952), displays views about nation, power and decline which would appeal, I think, to anyone interested in a psychoanalytically informed cultural history - of the sort provided in John Barrell's splendid *book The Infection of Thomas De Quincey*; in this regard I warmly recommend a perusal of White's disquisition on the importance to the polite society of Augustan England of the erotics of the ear, chapter fifteen of *The Age of Scandal*.[14] In particular, however, I want to stress that in all White's accounts of his various versions of an idealised England, he also expressed partial alienation - whether it be from the heroic England of Arthur's prime, or the polite social world of Augustanism, or the beauty and cruelty of the pursuit of field sports in the countryside. With his heroes and heroines - Lancelot and Guinevere for instance - he is always ambivalent, always cruel; repletion, success, is never more than fleetingly attained. One constant theme of *The Once and Future King*, which underlines the impossibility of the fiction he yearns for of an adequate account of England and Englishness, is the tension between Arthur and his Celtic relations led by Morgause and Gawaine. White himself embodied these tensions. He spent a great deal of time in Ireland as a deliberate attempt to escape from England; he lived there throughout the Second World War, to which he was again very ambivalent, though it helped him to finish *The Once and Future King* (Tolkien's *Lord of the Rings* is also a product of, and stimulated by, the war years). Ireland was for him the ultimate symbol of the impossibility of the dream of an ideal England; which itself folds back in White's mind through the matrix of the end of happy family life, after his parents split up when he was 18. However, he was deeply ambivalent about Ireland; his views of the Irish were never unproblematically positive, and he parodied cruelly the family with whom he stayed in his 1947 fantasy novel of a new flood, *The Elephant and the Kangaroo* (in which he also parodies himself, as he does in many of his texts). Again, here, the writing blends the personal with the political, stressing that psychic wholeness is as unrealisable as coherent national identity.

4. Arnold Bax

Finally I turn to the composer and writer Arnold Bax; or perhaps I should say the composer Arnold Bax and the writer Dermot O'Byrne. Bax was born in 1883 to a very prosperous family; studied at the Royal Academy of Music; and immediately embarked on a career as professional composer. He lived and worked in a series of rented houses and rooms; an early marriage only lasted four years. He composed much for the piano, including three sonatas, and much for the orchestra, including seven symphonies. Bax was at the Royal Academy at a time of great import for the revival of specifically English styles of composition; following Stanford, Parry and Elgar, composers like Cyril Scott, Rutland Boughton and Ralph Vaughan Williams were trying to make specifically English music, using folk and Tudor musics as prime sources.[15] Bax didn't quite do this. Early on, he was happy to follow Wagner and Richard Strauss as models; though he did have a complex dialogue with folk music, the folk melodies he emulated were almost all Irish. Bax was appointed Master of the King's Music in 1942, to the anger of the Vaughan Williams lobby.[16] But his reputation was already on the wane, and the taste of the BBC was increasingly for European Modernism: a taste which was confirmed in the 20 years after Bax's death in 1953, to the virtual exclusion of Bax's music. This exclusion has continued, to the annoyance of an increasingly vocal group of people, most of them conservative Little Englanders of the type currently called Eurosceptics, who think that English music should be promoted, and who are convinced that Bax was a Great Composer. Sales of recordings of his symphonies tend to uphold the view that there is a sizeable public for Bax's work - at the time of writing, however, it is a stranger to the concert hall.[17]

For one particular band of conservatives, then, Bax is a heroic Englishman, neglected by the ageing 1960s trendies who run the BBC and the Arts Council. But their construction of Bax as English hero is highly problematic. Like White, Bax was a loner: like him, he was obsessed by the Celtic areas, spending long periods in Ireland and Scotland. He was also obsessed with his own life, constructing it as a long fall from the paradise of youthful vigour (portrayed in the autobiographical *Farewell My Youth*); obsessed by various people, notably several younger women; and obsessed by the sea. While in his teens Bax first visited Ireland; the country and the poetry of Yeats made a deep impression on him, and he assumed a portable Irish identity: 'when I landed at Dunleary or Rosslare I sloughed off the Englishman as a snake its skin in the spring; and my other existence as a musician... as an ardent cricketer, even as a lover of women, became almost unreal. For now I was in love with Ireland and for the while needed no mortal mistress'.[18] He learned Irish Gaelic. Under the pseudonym Dermot O'Byrne he wrote short stories and poetry drawing on and reworking Irish folk tales and legends. He was known to Yeats' circle, early on, as a writer and Irish nationalist; at this time, unknown to them, he was also writing music deeply influenced by the same folk stories, and also by Irish music: 'In part at least I rid myself of the ghosts of Wagner and Strauss, and began to write Irishly, using figures and melodies of a definitely Celtic curve... at the same time... only once in my career as a composer have I made use of an actual folk-song'.[19]

While contemporaries were remaking English music by collecting folk tunes and hymns, and incorporating them into their music, Bax stayed every year in Ireland and wrote words and music which were deeply inflected by his assumed Irishness; including its hostility to England. The connection continues. His literary and musical remains are collected in a memorial room at university College Cork. In 1966 the Dublin government published a leaflet on the 50th anniversary of the Easter Rising, which was headed by one of Dermot O'Byrne's reactions to the event, part of a poem called 'Shells at Oranmore' - a poem which, in 1916, had been banned by British officials:

> Never before had such a song been sung,
> Never again perhaps while ages run
> Shall the old pride of rock and wind be stung
> By such an insolence winged across the sun,
> So mad a challenge flung![20]

This impersonation was successful enough for many to claim unproblematically that Bax was an Irish composer. The Bax family were in fact long-term Surrey residents of Dutch descent.   But I don't want to give the impression that Bax lived a fantasy life as an Irish writer, as if it were easy. In fact, he was well aware of the fantasy, of the impossibility of this particular fiction as it were, and after the tragic events of 1916 turned away from what he later recalled nostalgically as the 'ivory tower of my youth'.[21]

But this does not mean that he sat down and wrote in a more positively English style; like White, he remained in some way fundamentally alienated from England and Englishness, and like Tolkien, he turned to the North, to Scandinavia in particular, for a great deal of his musical inspiration. A great deal of Bax's early music is Irish-sounding; a great deal of Bax's work after the 1920s can be heard to move gradually away from these idioms and towards the sound-world of Sibelius. The constant absence in these creations is any sense of English music as such; Bax was convinced that

> a truly national art is unrealisable unless there exists a national life on which to found it. Imperialism has never been fecund in original artistic endeavour at any time in the world's history. We must turn to the small striving state with an intensive and self-contained social life and culture for an outpouring of art reflecting a national idea.[22]

The Vaughan Williams lobby was in a way right to be outraged that this musician should be appointed to the position of Master of the King's Music. Bax's music is not, as Vaughan Williams' was, about Englishness, but Britishness, in his own particular reading of British history in relation to the rest of Northern Europe: and by drawing for its inspiration on Celtic and Northern legend, rather than Christianity, as a main source of inspiration, it offers a kind of magical alternative history of Britain, in a way I think is similar to White's.

It is of course impossible to convey the sound of Bax's music in print. For the interested listener, I suggest the following works as illustrative of aspects of Bax's style. First a couple from the early and specifically Irish pieces. The opening of an orchestral work called *The Garden of Fand* (1916) - a title drawn from Irish legend - presents sea music portrayed via divided strings drifting against each other harmonically while solo instruments play short strands of melody clearly influenced by the modal shapes of Irish music. Another piece of Irish Bax, a more specifically political one, is the *Elegiac Trio* for flute, viola and harp, one of several pieces he wrote after the events of Easter 1916. After the horrors of the Easter Rising, and the First World war, Bax changed direction. It could be argued that he became disillusioned with the dreamy Celtic romanticism of *The Garden of Fand*-style writing, and indeed with musical Irishness. I don't think so - the regret for the loss of the ivory tower of youth remains profound - though we can see how the influence was challenged. The opening of the final movement of the *Third Symphony*, written in 1929, copies the rhythms of dance music for fiddle (violas) and bhodran drum (orchestral side drum). However, in the epilogue to this movement, and the symphony as a whole, the jaunty rhythms have been flattened out, and though there may be a Celtic inflection, the music also sounds more German or Scandinavian. What was happening, I think, was that Bax was beginning to express his amibiguity towards Englishness by moving away from folk-music modalities and towards the sound-world of the Scandinavian symphony, especially the sound-world of Sibelius. This move is clearly apparent from the start of Bax's *Fifth Symphony* of 1932, which reproduces exactly the rhythm, and the prevailing sense of forested gloom derived from Wagner's *Ring*, of the second movement of Sibelius's *Fifth Symphony* of 1922. But Irish music remained a constant, if less exclusive, reference point in Bax's work to the end: the sea and wind, Irish music, the rhythms of Sibelius and the North, are all conflated in the opening phrases of the *Seventh Symphony*, his last, first performed in 1939.

The critic Lewis Foreman, in a sleeve note to a recording of the Bax symphonies, writes of them as 'a world of epic legend inextricably tangled with personal experience, which surpasses even Tolkien's later achievement of manufactured saga in breadth and imaginative command'.[23] What we have here in the cycle of Bax symphonies is a history, a manufactured narrative, a new mythology; but unlike Tolkien's, this is a history for Britain, an alternative British history - very much a fiction of impossibility. And as with White's work there is always here a personal quest for place, for a geographically centred wholeness which will contribute to psychic wholeness, just adding to the impossibility of the task. Whatever its achievements, the counter-Renaissance and its vision of the North remains forever fragmentary, incomplete.

Andrew Blake

NOTES

1. See, for example, H. Carpenter, *The Inklings*, London: Allen and Unwin, 1978, for a preliminary discussion of the work of some of these writers as a group.
2. In the absence of academic criticism there have been some brief journalistic examinations of aspects of this phenomenon: see A. Gardner, 'Literary Giant or Monstrous Myth?', *The Times*, 28.12.91, pp.30-33; P. Popham, 'Of Orks and Squigs', *The Independent Magazine*, 22.5.93, pp.36-38; Jo-Ann Goodwin, 'In Defence of Fantasy', *The Independent on Sunday*, 25.7.93, pp.32-33.
3. For academic work on Tolkien see N. Isaacs and R. Zimbardo (eds), *Tolkien and the Critics*, Notre Dame, Indiana: University of Notre Dame Press, 1968; for video games, J. Fisher, 'Boys' Games', *Magazine of Cultural Studies* 5 (Autumn 1992), pp.13-15.
4. R. Jackson, *Fantasy*, London: Methuen, 1982.
5. But see A. Swinfen, *In Defence of Fantasy*, London: RKP, 1984; K. Filmer (ed), *The Victorian Fantasists*, London: Macmillan, 1984; K. Filmer (ed), *Twentieth Century Fantasists*, London: Macmillan.
6. E.J. Hobsbawm and T. Ranger (eds), *The Invention of Tradition*, Cambridge: Cambridge University Press, 1982; see also R. Colls and P. Dodds (eds), *Englishness, Politics and Culture 1880-1920*, London: Croom Helm, 1986.
7. 'Imagined communities' comes of course from B. Anderson, *Imagined Communities*, London: Verso, 1984. The phrase 'counter-Renaissance', however, is my own.
8. See B. Doyle, *English and Englishness*, London: Methuen, 1990.

9. For Tolkien's 'mythology' and one attempt to interpret it see J.C. Nitzche, *Tolkien's Art*; Tolkien's posthumous works now include six volumes of *Unfinished Tales*, edited by Christopher Tolkien and published London: Unwin Hyman.

10. M. Kellman, *T.H. White and the Matter of Britain: A Literary Overview*, Lewiston/Queenstown: Edwin Mellen Press, 1988.

11. *Ibid.*, pp.44-6.

12. S.T Warner, *T.H. White*, London: Jonathan Cape, 1967, reprinted Oxford: Oxford University Press, 1989, p.134.

13. T.H. White, *The Once and Future King*, London: Collins, 1958, reprinted London: Fontana, 1962.

14. See J. Barrell, *The Infection of Thomas de Quincey: A Psychopathology of Imperialism*, London: Yale University Press, 1991.

15. For two useful recent surveys of the cultural formation of twentieth century English music, see R. Stradling and M. Hughes, *The English Musical Renaissance 1860-1940: Construction and Deconstruction*, London: Routledge, 1993; and G. Boyes, *The Imagined Village: Culture, Ideology and the English Folk Revival*, Manchester: Manchester University Press, 1993. My forthcoming *Music, Culture and Society*, Manchester: Manchester University Press, will examine these issues in the context of the impact of European modernism and American and other popular musics on British musical life in the twentieth century.

16. See Stradling and Hughes, *op.cit.*, p.172.

17. See, for example, the splenetic correspondence in *The Independent* 18.1.92, 23.1.92, 28.1.92, 29.1.92, and 24.2.92.

18. A. Bax, *Farewell My Youth* (ed. L. Foreman), Aldershot: Scholar Press, p.41.

19. *Ibid.*, p.42.

20. The poem as a whole is in appendix 1 to L. Foreman, *Bax: A Composer and his Times* (Second Edition), Aldershot: Scholar Press, 1988.

21. Bax, in a radio interview re-broadcast on BBC Radio 3, 12.11.83.

22. Bax, *op.cit.*, p.103.

23. L. Foreman's notes to Bax symphony recordings, Chandos CD 8906-10 (1988).

3.

RE-THEORISING TEXTUAL SPACE:
FEMINIST SF (AND SOME CRITICAL LIMITATIONS)

Despite the growing body of feminist scholarship accruing around the science fiction narrative, until recently critics have placed so much emphasis upon the significance of its political content that the importance of politicising the narrative structure has almost entirely been overlooked. Historically, this shortcoming has tended to characterise a lot of fantasy criticism and may in part explain why comparatively little of it is, even today, genuinely interested in engaging with contemporary literary theory. But when this occurs within the otherwise highly theoretical framework of feminist scholarship, it functions as a profound and surprising limitation.

The problem revolves, it would seem, around the notion of narrative closure and, at least in part, the relationship between this and generic enclosure. It is important to recognise, when dealing with SF, that a conventional work of fantasy functions via 'an intellectually closed system,'[1] a point that some fantasy critics remain unwilling to accept. Thus although it may present the reader with a fictional world in which certain (or even many) of the conventions of empirical reality are challenged (perhaps irrevocably), it does so in a manner that prioritises internal coherence and allows for the consolationist possibilities of narrative closure which keep fantasy on a safely distanced level. Evidently, any critic wishing to claim that feminist SF is endowed with special revolutionary properties simply because it is feminist SF will, therefore, either have to overlook this issue of closure altogether, or make claims for radical content as an intrinsically destabilising narrative device that challenges even the bonds of the formula mode. There is an element of truth in the latter, insofar as closure is at least partially dependent upon narrative consolation for effect.

Thus, as Sarah Lefanu asserts, 'Feminist SF... is part of science fiction while struggling against it'.[2] As we all know, speculative fictions aim to overstep their own narrative limits by means of defamiliarisation techniques which will disturb the reader's relationship with the real in a manner that should problematise consolation. But surely we must grapple with closure in a more rigorously textual sense if the workings of this are to be fully explored. One of the debates that finally seems to be emerging into the arena of feminist science fiction studies is how to adopt a theoretical approach that will enable critics to destabilise and open up the relationship between narrative textuality and generic identity.

As long ago as the end of the 1970s, Rachel Blau DuPlessis[3] took the first steps towards this in arguing that certain works of feminist SF offer women a means of 'writing beyond the ending' in a speculative sense. This she connected explicitly with the literary device of futurism, a projection which, she argued, prevents the reader's sense of her own 'space' within the text from remaining static and 'unsullied'. Instead we are left with a sense of unfinished business, she claims, simply because we have moved ahead of the real-time present. The importance of this in ideological terms, of course, is that 'If the future is no longer a resolved place, then in the same way, the past - history itself - no longer has fixity or authority'.[4] This is a position with which, fifteen years later, Jenny Wolmark might be expected to concur, her more recent book on feminist SF and the postmodern[5] offering an interesting and reasonably rigorous approach to concepts such as temporal instability and its potential for destabilising the narrative subject. Both DuPlessis and Wolmark are clearly looking to challenge the assumption that feminist SF operates primarily through textual cohesion and narrative resolution. Ultimately, however, rooted as both studies are within quite fixed (although in both cases unspecified) notions of the parameters of genre fiction, both have to fall back   inevitably   upon   the content-related issues that shore up these demarcations. DuPlessis, for example, concludes by claiming that by means of the 'apologue' mode feminist writers interrogate the limitations of the present, in the process pushing us towards the alternative territory of an unstable and thus discursive future.[6] This is a point that Wolmark also implies when she equates the utopian mode with the 'radical possibilities' of interrogative texts.[7]

But while this is undoubtedly true on the level of content, the apologue/utopia necessarily adopts a static narrative framework that must always be primarily dependent upon structural closure for success. Inevitably, the allegorical premise of the singular narrative stance. The expectations are that the reader will agree with the ideological premise instilled within the narrative and very little in the way of narrative pleasure is available as an alternative if we fail in this. We may resist the framework set up within a utopian narrative, but in the process we would be far more likely to reject the entire text out of hand than be prepared to radically interact with it, unless a more interrogative attitude towards our whole understanding of utopian fiction is adopted. At their worst, feminist readings of the utopia offer us no more than politically correct wish-fulfilment narratives, in the process falling into the trap of revalorising an (albeit alternative) institutional order by providing us with reassuring placebos. All too easily in these terms, closure simply functions as ideological enclosure. In contrast to this we need to look at how we can challenge our desire for gratification in reassuring forms and steel ourselves for a confrontation with narrative dis-ease whilst maintaining a political edge. If feminist criticism of SF is to genuinely engage with the powerful creative potential of the best of its narratives, it must read them as narratives, not as manifestoes.

One of the most important issues that critics of feminist SF still have to thoroughly address is the relationship between the spatial and the liminal, something Wolmark acknowledges in arguing that the spatial is a significant site of discursive narrative practice. However, a problem arises when she attempts to positively reclaim concepts of enclosure as 'feminised space' by means of a feminist rereading within the terms of which,

> ...dominant textual metaphors of boundaries and walls indicate unresolved textual ambiguities regarding the reconceptualising of gender...[whereby] the city provides a new space in which the female self is no longer contained by masculine assumptions about gender.[8]

This is an interesting perspective and one for which Gaston Bachelard's work on space provides a precursor,[9] claiming that the inside and the outside, although divided from each other, are constantly in a dialectical relationship that actually challenges the fixity of limits altogether. Nevertheless, within the terms of a feminist argument this remains a difficult issue, as we shall come on to see. And yet undoubtedly space is an especially problematic concept for women, precisely because we have historically been denied space (and time) for ourselves and the metaphors of SF largely enable women to speculate upon strategies for rethinking such issues in a positive sense. In this context 'Outer space' can therefore frequently function as 'Other space', a blank page upon which women can reinscribe cultural notions of the self. This is a point that brings Luce Irigaray's controversial words to mind: '...it is useless, then, to trap women in the exact definition of what they mean... they are already elsewhere'.[10]

Some of the most innovative and exciting approaches to current feminist scholarship as an interdisciplinary notion function through such radical rereadings of the gender dimensions of space (be that space political, philosophical, architectural or geographical).[11] That such rereadings frequently involve a deconstruction of the linear akin to the type of reading Bachelard offers is undeniable, something that feminist SF does indeed need to address if it is to offer a thorough critique of masculinist notions of space as 'the final frontier', or as 'virgin territory' lying in wait to be penetrated. But although Wolmark believes that the spatial itself can radically interrogate limitations (including genre limitations), the feminist utopia that positions women within walls is no utopia at all. Not only might separatism be argued to reinforce rather than interrogate limits but, and more significantly, 'shutting women up' inevitably silences rather than revolutionises any challenge to textual (en)closure. Such an approach does not advocate woman's new space, it returns us to our traditional place: the four walls of the home. If feminist readings are to succeed in utilising the medium of textuality in order 'to reach toward the woman trapped on the other side of the mirror/text and help her climb out',[12] then we also need to rethink narrative space as something far more liberating than such metaphors of closed door domesticity permit.

Mari McCarty seems to recognise this in calling for the female narrative to identify with a 'boundary zone' that will, in being taken up voluntarily, reconceive itself as 'infinitely-expanding space'.[13] This stance of transgressive marginality, rather than theorising space as a limit, retheorises the limit as a space in a manner that frees texts from the stultifying enclosures of genre theory, rather than re-anchoring them in old frameworks which render them 'creation[s]... "penned up" or "penned in"'.[14] It is by now quite common for the ideological stance taken by feminist SF to be positively equated with an intrinsically transgressive potential, but few critics fully harness the theoretical intricacies of transgression to serve their (or the genre's) own ends as far as the issue of narrative form is concerned. Even Wolmark primarily restricts her reading of formal transgression to a consideration of the role played by overlapping generic modes as a means of rethinking the relationship between gender, genre and feminist SF.[15] In this respect she unwittingly restrains the gender/genre debate within the auspices of a consolatory narrative argument, as we shall come on to see. Undoubtedly such generic intersections are as common to feminist SF as they are to any other popular form and they do provide a creative stimulus which might otherwise be lacking in some cases. But they cannot provide a means of utilising gender in order to destabilise genre. Nor, in fact, can such intersections genuinely transgress generic limitations *per se.* Rather they simply call into question the fixity of those shared points on the limit where all popular forms interconnect.

In order to fully explore the difficulties intrinsic to the relationship between feminist SF narratives and transgression, we perhaps need to adopt a two-stage approach. Firstly we need to begin by accepting that an inherently paradoxical stance needs to be adopted when wrestling with (as opposed to working within) the constraints of genre theory. If we see feminist genre fiction as nothing more than a narrative contract based upon collective ideological gratification, we seem to be left with little option but to read it from a stance of anti-theoretical textual conformity (even if this is an alternative conformity couched within a feminist discourse). In the process we are also likely to reduce genuine literary creativity to what Nicci Gerrard refers to as 'the porridge of standardisation'.[16] More interesting possibilities emerge when postmodern readings of transgression and narrative practice acknowledge the presence of genre boundaries simply as a means of problematising the consolationist aspects of the generic form and, in its turn, the relationship between genre and gender.

According to Michel Foucault, transgression inhabits:

> ...that narrow zone of a line where it displays the flash of its passage... a line which closes up behind it in a wave of extremely short duration, and thus it is made to return once more right to the horizon of the uncrossable.[17]

Under the terms of this rather more complex reading, transgression becomes a concept voiced solely in terms of anti-consolationist narrative tensions. Rather than relating to intersecting or over-lapping formulae, here we are dealing with the articulation of a generic positioning that takes up its identity through an interrogation, not merely an acceptance, of the very limits that simultaneously structure and destabilise that narrative identity. Although more problematic and less reassuring, surely this is more in keeping with the interrogative narrative strategies adopted by the more interesting examples of feminist science fiction. Texts such as Joanna Russ' *The Female Man*, Angela Carter's *The Passion of New Eve* and Mary Shelley's *Frankenstein*,[18] for instance, can all be situated in relation to an awareness of the literary category known as feminist SF and it would be a wilful denial to claim otherwise. However, only a reductionist reading could perceive these narratives as nothing more than feminist SF. In essence the power of these novels derives from textual excess, a narrative overspill that not only defies any one generic categorisation (as Wolmark might argue), but any totalising assimilation in generic terms at all. This, paradoxically, allows for genuine innovation and deviation from the label 'feminist SF' whilst retaining an intrinsic relationship with it.

This, it seems to me, aligns itself quite well with some of the most exciting and dynamic aspects of feminist literary theory elsewhere. It certainly aligns itself with a stance that Hélène Cixous and Catherine Clement have perceived to be central to feminist poetics when they refer to the woman writer's experience of the writing process as 'the crossing, entry, exit, sojourn, of the other that I am and am not... that tears me, worries me, alters me... the unknown...'[19] That Cixous and Clement associate the power of the creative word with a crossing over into unknown territory should remind us of the similarities this position holds with the concerns of feminist SF on the level of content. But also, the articulation of this positionality in liminal terms links the act of writing with a recognition of the centrality of a precariousness that is deeply unsettling to conformist notions of fictional form. In addition, their choice of terms is worthy of comment. The bodily puns that reside in the words 'tears' (ripping and crying) and 'worries' (fretting and gnawing) contribute, in themselves, to a destabilising of the self that is not simply one of alteration but also one of altercation, or the multiplicity of voices that reside within the text and open up this body of work to contradiction and pluralism. Once such notions are linked in with Patricia Parker's work on the grotesque body and narrative dilation,[20] the full extent of the revolutionary potential inherent in this complex interaction between content and form, text and reader starts to emerge.

Parker argues that the motif of the dilated female body is frequently inscribed within texts of the Renaissance period in such a way as to function as an 'obstacle *en route* to completion and ending'.[21] In response to this the narrative structure is forced into a creative attempt at 'controlling the implicitly female, and perhaps hence wayward, body of the text itself' if closure is to be reached at all.[22] Despite its apparent historical specificity, this approach can help to inform a feminist rereading of the problematics of contemporary genre theory. When we speak of the 'body' of a text we imply, through that comparison, a complex entity which is only precariously held in tension between fixity and revolt (something that, as far as each individual text is concerned, facilitates originality). On an anatomical level, we need to take at 'face value' the assumption that our bodies have an apparently recognisable and constant form. But we are simultaneously aware (though we generally suppress this knowledge) that perpetually undercutting and destabilizing this apparently reassuring outline is the continual physiological process of cellular flux and change that reminds us 'The characteristic feeling accompanying transgression is one of intense pleasure... and of intense anguish...'[23] But this recognition, though sometimes disturbing, should not in itself deter us/ One of the characteristics which makes feminist theory innovatory, exciting and challenging is its willingness to face up to and (more importantly) create out of contradictions, disputes and pluralism. Like the fantastic, feminism also takes its impetus from its radical and continual interrogation of limits, not merely the spaces enclosed by those limits. After all, if 'feminist thought, is poised on the divide that joins and distinguishes... oppression and resistance..., hegemony and marginality, sameness and difference...',[24] then that seems a position most worthy of appropriation by liminal readings of feminist SF.

Lucie Armitt

NOTES

1. W.R. Irwin, *The Game of the Impossible: A Rhetoric of Fantasy,* Urbana: University Illinois Press, 1976, p.189.

2. S. Lefanu, *In the Chinks of the World Machine: Feminism and Science Fiction,* London: Women's Press, 1988, p.5.

3. R. Blau DuPlessis, 'The Feminist Apologues of Lessing, Piercy, and Russ,' *Frontiers,* 4(1), 1979, pp.1-8.

4. *Ibid.,* p.2.

5. J. Wolmark, *Aliens and Others: Science Fiction, Feminism and Postmodernism,* Hemel Hempstead: Harvester Wheatsheaf, 1993.

6. Du Plessis, *op.cit.,* p.7.

7. Wolmark, *op.cit.* p.11.

8. *Ibid.,* p.95.

9. G. Bachelard, *The Poetics of Space,* Boston: Beacon Press, 1969. See especially p.211 with regard to this issue.

10. L. Irigaray, *This Sex Which is Not One,* Ithaca: Cornell University Press, 1985, p.29.

11. See, for example, P. Ryan, 'Black Women Do Not Have Time to Dream: The Politics of Time and Space,' *Tulsa Studies in Women's Literature* 11(1), 1992, pp.95-102; J. Moore, 'An Other Space: A Future for Feminism', in *New Feminist Discourses* (ed. Isobel Armstrong), London: Routledge, 1992, pp.65-79; and her *Matrix Making Space: Women and the Man Made Environment,* London: Pluto, 1984.

12. As suggested by S. Gilbert and S. Gubar, *The Madwoman in the Attic: The Woman Writer and the Nineteenth Century Literary Imagination,* Yale: Yale University Press, 1984, p.16.

13. M. McCarty, 'Possessing Female Space: "The Tender Shoot",' *Women's Studies* 8, 1981, pp.367-374.

14. Gilbert and Gubar, *op.cit.*, p.68.

15. See, for example, Wolmark, *op.cit.*, p.68.

16. N. Gerrard, *Into the Mainstream: How Feminism has Changed Women's Writing*, London: Pandora, 1989, p.117.

17. M. Foucault, 'A Preface to Transgression' (trans. Donald F. Bouchard and Sherry Simon), in *Language, Counter Memory, Practice: Selected Essays and Interviews* (ed. Donald F. Bouchard), Ithaca: Cornell University Press, pp.29-52; 33-4.

18. J. Russ, *The Female Man*, London: Women's Press, 1985; A. Carter, *The Passion of New Eve*, London: Virago, 1982; M. Shelley, *Frankenstein*, Harmondsworth: Penguin, 1985.

19. H. Cixous and C. Clement, *La Jeune Née*, Paris: Union Génerale d'Editions, 1975, p.158. Cited and translated by P. Salesne in 'Hélène Cixous' Ou l'art de l'innocence: The Path to You', in *Writing Differences: Readings from the Seminar of Hélène Cixous* (ed. S. Sellers), Milton Keynes: Open University Press, 1988, p.124.

20. See P. Parker, *Literary Fat Ladies: Rhetoric, Gender, Property*, London: Methuen, 1987.

21. *Idem.*

22. S.R. Suleiman, 'Pornography, Transgression and the Avant-Garde: Bataille's Story of the Eye', in *The Poetics of Gender* (ed. N.K. Miller), New York: Columbia University Press, 1986, pp.117-136 (p.120).

23. *Idem.*

24. As claimed in T. de Lauretis, 'Eccentric Subjects: Feminist theory and Historical Consciousness,' *Feminist Studies*, 16(1),1990, pp.115-5 (p.115).

4.

SCIENCE FICTION AS POSTMODERNISM:
THE CASE OF PHILIP K. DICK.

There is a moment in Fredric Jameson's hugely influential *Postmodernism: Or the Cultural Logic of Late Capitalism*[1] where he argues that cyberpunk is 'the supreme literary expression if not of postmodernism, then of late capitalism itself'. This is one of several attempts in recent years to forge a link between cyberpunk, its parent mode of science fiction and postmodernism; it can be traced in such events as the 1989 conference at Leeds, *Fiction 2000*,[2] in special issues of *Critique* and *The Mississippi Review*, the latter forming the basis for Larry McCaffery's *Storming the Reality Studio*.[3] Science fiction was once just seen as part of mass culture rather than the literary canon, and therefore not worthy of serious academic study, but one of postmodernism's characteristics is to overturn such hierarchies. Another reason for this increase in interest is that science fiction, despite its often nebulous boundaries, has a definite repertoire of tropes, languages and situations known to its readers which is open to pastiche and imitation, a common strategy in postmodern art. Cyberpunk - a mixture of film noir thrillers, designer labels, voodoo, street culture, drugs and a romantic view of the power of computers - has done much to make such borders even more nebulous.[4]

One of the authors seen as a spiritual father of cyberpunk, Philip K. Dick, has been treated as a postmodern author in his own right. Several critics have drawn upon postmodernism to explore Dick, and some have indeed drawn upon Dick to explain postmodernism. Such characteristics of his work as his generic status, his ontological playfulness and his philosophical depth all combine to make him an iconic figure for many postmodernists.[5] But part of this interest in Dick has led to a series of misreadings, falsifications of Dick's work, which might in turn lead to a questioning of whether Dick is postmodern after all. The aim of this chapter is to examine some of the postmodern readings of Dick, and to attempt a more accurate reading of two of his novels - *A Scanner Darkly* and *VALIS* - within the postmodern arena.

Although I do not propose to give a strict definition of postmodernism - which would take an entire book in itself - I do wish to consider briefly what sort of postmodernism incorporates Dick. Jameson wrote about Dick in an article published in 1976, and returned to him in his 1989 article 'Nostalgia For the Future' which now forms chapter nine of *Postmodernism: Or the Cultural Logic of Late Capitalism*; according to Jameson, Dick 'used science fiction to see his present as (past) history'.[6] Such a blurring of categories of past, present and future contributes to a sense of the end of history, which Jameson sees as characteristic of postmodernism. The French theorist Jean Baudrillard is saturated with Dickiana in his explorations of reality mediated by television, of the hyperreality of Disneyland and of consumer culture. It is feasible that Baudrillard's use of the term 'simulacra' was inspired by Dick's use of the word, for example in *We Can Build You* and *The Simulacra*.[7]

But whilst these two theorists appear to be fruitful for a reading of Dick, there are others who are quite plainly wrong. For instance, Brian McHale claims that in *The Man in the High Castle*, 'the parallel world of a parallel world is our world,'[8] when a careful reading shows that this is not the case. The Nazi-dominated world described in the novel may well be a parallel world, but the world described in the novel within the novel is distinct from ours. Another example is an essay by Veronica Hollinger, which sees Dick as part of a project of 'anti-humanist SF',[9] that is, he is part of a literature that celebrates the end of the flesh-based individual human being and its replacement by computer implants or networks and so on. In fact, Dick's characters often show a horror at the possibility of such a change. If postmodern science fiction, if not postmodernism itself, is to be characterised as anti-humanist, then Dick is not a part of it. The related idea of the death of the individual is found in an essay by Eric S. Rabkin, which accuses Dick of: 'having the irrational expectation that in our world the individual still matters'[10], and continues by accusing him of going mad. Rather than celebrating the death of the subject, of the self, of the I, Dick explores the survival of the subject, despite the questionable or inauthentic nature of any surrounding reality. This may well be irrational, but it permeates the PhilDickian canon.

The underlying ethics of the individual's right to exist and the corresponding demands levelled on that individual by others is lacking from almost all of the postmodernist discussions of Dick. To the extent that this ethical dimension is excluded from postmodernist thought itself, it is clear that this current chapter can be situated in opposition to postmodernism. But there are other sorts of postmodernist thought, which do incorporate ethics. In particular, I want to consider the ideas of Emmanuel Levinas; since Levinas has been discussed and considered by thinkers such as Lyotard, Irrigaray and Derrida,[11] all broadly within the arena of postmodernism, Levinas' ideas are still part of the postmodernist debate. In using the ideas of Emmanuel Levinas to discuss two late novels by Dick, he in turn is returned to the postmodern arena, but in a new, ethical, light.

However, before I discuss Levinas' ideas in relation to Dick's fiction, I'd like to digress with an anecdote which I hope can be used to form the basis of a helpful analogy. One day in early March 1992, ten years and a day after Dick's death, I was waiting to catch a bus back from the Science Fiction Foundation which was then situated in Barking. I noticed a security camera protecting the car park. The camera was surrounded by barbed wire, presumably to prevent it from being stolen. At first I wondered why there was not a second camera, to protect the first, but then I realised that would be at risk as well and so there would have to be a third camera to protect the second, and so on. Alternatively the two could be focused on each other, to give mutual protection, but then neither would be able to fulfil the function of safeguarding the car park.

At the end of this disturbingly PhilDickian chain of thinking I remembered *A Scanner Darkly*. In the near future in California, the problem of drug abuse has worsened. The Drugs Enforcement Agency relies on tip-offs, undercover agents and complicated monitoring equipment. An agent codenamed S. A. Fred is assigned to spy on Bob Arctor, a drug user who sporadically disappears and seems to have more money than he should have, and is therefore suspected of being a dealer. However the bugs that Fred has installed in Bob's house cannot show the whole story that the reader knows and Fred quickly forgets: Bob is in fact Fred's undercover identity. His disappearances are on agency business and the money is his pay for being an agent.

As a result of using the drug Substance D and the schizophrenic pressures of his work, the personalities of Fred and Bob become two separate people. This is because, as one of Fred's superiors warns Fred: 'In many of those taking Substance D, a split between the right hemisphere and the left hemisphere of the brain occurs'.[12] Dick's ideas of the split brain draw on research conducted in the sixties and seventies by Robert Ornstein and others which suggested that the two halves of the brain were virtually separate brains, the left half specialising in linguistics and logic and the right dealing with imagination. In *A Scanner Darkly* the split is such that Bob is using the right side of the brain and Fred the left.

To return to my analogy of the camera, Fred's mission can be compared to a camera videoing its own monitor. The result, naturally, is feedback. Both Fred and Bob occasionally receive flashes from the other side of their brain, represented in the text by the indented passages about split brain theories or poems in German.

The reader shares his - or should I say their - feeling of dislocation. *A Scanner Darkly* is a novel which deals with the breakdown of the self, but it would be a callous reader who feels that it celebrates this. Amongst the self-degradation of drug abuse are moments of sublime charity for others, which allows some hope for the continuation of the human race.

As I have suggested above, I will approach the problem of self-identity and relations with others through the ideas of Emmanuel Levinas.[13] Levinas was born in 1906 in Lithuania and studied philosophy at Strasbourg. He visited Fribourg to attend lectures given by the phenomenologist Edmund Husserl. Husserl's theories argue that it is impossible to separate perception of the world from the perceiver. Levinas wrote the first book in French on Husserl[14] and co-translated Husserl's *Cartesian Meditations*. Another influence upon Levinas was Martin Heidegger's *Sein und Zeit*, which makes a distinction between entities or beings (*Seiendes*) and the actuality of existence or Being (*Sein*). A being is thrown into Being, and may also be thrown out of Being, that is, die. This Being-towards-death causes an anxiety in the being, from which it prefers to be distracted. The being can turn to care or solicitude in one of three forms: for things or objects, for other people, and for itself. Objects within the world are to be considered as tools, to be grasped and used in these caring processes. Heidegger thus links the nature of the authentic reality with the status of the individual human being. Whilst the entity and Being are distinct terms, the entity can only make sense in terms of Being and Being is only an issue for a (given) entity. Through a synthesis of Husserl and Heidegger, and a partial rejection of them both, Levinas became a thinker in his own right and an influence on thinkers such as Sartre. The importance of Levinas' work is amplified when considered in relation to a thirty year debate he has maintained with Derrida.[15]

According to Levinas, the self experiences a lack within itself. The self, as observer of the world, exists in solitude. The world of utilizable objects or tools is mastered by the self, and can be considered as an extension of the self. The self is engaged in self-contemplation, and so it risks the feedback effect of the self observing the self observing the self and so on, much as S. A. Fred did. The only way out of this closed cycle is to have recourse to the not-self, to the Other. However if the Other is in turn grasped, treated as an object, then it would still be an extension of the self rather than being separate from the self and so the feedback effect would remain. Therefore the radical alterity, the radical strangeness of the Other has to be maintained.

The self is in a peculiar ontological position: since it can only perceive that which is not itself or an extension of itself, it cannot perceive the perceiving part of itself. The self can therefore be said to be absent to itself. In my analogy of the camera, the camera can only video that which is not itself, it cannot video itself. Therefore the camera is not present to itself, without the distortions of mirrors. However both the self and the camera *are* there since something is obviously being perceived. So what is - if such a verb of being remains relevant - the ontological status of the self? As the self is neither present nor absent to itself, it is what Levinas terms 'otherwise than being'. The I occurs in a kind of ethical non-space which is not existence, which is somehow prior to existence.

The I, as the basis of perception has an encounter or a face-to-face meeting, with the Other, which calls the status of the I into question. The Other says in its face 'Here I am' and 'Thou shalt not kill'. The I has a Responsibility for the Other, for the naked face of the first individual to come along. A responsibility that goes beyond what I may or may not have done to the Other or whatever acts I may or may not have committed, as if I were devoted to the other man before being devoted to myself. Or more exactly, as if I had to answer for the other's death even before being. A guiltless responsibility, whereby I am none the less open to an accusation of which no alibi, spatial or temporal, could clear me.[16] Naturally this demand can be rejected, murders can be committed, but that is hardly ethical behaviour. The relationship is asymmetric, because the I is the basis of perception and the Other is infinitely other.[17]

This should be contrasted to the I and Thou relation described by the German Jewish theologian Martin Buber.[18] He suggested that the I exists in relation to the Thou, that the I becomes the I through contact with the Thou, but the Thou becomes the Thou in relation to the I. Here the model is of two cameras trained on each other, each guaranteeing the other's existence. However Levinas maintains that the relation is asymmetric. The I has concern for the Other without reciprocating Other's concern for the self; the I is not the Other's Other. In my analogy this would be one camera protecting the other despite the risk to itself.

Compare this model to the novel *VALIS*. Horselover Fat has a series of mystical experiences, during which he believes he has encountered God. He believes that the world of the 1970s is actually a fake, that the true date is around 70 AD, the period of the early apostles. His friends, Kevin, David and Phil Dick believe that he has gone mad, and according to Phil the narrator, Horselover's madness is triggered - or his nervous breakdown begins - when he attempts to prevent Gloria's suicide. Horselover's aid to Gloria is rebuffed, and he does not prevent the suicide, but he has at least made the attempt. After this, Horselover demonstrates his concern for Sherri, who is dying of cancer, which hardly helps his mental state. However his concern remains for her, despite the cost to himself. This is clearly, in the words of Levinas, 'A responsibility that goes beyond what I may or may not have done to the Other or whatever acts I may or may not have committed, as if I were devoted to the other man before being devoted to myself' This is the ethical demand which justifies Horselover's existence, despite the fact that he fails to keep the woman alive, and despite the fact that it contributes to his nervous breakdown.

Phil the narrator shows concern at Horselover's concern for Sherri, and in fact is scathing about it:

> [Horselover] had become a professional at seeking out pain; he had learned the rules of the game and now knew how to play.... [Sherri] expressed fury and hatred, constantly, at the doctors who had saved her.... Fat said to himself in the depths of his fried mind, I will help Sherri stay healthy but if and when she gets sick again, there I will be at her side, ready to do anything for her.[19]

In this attempt to look after other people, Horselover can only bring pain upon himself. At times his suffering is as much as those he shows concern for, which is also a Levinasian idea; the concept of substitution, the responsibility 'which can be carried to the point of being substituted for the other person'.[20] Horselover is faced by ethical demands from all sides, contributing to a nervous breakdown, but paradoxically leading to the creation of a self which can care. Horselover must receive these demands; this is not the paranoia of a fantasist, but a set of very real demands: 'the idea that I am sought out in the intersidereal spaces is not science-fiction fiction, but expresses my passivity as a self'.[21] Levinas' theories could be boiled down to the idea that the self is constituted by paradoxically being non-self-identical; that is, the self is constituted by constantly being called into question. The self, having broken free from itself, must not return to the exact same point. In Dick, where the world which surrounds the characters always contains the possibility of its own illusory nature, the ontological status of the self is naturally questioned and undermined. Scott Durham[22] has argued that this demonstrates the death of the subject; on the contrary, I would argue that it demonstrates the attempts of the subject to survive.

Christopher Palmer takes a similar view in one of the more perceptive postmodernist essays about Dick. Palmer argues that Dick's novel *VALIS* is: 'the record of a painful blockage... The achievement of VALIS is to suggest how painful it can be when the pursuit of the ethical collides with the proliferating textuality of meaning'.[23] I largely agree with this, although Palmer fails to explore the ethics he raises. I have already shown how Horselover's concern situates the novel within the realm of Levinasian ethics. However the novel, as Palmer's comment about 'the proliferating textuality of meaning' suggests, is more complicated than I have hitherto allowed.

First I will suggest two ways in which the novel itself produces multiple meanings or readings. To start with the title and the precise nature of *VALIS*, does the title refer to the metaphysical entity defined in the (fictional) Great Soviet Dictionary of 1992, quoted at the front of the book? Or does it refer to the movie *Valis* within the novel, or the satellite *VALIS* within the movie? Is *VALIS* the entity which has spoken to the movie makers, or are they just cranks? Is this entity the one which has contacted the novel's protagonist, Horselover Fat? Indeed is the title of the novel *VALIS*, as it is on the spine and title page, or *Valis*, as it is on the front cover?[24] Then there is the nature of the author, who is usually viewed as the arbiter of acceptable meanings of the work. Is the author Philip K. Dick identical to the novel's narrator, Phil Dick, and is this the same Philip K. Dick who wrote the other novels and short stories? Is this the same Phil Dick who narrates two thirds of *Radio Free Albemuth*?

Even without the potential confusion of author and narrator, the position of the latter is problematic. The narrator constitutes himself by using the pronoun I, and shows concern for his friend Horselover Fat, as well as repeating Horselover's theories about the nature of God and the universe, at the risk of ridicule to Horselover. But early in the novel the narrator admits: 'I am Horselover Fat, and I am writing this in the third person to gain much-needed objectivity'.[25] As *in A Scanner Darkly*, there is a divided protagonist; here it is taken to the extreme that the two may talk to each other. To return to the split brain theory explored in the earlier novel, Horselover with his theories of having met God could be seen as the right side of the brain, Phil who reports them is the logical left side. This division of identity may be taken further; Robert Galbreath has suggested that two other characters in the novel, Kevin and David, may be further alter-egos.[26]

The novel is structured by Horselover's continual 'pursuit of the ethical', which is simultaneously a quest for identity and for God, as well as a quest for compassion. Horselover shows compassion for Gloria and Sherri. Phil shows compassion for Horselover. Outside of this the author Philip shows compassion for his characters. It is tempting, having read various essays, letters and diary entries by Dick, as well as interviews which suggest his experiences are similar to

Horselover's, to confuse Dick-as-author and Horselover and then argue, as Rabkin has done, that, 'Frankly, I think he did go insane'.[27] But to limit speculation to the novel itself, it is not certain whether God has been encountered or not. Indeed the novel advances several other competing explanations for the experience - Russian experimentation, an alien invasion and so on - without endorsing any particular theory. Whilst the ontological status or reality of the events are open to question, the compassion remains constant.

The events may have been inspired by chemical experimentation by Dick. In the April 1974 issue of *Psychology Today* - which would have been available in early March - he found an article discussing the use of vitamins to control schizophrenia. Dick tried the recipe the article gives and the results were important enough to be described in *A Scanner Darkly* and quoted in *VALIS*: 'For about six hours, entranced, ... [he] had watched thousands of Picasso paintings replace one another at flashcut speed, and then he had been treated to Paul Klees, more than the painter had painted during his lifetime'.[28] In one essay Dick suggested that the experience may have been his left and right hemispheres 'communicating in a Martin Buber I-and-Thou dialogue'.[29] However it must be remembered that Levinas is a more accurate model than Buber's thought as the dialogue is not symmetric; in *VALIS* the logical side is able to comment on the irrational.

In using the ideas of Levinas to discuss the relationship between characters, the author and the reader, I am aware that to some extent I am necessarily misrepresenting both Levinas and Dick. It is necessary to maintain the difference between the two. The similarities are understandable, since both grew up with a knowledge of Western philosophy, had an interest in Christo-Judaic materials and produced an ethics which does not presuppose an ontology. The difference comes when Dick has his characters show concern for several others, whereas primarily Levinas writes of a single I-Other encounter, the pre-original face-to-face. In my reading of *VALIS* I have set up a nexus of relationships, a series of cameras, which could be designated as, for example, Reader < Author < Phil Dick < Horselover Fat < Sherri Solvig. But Levinas only writes of two points in the chain; in an interview he has argued: 'with the appearance of the third - the third is also a face, one must know whom to speak to first. Who is the first face? And, in this sense, I am led to compare the faces, to compare the two people. Which is a terrible task'.[30] With the appearance of a third face, decisions between people must be made, and systems of justice and society must be developed. The choices and the crises they pose to the I may well constitute the painful blockage of which Palmer writes. It is when this judging of concerns begins that ontology becomes relevant.

Another similarity between Levinas and Dick is that they do not discount the possibility of the existence of God. In Levinas there is the underlying infinitely Other, which is God. More than any other Other this may not be grasped or reduced to the same, as God is infinitely high, infinitely transcendent, and therefore forever out of sight; at the same time it is possible to have a concern for God. This can be seen in *VALIS* with the discussions of a healer who must be healed, a saviour who must be saved. It is also tied in to Horselover's continuing quest for him; Horselover's identity seems to be tied up in the search. Only by infinitely prolonging his search and therefore his concern, can he maintain his identity. Levinas uses the image of: 'the story of Abraham who leaves his fatherland forever for a yet unknown land, and forbids his servant to even bring his son to the point of departure',[31] and Horselover's endless quest could seen as leaving his fatherland forever. Dick and Levinas are the same but different; they meet 'in the heart of a chiasmus',[32] where two distinct items converge yet remain always separate.

I am aware that I have only scratched the surface of the novel *VALIS*, but I have perhaps provided a framework for further study; indeed, I have found that Dick's writings are permeated with Levinasian ethics. This ethics operates on the edge of postmodernism, being discussed by and used in discussions of thinkers who are more obviously postmodern, such as Derrida, Lyotard and Irrigaray. It seems more useful to examine how Dick justifies the individual subject, and the importance of each individual's actions in respect of others, rather than forcing Dick into a Marxist or post-marxist model of postmodernism as late capitalism, where groups seem to be more important than individuals.

For this an ethics is needed, such as the one provided by Levinas. True, Dick does have things to say about existence and ontology, as well as capitalism, but this has been often privileged at the expense of ethics in previous postmodernist critiques of Dick. This is a hierarchy I hope I have gone some way towards overturning. Dick's science fiction is a postmodern one, to the extent that he explores the implications of a postmodern ethics.[33]

Andrew Butler

NOTES

1. Fredric Jameson, *Postmodernism: Or The Cultural Logic of Late Capitalism*, London and New York: Verso, 1991.

2. Collected by George E. Slusser and Tom Shippey, *Fiction 2000: Cyberpunk and the Future of Narrative*, Athens, GA: University of Georgia Press, 1992.

3. Larry McCaffery, *Storming the Reality Studio: A Casebook of Cyberpunk and Postmodern Science Fiction*, Durham and London: Duke University Press, 1991. The special issues are: *The Mississippi Review* 47/48, 1988 and *Critique* 33(3), 1992.

4. Bruce Sterling, the propagandist who did more than anyone else to map a cyberpunk movement, has even coined the term *slipstream*, an anti-genre which is neither science fiction, fantasy nor the literary mainstream, further erasing the boundaries of both. Authors labelled as slipstream include J. G. Ballard, William S. Burroughs, Borges and Rushdie.

5. This is in addition to his status as one of the authors of Blade Runner, a key postmodernist film. The Philip K. Dick texts used in this chapter are: *The Simulacra*, London: Methuen, 1977a; *The Three Stigmata of Palmer Eldritch*, New York: Manor Books, 1977b; *A Scanner Darkly*, London: Panther, 1978; *The Divine Invasion*, London: Corgi, 1982; *We Can Build You*, London: Grafton, 1986; *Radio Free Albemuth*, London: Grafton, 1987a; *VALIS*, Worcester Park: Kerosina, 1987b; *The Dark Haired Girl*, Willimantic, Ct: Mark V. Zeising, 1988.

6. Jameson, *op.cit.*, p.296. The previous articles by Jameson are: 'After Armageddon: Character Systems in Dr. Bloodmoney', in Richard D. Mullen and Darko Suvin (eds), *Science-Fiction Studies: Selected Articles on Science-Fiction 1973-1975*, Boston, Mass: Gregg Press, 1976; and 'Nostalgia for the Future', *South Atlantic Quarterly* 88, 1989, pp.517-37. The latter has a few minor differences from its later appearance as chapter 9 of Jameson's 1991 book.

7. Baudrillard indicates that he has read *The Simulacra* and some short stories in *Simulations* (trans. Paul Foss, Paul Patton and Philip Beitchmann), New York: Semiotext(e), 1983. He cites the French edition of *We Can Build You (Les Bals Des Schizos)* in *Seductions* (trans. Brian Singer), London: Macmillan, 1990. See also his 'Simulacra and Science Fiction', *Science Fiction Studies* 18(3), 1991, pp.309-13.

8. Brian McHale, *Postmodernist Fiction*, New York and London: Methuen, 1987, p.61.

9. See, for example, *The Three Stigmata of Palmer Eldritch*, where the absorption of humans by the partly artificial Eldritch is presented as nightmarish. The Hollinger essay is collected in McCaffery, *op.cit.*

10. Eric S. Rabkin, 'Irrational Expectations; or, How Economics and the Post-Industrial World Failed Philip K. Dick', *Science Fiction Studies* 15(2), 1988, pp.161-72 (p.171).

11. Essays by Lyotard and Irrigaray can be found in Richard A. Cohen (ed), *Face to Face with Levinas*, New York: State University, 1986.

12. Dick 1978, *op.cit.*, p.103.

13. Levinas' most important works are *Totality and Infinity: An Essay on Exteriority* (trans. Alphonso Lingis), The Hague: Nijhoff, 1979 and *Otherwise Than Being*. There is a useful collection edited by Sean Hand, *The Levinas Reader*, Oxford: Basil Blackwell, 1989. A lucid introduction is provided by editor and translator Alphonso Lingis in Levinas' *Collected Philosophical Papers*, Dordrecht: Nijhoff, 1987. I also recommend the interviews in *Ethics and Infinity: Conversations with Philippe Nemo*, Pittsburgh, Pa: Duquesne University Press, 1985 and in Cohen, *op.cit.* There is another strand to Levinas' work, that of Talmudic exegesis, which is briefly considered by Georg Schmid in 'The Apocryphal Judaic Traditions as Historic Repertoire. An Analysis of *The Divine Invasion* by Philip K. Dick', *Degrès Revue de Synthèse à Orientation Semiologique* 51, 1987, F1-F11.

14. Emmanuel Levinas, *The Theory of Intuition in Husserl's Phenomenology* (trans. André Orianne), Evanston, Ill: Northwestern University Press, 1973.

15. References to Levinas are scattered throughout Derrida's work, but the most important essays are 'Violence and Metaphysics: An Essay on the Thought of Emmanuel Levinas' in *Writing and*

Difference (trans. Alan Bass), London and Henley: Routledge & Kegan Paul, 1978, and 'At This Very Moment in This Work Here I Am' in Robert Bernasconi and Simon Critchley (eds), *Re-Reading Levinas*, Bloomington and Indianapolis: Indiana University Press, 1991. Levinas' responses include 'Wholly Other', also in the latter volume, and 'God and Philosophy' in Levinas (1987), *op.cit.* and Levinas (1989), *op.cit.* See also Simon Critchley, *The Ethics of Deconstruction*, Oxford: Basil Blackwell, 1992.

16. Levinas (1989), *op.cit.*, p.83.

17. In his early works, Levinas argues that the Other is higher than the self, but this is difficult to comprehend as this is not meant to be taken as a spatial and therefore ontological relationship. His later writing, *Otherwise than Being* and after suggests that the self contains a trace - a residue of that which has never been present - of the Other. This new idea, labelled proximity, remains ontological. See 'The Trace of the Other' in Mark C. Taylor (ed), *Deconstruction in Context*, Chicago: Chicago University Press. Derrida has argued that western metaphysics is obsessed with ontology and presence. For example, in Plato speech (where the speaker is present) is privileged over writing (where the writer is absent). Levinas' use of ontological terms whilst rejecting ontology is seen by Derrida as symptomatic of the difficulties of breaking with western metaphysics.

18. Buber posits two relations, that between the I and objects, or the I-It, which is one-way, and the mutual I-Thou relation with other people. Martin Buber, *I and Thou* (trans. Walter Kaufmann), Edinburgh: T. and T. Clark, 1970. See objections to this in Levinas (1989), *op.cit.*, pp.59-74.

19. Dick (1987b), *op.cit.*, p.73.

20. Levinas (1989), *op.cit.*, p.84.

21. *Ibid.*, p.105.

22. Scott Durham, 'P.K. Dick: From the Death of the Subject to a Theology of Late Capitalism', *Science Fiction Studies* 15(2), 1988, pp.173-86.

23. Christopher Palmer, 'Postmodernism and the Birth of the Author in Philip K. Dick's *VALIS*', *Science Fiction Studies* 18(3), 1991, pp.330-42 (p.340).

24. This specifically refers to the hardback edition published by Kerosina in 1987. However the Harper Collins paperback makes a similar distinction.

25. Dick (1987b), *op.cit.*, p.11.

26. Robert Galbreath, 'Salvation-Knowledge: Ironic Gnosticism in *VALIS* and *The Flight to Lucifer*' in Gary K. Wolfe (ed), *Science Fiction Dialogues*, Chicago: Academy Chicago, 1982. With regard to Levinas this would need some clarification. The Other is not just an alter-ego (literally other-self), nor is it some dark side of the self's psyche. The Other, whether infinitely high or contained by the self within a trace, is separate to the self. In Dick, particularly in *A Scanner Darkly*, the self has been split into several different selves.

27. Rabkin, *op.cit.*, p.170.

28. Dick (1978), *op.cit.*, p.24 and (1987b), *op.cit.*, p.107. The article read by Dick is by Harvey M. Ross, 'Orthomolecular Psychiatry: Vitamin Pills for Schizophrenics', *Psychology Today*, April 1974.

29. Dick (1988), *op.cit.*, p.222. Dick's metaphysical experiences of 2nd March, 1974 are largely beyond the scope of this chapter, but are discussed at length in the biography by Lawrence Sutin, *Divine Invasions: A Life of Philip K. Dick*, New York: Harmony, 1989.

30. See Robert Bernasconi and David Wood (eds), *The Provocation of Levinas: Rethinking the Other*, London: Routledge, 1988, p.174.

31. Levinas (1986), *op.cit.*, p.348.

32. Cited from 'Wholly Other' in Critchley, *op.cit.*, p.13. Levinas was referring to his own encounter with Derridean thought.

33. Finally, I wish to record a debt to Roger Luckhurst. Several of my ideas about postmodernism and autobiography grew out of discussions with Roger; the responsibility for what violence I have done to these is, of course, my own.

II. EXTRAPOLATION

5.

UTOPIAS AND HETEROTOPIAS.
THE 'CULTURE' OF IAIN M. BANKS

Utopias afford consolation: although they have no real locality there is nevertheless a fantastic, untroubled region in which they are able to unfold; they open up cities with vast avenues, superbly planted gardens, countries where life is easy, even though the road to them is chimerical. *Heterotopias* are disturbing, probably because they make it impossible to name this and that, because they shatter or tangle common names, because they destroy 'syntax' in advance, and not only the syntax with which we construct sentences but also that less apparent syntax which causes words and things (next to and also opposite one another) to 'hold together'. This is why utopias permit fables and discourse: they run with the very grain of language and are part of the fundamental fabula; heterotopias... desiccate speech, stop words in their tracks, contest the very possibility of grammar at its source; they dissolve our myths and sterilise the lyricism of our sentences.

(Michel Foucault, *The Order of Things*, cited 'Appendix B. Ashima Slade and the Harbin-Y Lectures : Some Informal Remarks toward the Modular Calculus, Part Two', in *Triton*, by Samuel R. Delaney).[1]

The narration, in fact, doubles the drama with a commentary without which no mise-en scéne would be possible. Let us say that the action would remain, properly speaking, invisible from the pit - aside from the fact that the dialogue would be expressly and by dramatic necessity devoid of whatever meaning it might have for an audience: - in other words, nothing of the drama could be grasped, neither seen nor heard, without, dare we say, the twilighting which the narration in each scene casts on the point of view that one of the actors had while performing it?

(A 'now famous epigraph from Lacan'. Subject of 'a series of exhaustive readings' by Gene Trimbell (The Spike) in her articles on the theatre (collected under the title Primal Scenes). General Information File on 'The Spike', in *Triton*, by Samuel R. Delaney).[2]

* The terms, 'character', 'text', 'matrix' while possessing many meanings, all open into the technologies of print. The intimate connections between this form of communication and our culture should be borne in mind when considering this text and its textus... Text and Textus? Text, of course, comes from the Latin *textus*, which means 'web'. In modern printing, the 'web' is that great ribbon of paper which, in many presses, takes upwards

of an hour to thread from roller to roller throughout the huge machine that
embeds ranked rows of inked graphemes upon the 'web', rendering it into
a text. All the uses of words 'web', 'weave', 'net', 'matrix' and more by
this circular 'etymology' become entrance points into a *textus*, which is
ordered from all language and language-functions, and upon which the text
itself is embedded. (p333)
Appendix A. From the *Triton* Journal : Work, Notes and Omitted Pages.
Triton. Samuel R Delaney. 1976 (Grafton 1992)

One.

Foucault's reflections on the heterotopic, and Lacan's 'enigmatic
remarks' are dispersed, and displaced through their incorporation into Samuel
Delaney's novel *Triton*, reaching those for whom *The Order of Things* and
Écrits have a dubious 'reality status'. Within the frame of the novel, there is
no necessity for either 'Foucault' or 'Lacan' to exist 'outside the text'. These
statements become a part of the workings of the text, which the reader
incorporates into a part of their experience of reading the text, and indeed the
genre. I will use these statements to interrogate some of the workings of the
'Culture' novels of Iain M. Banks, and the relationships between topography
and 'character'. In SF, the necessity of constructing topoi, not merely
landscapes, but entire societies, brings into play a diversity of neologisms, a
diversity of identities and identifications. Delaney has argued that

> the science-fictional enterprise is richer than the enterprise of mundane
> fiction. It is richer through its extended repertoire of sentences, its
> consequent greater range of possible incident, and through its more varied
> field of rhetorical and syntagmatic organisation.[3]

In 'A Cyborg Manifesto: Science, Technology, and Socialist-Feminism
in the Late Twentieth Century', Donna J. Haraway draws upon diverse feminist
science-fiction texts to elaborate upon her 'cyborg myth' of 'transgressed
boundaries, potent fusions, and dangerous possibilities'. She suggests that 'a
cyborg world might be about lived social and bodily realities in which people
are not afraid of their joint kinship with animals and machines'.[4] Haraway's
richly suggestive text is an attempt to think beyond binaries, in a postmodernist
way, while still retaining the ethics of resistance to oppression. The notion of
heterotopias can be constructed within this intersection between the sets of
'SF' and 'critical theory'. Just as in *Triton* the critical theory forms a part of
the text, - and is thus 'relativised', so in 'A Cyborg Manifesto', SF provides not

illustrations of a particular politics or theory, but the very terms through which this politics is thought, and opens up possibilities for thinking otherwise.

This intersection between critical theory and fiction may not be perhaps the 'hard science' that popular belief has linked with the 'fiction', but is science in its widest sense of 'knowledge', linked with the speculative (which is another working of SF) not the empirical. The topographical 'writing the place', or 'the place as written' intersects with the anatomical mapping of the surface of the body, and both move to topology as a topographical study of a particular place, - a specificity; to mathematical analogy which permits the study of geometrical properties and spatial relations unaffected by the continuous change of shape or size of figures, or even more relevantly for this study, the algebraic study of limits in sets regarded as consisting of a collection of points. I will be considering too, the properties of a 'textus', and its limits. SF, Delaney points out, can be seen as a textus, within which

> It is the scatter pattern of elements from myriad individual forms,... that gives their respective webs their densities, their slopes, their austerities, their charms, their contiguities, their conventions, their clichés, their tropes of great originalities here, their crushing banalities there. The map through them can only be learned, as any other language is learned, by exposure to myriad utterances, simple and complex, from out the language of each. The contours of the web control the reader's experience of any given s-f text; as the reading of a given s-f text recontours, however slightly, the web itself, that text is absorbed into the genre, judged, remembered, or forgotten.[5]

It is with reference to these mathematical models that I wish to consider the *mise-en-scene* of the drama of Utopian/heterotopian fictions, and in my concluding remarks, reflect upon what might be the 'narration' which doubles the drama - providing its textual *a-priori*, and marking the limits of the drama.

SF, from one of the earlier texts which contribute to the matrix of the conception of this textus, Mary Shelley's *Frankenstein*, has been marked with the incorporation into the text of 'science' and its parameters, of philosophy viewed from the perspective of the 'outsider' who offers a narration on the drama which is Western philosophy. Thus the monster reads Western literature and from this material constructs an Ideal Image of human beings. The consequences of the encounter between these illusions and the realities of his existence as monstrosity form the narration of the drama of his existence. This play then between 'the ideal', the 'utopian', and its negation or relativisation, exists in what Delaney identifies as 'the web of possibilities, the *textus*'.

Two.

The Culture novels of Iain M. Banks play with the oppositions of the 'Utopian' and the 'heterotopian'. The possibilities of a society without want, of joy and fulfilment are evoked, indeed described with considerable élan, yet the complexities and contradictions of the Culture when it encounters other cultures, who do not share its existence, form the action of the text.

All Iain M. Banks' science fiction novels work in the encounter of cultures, and in the first three, *Consider Phlebas* (1987), *The Player of Games* (1988), and *Use of Weapons* (1990), between 'the Culture' (the advanced symbiotic machine-humanoid or 'cyborg' society) and other, less sophisticated, religious, cultures. Even his most recent novel, *Against a Dark Background* (1993), is defined by being a 'non-Culture' novel, and the fragmented, isolated, decadent, and cyclical world of Golter is driven by the exploration of a society which unlike the Culture does not and cannot progress to a stable high level civilisation. In his earlier non-SF (or half/half) fictions, *Walking on Glass* (1985), and *The Bridge* (1986) he explores the intersection between the 'realist', or in Samuel Delaney's phrase 'the mundane', and the science-fiction, and/or sword and sorcery genres. In these two novels the 'reality status' of 'other worlds' is left ambivalent. In the short story *'The State of the Art'* (1989) the Culture encounters Earth c.1988, and as in *'A Gift from the Culture'* (1987) there is a dissident culture person who 'goes native'.[6]

The Culture is very much constructed as a Utopian civilisation. The humanoids have advanced gene technology, are able to change sex, with full reproductive capacity, have a greatly heightened sexual performance and orgasmic response, and a life span of some four hundred years. They live in harmony with the machines. 'Indeed, a case could be made for holding that the Culture was its machines, that they represented it at a more fundamental level than did any single human or group of humans within the society'. Some of the machines are 'so smart that no human was capable of understanding how smart they were (and the machines themselves were incapable of describing it to such a limited form of life)'.[7] The machines, who are quirky individualists, range from ships, which name themselves with such titles as the *Size Isn't Everything* and *Very Little Gravitas Indeed*, through 'drones' who are of various stages of technological development and function (and tend to have humanoid-type names, such as Chamlis Amalk-ney and Skaffen-Amtiskaw), to 'circuits in a micromissile hardly more intelligent than a fly'.[8] The efficiency of the machines leaves 'the humans in the Culture free to take care of the things that really mattered in life, such as sport, games, romance, studying dead languages, barbarian societies and impossible problems'.[9]

Banks skilfully draws upon the repertoire of SF, in its developments of ideas of language, worlds and perspective. The Culture is a utopian liberal constellation of tolerance and difference, of sexual and personal freedom, where 'need' does not exist, where there is no ownership. It is an advanced communist utopia, where Wilde's celebrations of machines, and Trotsky's celebrations of the potential of human beings to alter and construct their environment are elaborated and developed. The novels represent an exploration, not only of this state of existence, but of its limitations, and contradictions. If this rational, but not rationalistic, civilisation existed, what would the inhabitants and edges be like? How would it survive encounters with hostile forces? Indeed, if a utopia is placed in a 'universe' of conflict, it is not then 'heterotopic' within the text, and open to challenge, to critical readings.

'Utopia' as a term is necessarily ambivalent; within our cultural heritage and indeed in Banks' novels, it operates across two terms. The one is the imposition of a certain 'Culture' upon all, whether they wish it or not - an imperialist formulation of one destiny and one state of being. One which offers too, a consolatory fiction. Hence Foucault's formulation, and the reluctance of many to speak of 'Utopia'. The other is the desire to imagine a world beyond greed and oppression, a world where we are not limited by our class, our race, our gender, where physical and cultural needs are fulfilled. A place from which we can imagine this state of being and criticise 'how it is here and now'. A device which stops the other consolatory fiction of 'that is how it is and nothing will change it' dead in its tracks. It is through the construction of multiple other worlds, heterotopias, that this utopian project takes place. As Delaney points out, in SF,

> The deposition of weight between landscape and psychology shifts. The deployment of these new sentences within the traditional s-f frame of 'the future', not only generates the obviously new panoply of possible fictional incidents: it generates as well an entirely new set of rhetorical stances: the future-views-the-present forms one axis against which these stances may be plotted: the alien-views-the-familiar forms the other.[10]

It is not that one term can 'disappear', can be eliminated by the other, but this terrain must be worked across, explored, considered, examined. The topography, a writing of worlds, marks the movement between the two poles of topics.

Banks' Culture novels explore the edges of the 'Culture', the oppositions and resistances to a tolerant, liberal utopia, through variously an opponent, a dissatisfied Culture person a(n apparently) dissident machine, a contracted trouble-shooter. As with his 'mundane fiction', he explores the psychology of disgust, self-deception, and despair. Yet the science-fiction genre moves these explorations into a different register, through the interaction between cultures, the exuberant and joyful inventiveness of Banks' Culture. In part, the construction of the Culture and its inhabitants works as an interrogation of our inequalities, of gender, ethnicity, pushing it to biological/machine based beings. It permits an extended repertoire of interactions and peculiarities, and questioning; including the rhetorical stance, for example, of 'enemy-views-the-Culture', or 'Culture-person-views-gendered-imperialist-culture'.

Banks' novels work through the construction of worlds, which operate in two modes; firstly the utopian project/heterotopian project, and both of these are linked with the construction of character, as well as 'worlds'. Thus, as Frankenstein's monster asks 'who am I?', so do these questions place themselves for the characters. It is through the construction of (some kind of) consecutive, continuous identity, that the construction of difference can also exist. After all, if 'identity' is non-existent, or exceedingly multiple and fragmented, it can offer no points of comparison, no challenges to the 'syntax' of common sense of each world. It is the movement through different worlds that constructs difference and thought. Banks' interest in guilt and the legacies of the past is most evident in *Use of Weapons* where the identity of Cheradine Zakalwe is gradually uncovered through flashbacks and his quest for his sister. The movement through different worlds is refracted through Zakalwe and Diziet Sma, and in a way the focus of the text is less the conflict of different worlds, as much as the orchestration of history by the Culture, and the movement through to revelation and death of Zakalwe. I will therefore concentrate on the first two 'Culture' novels which set up the terms through which this text works.

Brian McHale has argued that 'SF, ...like postmodernist fiction, is governed by an ontological dominant, by contrast with modernist fiction or, among the genres of 'genre' fiction, detective fiction, both of which raise and explore issues of epistemology and are thus governed by an epistemological dominant'.   He clarifies this by indicating the questions asked by 'epistemologically-orientated fiction (modernism, detective fiction)' as 'What is there to know about the world? Who knows it and how reliably? How is knowledge transmitted, to whom, and how reliably? etc.,' and by 'ontologically-orientated fiction (postmodernism, SF)' as 'What is a world? How is a world constituted? Are there alternative worlds, and if so how are they constituted? How do different worlds, and different kinds of world, differ, and what happens when one passes from one world to another? etc.'[11] It is that which puts the question of 'being' in the 'world/worlds'. Who am I? What am I? How can I exist? are the questions of Frankenstein's construction, and they echo throughout the *textus*.

McHale,   following   Christine   Brooke-Rose,[12]   argues   that 'characterisation' in SF is generally '"thin", "shallow", and impoverished, strictly subordinated to the foreground category of "world"'.   This characterisation of the genre seems itself to be somewhat impoverished.   One might cite Asimov's Robot trilogy, most of the work of Samuel Delaney, and Joanna Russ as refutations of this.   Indeed the argument that SF actually enables a greater range of 'characterisations' and narrative *mise-en-scene* than does 'mundane fiction' is a serious one, particularly for those who would wish to challenge the still dominant white-male point of view. Samuel Delaney has pointed out that,

> The hugely increased repertoire of sentences science fiction has to draw on... not only allow the author to present exceptional, dazzling, or hyper-rational data, they also, through their interrelation among themselves and with other, more conventional sentences, create a textus within the text which allows whole panoplies of data to be generated as syntagmatically startling points. Thus Heinlein, in *Starship Troopers*, by a description of a mirror reflection and the mention of an ancestor's nationality, in the middle of a strope on male make-up, generates the data that the first person narrator, with whom we have been travelling now through two hundred and fifty-odd pages (of a three-hundred-and-fifty page book), is non-white.[13]

Haraway, following Katie King, argues that the 'pleasure in reading these fictions is not largely based on identification'.[14]   Texts like Joanna Russ' *The Adventures of Alyx* or *The Female Man* provide 'heroic quests, exuberant eroticism, and serious politics', while 'the characters refuse the reader's search for innocent wholeness'. It depends, I suppose, on what one means by 'identification'. It is the opening up for those 'marginal' subject positions of the possibility of not being defined by one's 'gender' or 'race', but as an *actant* in a narrative, a quest, a romance. A subject position not always available; that is, identified subjects of the narratives both intersect with our 'real identities', and challenge our understanding of the available repertoire of actions available. As Delaney elaborates upon *Stormship Troopers*, despite 'the surface inanities of this novel,... its endless preachments on the glories of war, and its pitiful founderings on sublimated homosexual themes...'

> What remains with me, nearly ten years after my first reading of the books, is the knowledge that I have experienced a world in which the *placement* of information about the narrator's face is *proof* that in such a world the 'race problem', at least, has dissolved. The book as text - as object in the hand and under the eye - became, for a moment, the symbol of that world. In that moment, sign, symbol, image and discourse collapse into one, non-verbal experience, catapulted beyond the *textus* (via the text) at the particularly powerful trajectory only s-f can provide...[15]

It is not then the case that 'identity' becomes irrelevant, or even necessarily 'thin', but rather through the genre, it opens up points of entry into discourse, for those positioned outside it. Then the problematising of prioritising one specific identity, even to interrogate it, generally 'the white man', but occasionally 'the white woman', comes into its own, and challenges those divisions between 'man or woman, human, artefact, member of a race, individual entity or body'.[16] Thus it is not the 'thin' characterisation, but rather the plurality of identities available, which form the utopian component of the genre. The splitting and fragmentation associated with modernism is displaced, replaced, but not necessarily eliminated by the diversity of the ontological pluralities of SF/postmodernism.

Three.

Consider Phlebas takes its title from that section in *The Waste Land:*

> Gentile or Jew
> O you who turn the wheel and look to windward,
> Consider Phlebas, who was once handsome and tall as you.

As we might expect, from this pre-text, a dominant reading can be constructed which is that this is a text very much about identity, its lack, its movement through different worlds, a world of alienation and anxiety. The central protagonist is Bora Horza Gobuchul, a 'Changer', who is of a species which has the capacity to change its appearance. In addition, they possess poisoned nails, teeth, and spit, generally useful attributes for a secret agent. He is working in the service of the near immortal, tri-ped Idirans who are fighting a semi-religious defence of their culture in a war against the Culture. Hoza sees them as a point of resistance against the Culture.

The preface describes the construction (birth) and flight from enemy forces of a 'young Mind', a mega-intelligent machine, who takes refuge on 'Schar's World, near the region of barren space between two galactic strands called the Sullen Gulf, and it was one of the forbidden Planets of the Dead'[17] guarded from the Idiran-Culture war by the Dra'Azon, 'a pure-energy superspecies' as a monument to death and futility, on account of the inhabitants having destroyed themselves with biological weapons.

The first chapter relates the escape from imminent death of Horza as he is rescued by the Idirans, and is given his assignment to find the Mind, as it is his society which is the base on Schar's World. As he lived there for a while, and has an ex-lover living there, Horza has additional reasons for undertaking the quest. Much of the novel is a narration of Horza's exciting adventures on the way to, and on Schar's World, generally on an ancient space-ship. This is interset with the Mind's reflections as it waits for rescue from the Culture, or capture by the Idirans.

> It knew to the smallest imaginable fraction of a second how long it had been in the tunnels of the Command System, and more often than it needed thought about that number, watched it grow inside itself. It was a form of security it supposed; a small fetish, something to cling to.[18]

It reflects on its strategies of survival, and its problems.

> Better than nothing, though. Better still to have problems than to let death eradicate them all...
> There was, however, another less immediately relevant, but more intrinsically worrying, problem it had discovered, and it was implied in the question: who was it?[19]

Due to its situation, of having to exist in 'real-space' and not 'hyperspace', its thinking has slowed down.

> As for thinking, as for *being itself* - ...It wasn't its real self. It was a crude
> abstracted copy of itself, the mere ground plan for the full labyrinthine
> complexity of its true personality...
> So *who was it*?
> Not the entity it thought it was, that was the answer, and it was a
> disconcerting one...
> *But think positively. Patterns, images, the telling analogy...*
> If it was not itself, then it *would* not be itself.[20]

The third perspective in the novel is from the Culture or, more specifically, Fal'Ngeestra, who is a Culture Referrer, who could equal the Culture's Minds in 'accurately assessing a given set of facts', being 'one of those thirty, maybe forty, out of eighteen trillion who could give you an intuitive idea of what was going to happen, or tell you why she thought something which had already happened had happened the way it did'.[21] She is in part responsible for considering the Idiran War, and specifically the possibilities of rescuing the trapped Mind. She attempts to consider the perspective of the Idirans, and their reaction to the Culture. As she sees it, it is one of contempt for

> a mongrel race... (with a) rowdy upbringing full of greedy, short-sighted
> empires and cruel wasteful diasporas,... pathetic, fleshy things, so short
> lived, swarming and confused,.. worse to come... We meddle with the
> code of life itself... And, ...worst of all, not just producing, but embracing
> and giving ourselves over totally to the ultimate anathema: the Minds, the
> sentient machines: the very image and essence of life itself, desecrated.
> Idolatry incarnate.
> No wonder that they despise us. Poor sick mutations that we are, petty
> and obscene, servants of the machine devils that we worship. Not even
> sure of our own identity: just who is Culture? Where exactly does it begin
> and end? Who is and who isn't?... too many claiming some kind of
> independence. No clear boundaries to the Culture, then; it just fades away
> at the edges, both fraying and spreading. So who are we?[22]

Horza's hatred and fear of the Culture is based on his dislike of machines (Banks has good fun with his encounter with the rather queeny drone or 'Accredited Free Construct' Unaha-Closp, with whom Horza is forced to interact) and the gene technology of the Culture, as un-natural. Fal'Ngeestra locates this hostility in a repressed awareness of his own gene-altered ancestry, 'the product of careful thought and genetic tinkering and military planning and deliberate design... and war'.[23] Here is the creation of a sub-species for war purposes. The struggle to act, to comprehend, marks Horza's existence in the text, and it is perhaps in tribute to that the mind takes his name, and indeed narrates the story. For the Changer exists as sentient weapon of war, and bears more than a passing resemblance to John Le Carré's Perfect Spy, becoming blank in death.

> The face of the man on the stretcher was as white as the snow, and as blank. The features were there: eyes, nose, brows, mouth; but they were somehow unlinked and disconnected, giving a look of anonymity to a face lacking all character, animation and depth. It was as though all the people, all the characterisations, all the parts the man had played in his life had leaked out of him in his coma and taken their own little share of his real self with them, leaving him empty, wiped clean.[24]

The Mind is rescued by the Culture agent Balveda. The narrative is followed by extracts from 'A Short History of the Idiran War (English language/Christian calendar version, original text 2110 AD, unaltered) edited by Parharengysia Listach Ja'andeesih Petrain dam Kotoklo. The work forms part of an independent, non-commissioned but Contact-approved Extro-Information Pack', and a 'Dramatis Personae' section, which tells us of what happened to the characters after the close of the action. (This has lots of 'in-jokes', aka 'inter-textual references', to other SF novels, and mundane existences). The Mind serves in the war, and afterwards goes on to general service 'taking its slightly unusual name with it'. Many, many years later, the Epilogue tells us, Gimishin Foug, 'a great-great-great-great-great-great-grand niece of Perosteck Balveda (as well as a budding poet)' travels. She asks the ship its name. It replies that it is the Bora Horza Gobuchul.

> That's a weird name. How did you end up calling yourself that?
> The remote drone dipped one front corner slightly, its equivalent of a shrug. It's a long story...'
> Gimishin Foug shrugged;
> 'I like long stories'.[25]

Who is telling us this story? Is it the Bora Horza Gobuchul? Gimishin Foug? If the former, it has some claim to participatory action, in being the 'object of the quest'; if the latter, is it a point of relaying, similar to the Cashinahua conjured up in Jean-François Lyotard's The Postmodern Condition, who on hearing a narrative, have the power to relay it? In a way, it doesn't matter, except to note that it doesn't matter. Either way, we are asked to consider Phlebas, and by implication the Horza and the Changers, wiped out as a species during the final stages of the war, and indeed the Idirans, their culture fragmented and dispersed in defeat.

Four.

The framing narration of *The Player of Games* is the machine, Mawhrin Skel. In the final (brief) section 'The Passed Pawn', it admits to its multiple identities, by which it cajoled, pushed, blackmailed, guided, orchestrated the final conflict, and returned to safety, Gurgeh. It 'frames' him for the task of representing the Culture.

> This is the story of a man who went far away for a long time, just to play a game. The man is a game player called 'Gurgeh'. The story starts with a battle that is not a battle, and ends with a game that is not a game. Me? I'll tell you about me later...[26]

> There's still me. I know I've been naughty, not revealing my identity, but then, maybe you've guessed: and who am I to deprive you of the satisfaction of working it out for yourself. Who am I, indeed?...
> This is a true story. I was there. When I wasn't, and when I didn't know exactly what was going on... I admit that I have not hesitated to make it up. But it's still a true story.
> Would I lie to you?[27]

The Player of Games works from the framework of the internal perspective of the Culture. Jurnau Morat Gurgeh, bored with the Culture, approaches, is lured into, Special Circumstances, to play Azad, a game on which a three-gender, racially homogenous empire is based.

> It 'is used as an absolutely integral part of the power system of the empire... The idea... is that Azad is so complex, so subtle, so flexible, and so demanding that it is as precise and comprehensive a model of life as it is possible to construct. Whoever succeeds at the game succeeds in life...
> 'It doesn't have to be totally true,... but cause and effect are not perfectly polarised here; the set-up assumes that the game and life are the same thing... It becomes true; it is willed into actuality. ...Azad - the game - would appear to be the force that holds (the empire) together.[28]

Gurgeh travels to Azad, and succeeds in beating Azad at its own game. In the final stages of the game, on the Board of Form, Gurgeh realises that,

> The Emperor was out to beat not just Gurgeh, but the whole Culture. There was no way to describe his use of pieces, territory and cards: he had set up his whole side of the game as an Empire, the very image of Azad. Another image struck Gurgeh with a force almost as great; one reading - perhaps the best - of the way he'd always played was that he played as the Culture. He'd habitually set up something like the society itself when he constructed his positions and deployed his pieces; a net, a grid of forces

and relationships, without any obvious hierarchy or entrenched leadership, and initially quite profoundly peaceful.[29]

This relationship between the culture and the game-playing has been elaborated upon throughout the novel. So too has the relationship between language and culture. Thus, Gurgeh's colleague, the drone (machine) Flere-Imsaho, has anticipated this engagement, through observing the effects on Gurgeh of speaking the language of the empire, Eächic. Compared to Marain, 'a synthetic language, designed to be phonetically and philosophically as expressive as the pan-human speech apparatus and pan-human brain would allow', Eächic 'was an ordinary evolved language, with rooted assumptions which substituted sentimentality for compassion and aggression for co-operation'.[30] Through this cultural and linguistic exposure, Gurgeh begins to play 'like one of those carnivores he'd been listening to, stalking across the board, setting up traps and diversions and killing grounds; pouncing, pursuing, bringing down, consuming, absorbing...'[31]

Through the encounter between the Culture and Azad, Banks elaborates the gendered and ethnic structure of the latter. Gurgeh is briefed on the sexual/social structure of the Empire, and the three genders have just been described.

'...The one in the middle is the dominant sex.'
Gurgeh had to think about this. 'The what?' he said.
'The dominant sex', Worthil repeated. 'Empires are synonymous with centralised - if occasionally schematised - hierarchical power structures in which influence is restricted to an economically privileged class retaining its advantages through - usually - a judicious use of oppression and skilled manipulation of both the society's information dissemination system and its lesser - as a rule nominally independent - power systems. In short, it's all about dominance. The intermediate - or apex - sex... controls the society and the empire. Generally the males are used as soldiers and the females as possessions. Of course it's a little more complicated than that, but you get the idea.'
'Well.' Gurgeh shook his head. 'I don't understand how it works, but if you say it does... all right'. He rubbed his beard. 'I take it this means that these people can't change sex'.[32]

Banks uses the 'utopian' perspective of the Culture to challenge the taken-for-granted-ness of gender oppression, and elaborates upon the policy of gender oppression and ethnic cleansing pursued by the empire.

Azad is not the sort of place it's easy to think about coldly,... They have done things the average Culture person would find... unspeakable. A programme of eugenic manipulation has lowered the average male and female intelligence; selective birth-control sterilisation, area starvation, mass deportation, with the result that almost everybody on the home planet is the same colour and build.[33]

On Azad itself, during the course of the games, the 'library drone' - who is 'really' our narrator, Flere-Imsaho, takes Gurgeh out through the streets of Azad, to show the consequences of the society, which he has been playing at the abstract level of the game. Gurgeh is wrapped in a cloak, and seeks to help an old man who has been beaten up by apices,

> Do *not* touch him!
> The drone's voice stopped Gurgeh like a brick wall. 'If any of these people see your hands or face, you're dead. You're the wrong colour, Gurgeh. Listen; a few hundred dark-skinned babies are still born each year, as the genes work themselves out. They're supposed to be strangled and their bodies presented to the Eugenic Council for a bounty, but a few people risk death and bring them up, blanching them as they get older. If any of them thought you were one, ...they'd skin you alive.[34]

These tactics of de-familiarisation and estrangement work through the complexity of Gurgeh's positioning within the society of the Empire (and, by implication, our own): dark, and therefore marked as 'alien' and inferior; male, and thus inferior to the apex, although not a woman, which in Azad is a position from which one cannot participate beyond the first round of the games. Of course, one can read the construction of three genders onto the intersection of class/gender in our society, but with the genre, it is always both the estrangement (the construction of other systems) and the allegorical function. *Contra* those who claim the absolute relativisation of 'reality' and 'truth', there are few who would not recognise this reflection. It is both an analysis of our world, and something more. In the final process of playing Azad on the Board of Becoming,

> The board became both Culture and Empire again. The setting was made by them both; a glorious, beautiful, deadly killing field, unsurpassably fine and sweet and predatory and carved from [the Emperor] Nicosar's beliefs and his together. Images of their minds; a hologram of pure coherence, burning like a standing wave of fire across the board, a perfect map of the landscape of thought and faith within their heads. ...Nothing so subtle, so complex, so beautiful had ever been seen on an Azad board.[35]

The Culture, then is not untouched by its encounters; there is no pure opposition; the reason for Gurgeh being sent by Special Circumstances is to avoid a war - or occupation of the Empire by the Culture, whereby 'the Culture would lose by emulating those we despise; invaders, occupiers, hegemonists'[36] by destabilising the order of the Empire.

Five.

Banks' novels mark the limits of our own discourses and politics. Preceding the 'Consider Phlebas' citation heading the novel is a quotation from the Koran (2.190): 'Idolatry is worse than carnage'. The dates of the Idiran-Culture war are 1267-1367 AD. The extracts from *A Short History of the Idiran War* (English language/Christian calendar version, original text 2110 AD, unaltered) give accounts of the reasons for the war.

> It was, the Culture knew from the start, a religious war in the fullest sense...
>
> Faced with a religiously inspired society determined to extend its influence over every technologically inferior civilization in its path regardless of either the initial toll of conquest or the subsequent attrition of occupation, Contact could either disengage and admit defeat - so giving the lie not simply to its own reason for existence but to the only justificatory action which allowed the pampered, self-consciously fortunate people of the Culture to enjoy their lives with a clear conscience - or it could fight...
>
> For all the Culture's profoundly materialist and utilitarian outlook, the fact that Idir had no designs on any physical part of the culture was irrelevant. Indirectly, but definitely and mortally, the Culture *was* threatened ... [with] the destruction of its spirit; the surrender of its soul.[37]

The Culture is drawn up from the 'best self', and ideal image, of the West, a communist utopia of plurality, tolerance, and plenitude. It is a cyborg-world, in the doubling sense that Haraway evokes when she writes of the cyborg as 'text, machine, body and metaphor', and 'cybernetic organisms, - compounds of hybrid techno-organic embodiment and textuality'.[38] It runs with the grain of language, pushing the *fabula* to the point where it can only criticise our present existences. In the encounters with the Idirans and the Azad empire, it also questions the limits of the set, or web, from which such a utopia is constructed. The topography of imagined other worlds becomes then a geography, a writing of the earth, and a study of those shifting shapes, a geometric topology of those elements of the SF textus. The limits of the sets which mark our imaginings, our ability to think differently.

The Culture is essentially a postmodern, nineteen-eighties utopia, which witnessed not only the concluding stages of the post-war global arrangements, and the 'Cold War', but also the seemingly unstoppable globalisation of finance capital, consumer booms, and the homogenisation of space.[39] The rather different constellation of markers of the nineteen-nineties; the recessions, the Gulf War, the Rushdie *fatwah*, the break-up of the former Yugoslavia and Soviet Union are evoked in the construction of the rather different world of Golter, the polluted, politically unstable, and technologically degenerate world of *Against A Dark Background*. It is a world reminiscent of Tomi, that decaying city on the Black Sea, constructed in Christoph Ransmayr's *The Last World*,[40] a postmodern meditation on power, poetry, metamorphoses, and marginalities. Both of these texts are marked by an explicit juxtaposition of a poetics of space, with a politics of space.

McHale has indicated that

> this shared poetics of space is partly to be explained by the common
> historical origins of both SF and postmodernism in romance. In medieval
> romance the category of 'world', normally the unrepresentable, absolute
> horizon of all experience and perception, is itself made an object of
> representation through a particular metaphorical use of enclosed spaces
> within the romance world: castles, enchanted forests, walled gardens and
> bowers, etc. Such symbolic enclosures, functioning as scale-models or
> miniature analogues of worlds, bring into view the normally invisible
> horizons of the world, the very 'worldness' of world. Space, in other
> words, becomes in medieval romance an all purpose tool for 'doing'
> ontology - a means of exploring ontology in fiction, as well as (potentially
> at least) the ontology *of* fiction.[41]

I suggested earlier that Shelley's *Frankenstein* was an important component of the SF textual web. Like the later texts, it constructs disconnected worlds of climactic and physical extremes: the romantic sublime, but also written against those explorations of the globe by Europe. Shelley's discursive horizon is marked both historically (Frankenstein creates the monster through learning from old, discredited 'science') and culturally, through the incursion of Islamic texts, and the romance of the son of the family, in whose cottage the monster takes refuge. He is engaged to a young woman who, with her father, was forced to flee from anti-Semitism in Paris. It is an odd episode in the tale, whose function seems only to mark the limits of Christian discourse. It also recalls those oriental tales of the eighteenth and early nineteenth centuries, which Robert Mack has reminded us of, arguing that

> The spectacular effects of its 'enchanting' conventions - of its genies and
> its demons and its magic spells - are themselves the symptoms of a larger
> freedom and magic at work in these texts: the freedom of fictional
> explorations of alternative possibilities, of fearless sexuality, and of a
> possibility of expression beyond the limitations of ordinary, day-to-day
> life.[42]

The romance form emerged from the encounter between the Islamic and Christian cultures; the quest, the enchanted castle, the construction of a zone beyond the mundane indicate the complexity and the continuity of this form. That these continue throughout the media and histories of the genre can be indicated by comparing 'The Adventures of Sinbad' with 'Flash Gordon'. The movement between this textus and the 'post-modern' novel might similarly be considered via Cide Hammete Benengli, author of *Don Quixote*.

It is this encounter between the cultures of Islam and the West, whether secular or Christian, that I would like to indicate constructs an imaginary but also real terrain of desires, possibilities, and dangers. This is the reading that I would offer of 'Lacan's enigmatic epigraph'; that this is the narration doubling the drama of SF, rendering its *mise-en-scene* possible.

Carolyn Brown

NOTES

1. Samuel Delaney, *Triton*, London: Grafton, 1992, p.345.
2. *Ibid.*, p.50.
3. *Ibid.*, p.340.
4. Donna J. Haraway, *Simians, Cyborgs, and Women: The Reinvention of Nature*, New York: Free Association Books, 1991, p.154.
5. Delaney, *op.cit.*, pp.340-1.
6. Iain M. Banks, *Consider Phlebas*, London: Orbit, 1987; *The Player of Games*, London: Orbit, 1988; *Use of Weapons*, London: Orbit, 1990; *The State of the Art*, London: Orbit, 1991; *Against a Dark Background*, London: Orbit, 1993.
7. Banks (1987), *op.cit.*, p.86.
8. *Ibid.*, p.87.
9. *Ibid.*, p.87.
10. Delaney, *op.cit.*, p.339.
11. Brian McHale, *Postmodernist Fiction*, New York and London: Methuen, 1987, p.247.

12. Christine Brooke-Rose, *A Rhetoric of the Unreal*, Cambridge: Cambridge University Press, 1981.
13. Delaney, *op.cit.*, p.339.
14. Haraway, *op.cit.*, p.178.
15. Delaney, *op.cit.*, p.339.
16. Haraway, *op.cit.*, p.178.
17. Banks (1987), *op.cit.*, p.5.
18. *Ibid.*, p.178.
19. *Ibid.*, p.179.
20. *Ibid.*, p.179.
21. *Ibid.*, p.87.
22. *Ibid.*, pp.333-4.
23. *Ibid.*, p.336.
24. *Ibid.*, p.446.
25. *Ibid.*, p.471.
26. Banks (1988), *op.cit.*, p.3.
27. *Ibid.*, p.309.
28. *Ibid.*, pp.76-7.
29. *Ibid.*, p.268.
30. *Ibid.*, p.247.
31. *Ibid.*, p.247.
32. *Ibid.*, p.75.
33. *Ibid.*, p.80.
34. *Ibid.*, p.205.
35. *Ibid.*, p.274.
36. *Ibid.*, p.79.
37. Banks (1987), *op.cit.*, pp.451-2.
38. Haraway, *op.cit.*, p.212.
39. See David Harvey, *The Condition of Postmodernity*, Oxford: Basil Blackwell, 1989.
40. Christoph Ransmayr, *The Last World* (trans. John Woods), London: Paladin, 1991.
41. McHale, *op.cit.*, p.247.
42. Robert L. Mack, *Oriental Tales*, Oxford: Oxford University Press, 1992, p.xvii.

6

SILENCE AND AWKWARDNESS IN REPRESENTATIONS OF THE JEWISH HOLOCAUST, THE BOMBING OF HIROSHIMA AND NAGASAKI, AND A PROJECTED NUCLEAR HOLOCAUST

Ever since Himmler's declaration of the 'Final Solution', which resulted in the extermination of around six million Jews in various concentration, death camps and ghettos between 1941 and 1945, writers have been faced with the question of whether it is possible to represent the Holocaust. Some theorists have argued that language is powerless to describe the event, so it should only be represented with a reverential linguistic silence. For example, in *Language And Silence* George Steiner states that 'the world of Auschwitz lies outside speech as it lies outside reason'.[1] It is, according to Steiner, the product of an irrational ideology, and is beyond representation because language is based on a set of rational linguistic systems. His argument epitomises one common notion of linguistic silence which has arisen out of the Holocaust, but I wish to point out that it is questionable on two accounts. The conflation between speech and reason is simplistic. Language is not purely rational: linguistic systems are not perfect, and contain irregularities. It is also dangerous not to question the common conception of Auschwitz as 'irrational' when it was the clearly the product of a perverse form of logic. According to Nazi ideology the Jews 'stabbed Germany in the back', causing its defeat in World War One and keeping jobs Aryans should have, and so they needed to be disposed of as quickly and efficiently as possible (maps of Auschwitz show how carefully planned, systematic and controlled the killing was). Some revisionist critics have argued for another type of linguistic silence: literature should forget the Holocaust because it was simply an irrational blip, and therefore a forgivable event in German history. But the event was not beyond reason, but a product of perverted reason, which, as I shall demonstrate in this chapter, can be represented with the aesthetics of awkwardness.

Steiner goes on to argue that the Holocaust tends towards linguistic silence because it is part of a general 'revaluation of silence' in 'the modern spirit'.[2] He uses 'the epistemology of Wittgenstein' and 'the poetics of Beckett' to back up his argument, but the efficacy of his reading of these writers in the context of the Holocaust is questionable. He quotes the infamous line from *Tractatus*, 'whereof one cannot speak, thereof one must be silent' as proof of the inexpressibility of the event, but the appropriation is too easy. If it were impossible to 'speak' about Auschwitz, then it would logically follow that writers would have to be 'silent' about it. But this is not the empirical case: speech was central to the organisation of (and revolts against) the camp; theological, historical, literary (and so on) debates have raged about the Holocaust ever since its occurrence. Steiner manipulates the fragmented and disruptive nature of Samuel Beckett's plays as evidence of a crisis in language which the event initiated: the characters, according to him, struggle with language, and finally lapse into silence. In contrast, I believe that Beckett's poetics are more positive than Steiner suggests. The movement of the plays is from silence to language, not language to silence as he presumes. Familiar linguistic codes such as jokes, banter and even just wittering fill Beckett's plays and successfully combat the silencing of language inherent in his stage direction ('Pause'). Beckett's poetics, when placed in the context of the Holocaust, display the need to struggle against the temptation to represent it with linguistic silence.

I would also like to show how other writers have reacted against notions of linguistic silence. Critics have interpreted Theodor Adorno's references to the event in the essay 'Cultural Criticism and Society' as evidence of his supposed view that writers should be silenced after Auschwitz. Steiner asserts he said 'no poetry after Auschwitz', Alvin Rosenfeld that he thought it impossible to 'write poetry after Auschwitz', and James Young that he reviled 'Holocaust art'.[3] Their readings are careless. Adorno actually states that 'to write poetry after Auschwitz is barbaric'. He does not want to silence literature; on the contrary, he argues that post-Holocaust poetry should be of a particular 'barbaric' type. The etymology and conventional meaning of the word would suggest it is unrestrained, uncultured or rough in subject matter, but I believe Adorno is attempting to describe a new form of poetry which is stylistically and thematically *awkward*. The language is necessarily awkward because it struggles, and often fails, to find a language adequate to represent the horror of the Holocaust.

By extending Adorno's notion of 'barbaric' poetry to the whole of prose, it is possible to illustrate the different possible types of awkwardness. In Tadeusz Borowski's *This Way For The Gas, Ladies And Gentlemen*, the awkwardness lies in the chilling 'matter-of-factness' of the prose while engaging in a horrific event: 'between two throw-ins... three thousand people had been put to death'.[4] He depicts a disconcerting lack of emotion, but underneath the sparse prose lies a hint of helplessness and guilt: he cannot reconcile the privilege of the football game with the death of the victims. The language derives its awkward eeriness through an engagement with the grotesque: two seemingly irreconcilable concepts are juxtaposed, and the normality of the game contrasted with an act of genocide makes the latter appear more horrific. Even the mode in which the time-lapse is measured is awkward in its seeming arbitrariness: it could denote a space of anything between a few seconds and up to half an hour.

Gershom Shaked proposes that the only way to deal with the Holocaust is to 'turn to the grotesque', as 'only the grotesque can grapple with an emotional experience... beyond the power of human intelligence'.[5] I would contest his idea that it is beyond knowledge, but the grotesque does seem to be the style writers choose to tackle what they perceive as the awkward absurdity of the event. For example, in *The Watch* Carlo Levi faces the reader with the uncomfortable image of 'photographs of women weeping as they buried pieces of soap made from the bodies of their husbands and sons'.[6] The grotesque functions here by anticipating two opposite reactions in the reader: horror and laughter. The image is so absurd as to be funny if taken out of context, but a realisation of the horror of the indicated process of dehumanisation - and the impossibility of a conventional burial - immediately counteracts such a reaction.

In *If This Is A Man*, Primo Levi argues that existing language cannot help but appear awkward when juxtaposed with the reality of the Holocaust. Present linguistic resonances fail to encompass the extreme 'hunger', 'tiredness', 'fear' and 'pain' the inmates of Auschwitz suffered. He muses that if the camps had lasted longer, 'a new, harsh language would have been born,' but I would argue that his texts themselves deliberately try to forge an original 'barbaric' style. This is most evident in the 'The Truce':

> In those days and in those parts, soon after the front had passed by, a high wind was blowing over the face of the earth; the world around us seemed to have returned to primeval Chaos, and was swarming with scalene, defective, abnormal human specimens; each of them bestirred himself, with blind or deliberate movements, in anxious search of his own place, of his own sphere, as the particles of the four elements are described as doing so in the verse cosmologies of the Ancients.[7]

The language is most obviously awkward in its grammatical structure: the paratactic style compounds several possible sentences into one with the help of semi-colons, giving the impression that the words are written in haste during an epiphany. The use of adjectives is strange: allowing for the possibility of an erroneous translation, the piling together of words of similar meaning ('scalene/defective/abnormal') suggests Levi is groping for exactly the right word to describe the victims' predicament. The adjectives 'blind' and 'deliberate' create an awkward dichotomy: how is it possible for them to move both blindly and deliberately? The heightened tone of the passage is embarrassing, and the archaic words 'bestirred' and the references to 'Chaos' and 'the Ancients' make them appear as characters out of classical mythology.

Despite this evident stylistic awkwardness in Levi's work, Rosenfeld considers his writing to be purely 'documentary'.[8]   Yet heightened rhetoric conventionally has little to do with documentary art, belonging more obviously in the realms of fiction, drama and poetry.   This indicates another awkwardness inherent in Levi's texts: they transgress conventional constructions of genre. Rosenfeld has no conception of this, and sets up a false opposition between the 'documentary' and 'art'.[9] He perceives 'art' as distorting reality through metaphor, whereas the 'documentary' sticks to the facts of the Holocaust. But this notion of the 'truth' unimpeded by metaphor cannot be reconciled with Levi's portrayal of the victims. In reality they were obviously not 'particles of the four elements'. Rosenfeld's inability to spot the awkwardness of his style arises from the ease in which he accepts 'the truth'.

James Young questions the 'truthfulness' of the event. He believes there are no 'true' accounts, only individual and subjective representations, so the documentary should not be privileged over the unashamedly fictive.[10] Indeed, Young uncovers the essentially fictive nature of the documentary, or any other 'factually insistent narrative', by applying Roland Barthes' conception of the 'fetishisation of the real' to Holocaust literature. Barthes shatters the supposed objective nature of realist narratives by demonstrating how writers silence 'all traces of the I in their text'.[11]   This subverts Rosenfeld's conception of the documentary, and yet Levi himself never pretended to be objective in his novels: they are presented, even with an 'Author's Preface' before *If This Is A Man*, as his version of events.   However, the problem with Young's thesis is that by demonstrating the awkwardness of genre distinctions, and focusing on representations of the Holocaust, he virtually silences the referent. He argues that there can be no access to the real event, but this fetishisation of langauge is dangerously close to the Nazi's attempt to silence the referent through euphemism, and by actions such as destroying the crematoria and relevant documents at Auschwitz 'to eliminate all traces of the mass extermination'.[12] Texts may be awkward representations of reality, but the facts of the Holocaust still remain.

This occlusion of the referent by Young carries over into his criticism of Sylvia Plath's poetry. He argues she is 'not a Holocaust poet, simply because she does not write about the Holocaust'; she only writes about how the event is received in the world's abstract, 'collective consciousness'.[13] Yet there is no fixed, collective representation of the Jewish holocaust, only a myriad of different representations, behind which the referent remains intact. I shall now go on to discuss Plath's celebrated poem 'Daddy' in the light of my conception of the aesthetics of awkwardness.

The poem displays a disorientating use of metaphor: this is because the persona is a fuguist - someone who has completely lost their identity - and s/he desperately tries to re-construct it (or construct another) throughout the poem (I should stress here that I am using 's/he' in my discussion as there is no concrete evidence in the poem to suggest that the persona is definitely either male or female). The confusion this initiates can be illustrated in stanzas seven and eight. S/he has a vague notion of him/herself as a victim of oppression, so s/he attempts (unconvincingly, but not necessarily falsely) to identify with the Jews annihilated by the 'Final Solution'. However the identification is more confused than most critics have noticed. At the same time as s/he tentatively suggests 'I may be a bit of a Jew', s/he claims gypsy ancestress, weird luck and knowledge of tarot cards: s/he identifies with a completely different race, decimated as well by the 'Final Solution', which has origins in Hindu culture. By constructing him/herself as a victim, s/he then attempts to construct his/her father as an oppressor in order to complete the binary. This results in a similar confused mass of metaphors: 'daddy' is not only a Nazi, but also God, a member of the Luftwaffe (airforce) and Panzer (tank) division in the German army, a teacher, a devil, a witch doctor, a medieval torturer, and finally a vampire.

The persona attempts to return to a 'barbaric' form of language in order to re-invent 'daddy'. His/her identity is inextricably linked with his - as the opening image of the persona as the foot and 'daddy' as the shoe demonstrates - so by re-inventing him the persona simultaneously wishes to re-invent him/herself. S/he tries to remember the first snippets of language s/he learnt from him. Hence the poem begins in the form of a nursery rhyme: the first stanza is reminiscent of the specific tale which starts: 'There was an old woman who lived in a shoe/ She had so many children she didn't know what to do'. An 'oo' sound dominates the stanza, and runs throughout the whole poem. The persona conceives this as one of language's most basic sounds, as it articulates a child's love towards its parents (and vice versa, as in the nonsense phrase 'coochie-coochie-coo'). The sound then helps to construct the artifice of their identity. The persona needs a word to rhyme with 'you' in the sixth stanza, and comes up with 'Jew' in the seventh. S/he then repeats the word four times, as if the persona were a child able to understand and then play with a new phrase and concept.

The poem's 'oo' sound is counterbalanced by a 'k' sound. The persona perceives the latter as equally 'barbaric', as it articulates an opposite, basic emotion: hate. His/her hatred towards 'daddy' (perhaps for denying the persona an autonomous identity) is demonstrated in words such as 'black', 'kill', 'freakish' and 'Polack', and most obviously in the text's fragments of German, such as 'ich', 'Dachau' and 'swastika'. The presence of these German phrases is significant: the persona perceives a latent hatred in them. In the sixth stanza, Nazism is inextricably linked with the language in their conception of German as a 'barb wire snare'. This links with George Steiner's perception of a latent Nazism in the German language, which he outlines in the essay 'The Hollow Miracle':

> Nazism found in the language precisely what it needed to give voice to its savagery. Hitler heard inside his native tongue the latent hysteria, the confusion, the quality of hypnotic trance. He plunged unerringly into the undergrowth of language, into those zones of darkness and outcry which are the infancy of articulate speech... [he sensed] a rasping cadence, half nebulous jargon, half obscenity.[14]

I would argue that these 'barbaric' sounds can be found in many languages, not just German, and that Nazism forged confusion and hysteria out of the language, rather than simply articulating a hatred that was already there. For example the German verb 'ausschwitzen', meaning to sweat out (usually applied to animals) appears innocent enough, but in the context of the largest death camp 'Auschwitz' the word carries horrific historical baggage. However, the persona certainly remains worried that by re-constructing 'daddy' in the German language, s/he will inevitably construct him/herself as a Nazi. Articulation and inarticulation are linked in the image of 'choking': the persona struggles to learn the most basic German phrases, but when s/he does speak, s/he is tongue-tied due to the overwhelming hatred s/he detects in them. The persona is forced into a position where s/he has to choose between non-identity, and the possible identity of a Nazi. S/he chooses the former: in the infamous last line, 'Daddy, daddy, you bastard, I'm through', s/he frustratedly dispels the confused images of the father and him/herself, and lapses into the silence of non-identity.

Similar problems of representation to those I have discussed in relation to the Jewish Holocaust arise out of the bombing of Hiroshima and Nagasaki in 1945, and a projected nuclear holocaust. Some critics agree that these events are also impossible to represent for different reasons. For example, in the essay 'Armageddon from Huxley to Hoban', Thomas Morrissey argues that a projected nuclear holocaust is an 'important and unmanageable' theme, 'inexpressible' because it has not happened, and therefore there is no existing language capable of discussing it.[15] Moreover, the aftermath would destroy all texts and linguistic systems, so no one would be left to discuss it. This authenticist argument is weak: it is possible for writers to imagine what might happen without waiting to take part in it. David Dowling takes a different and common angle on linguistic silence by arguing that 'no language is appropriate to the holocaust' because of the sheer scale of its horror.[16] He applies Raymond Briggs's cartoon book *When the Wind Blows* to his theory: James searches for words but can only come up with 'Blimey' in the face of fall-out. Literary discourse is equally unhelpful: he quotes extracts from Tennyson's 'The Charge of the Light Brigade' and snippets of religious verse, but they crumble into silence as he dies of radiation sickness.

In his article 'Combat', Albert Camus declares that journalistic representations of the 1945 bombings should be 'full of silence' because of this lamentable and horrific nature of the holocaust.[17] A 'silent' newspaper would presumably consist of blank pages as a gesture of respect to the victims. However, the problem with a 'silent' newspaper is that it does not convey any news. In a reverential 'two minutes silence' the participants know who they are showing respect to, whereas it is possible that thousands of readers had not yet heard of the bombings in early August 1945. Already marginalised news would have been eradicated, leaving many ignorant of the event. Reverential silence commands respect, as Michael Freeman claims, but it 'denies all attempts at understanding' and therefore builds inhibitors to future holocausts.[18]

In his representation of the first atom bomb attack in *Hiroshima Diary*, the survivor Michihiko Hachiya demonstrates how linguistic silence is sometimes necessary to the victims, as opposed to the privileged, non-'hibakusha' (non-victim) perspective of the West. He argues that silence is a natural psychological reaction to an extreme situation with which humans cannot cope. His fellow survivors are initially stunned into speechlessness, and he is surprised to hear no moans of the injured, only complete silence; even a few hours later in a local hospital he asks 'why was everyone so quiet?'[19] Robert J. Lifton attributes this effect to psychic numbing, in which victims of the bombing cannot find an adequate emotional response to the apocalyptic imagery they receive, so they remain inarticulate.[20] Judging by the wealth of diaries, testimonies, poetry and so on which has arisen in Japan on the event, it is debatable how long this psychic numbing lasts. Ironically, such literature fills the silence it describes: in Hachiya's case, by writing in a hypotactic, documentary style he emphasises the horrific nature of the event behind the general atmosphere of inarticulacy.

In the essay 'The Future of Nuclear Criticism', Richard Klein argues that linguistic silence is necessary on a global scale - regardless of cultural difference - in the context of a future nuclear holocaust. He laments that the existing post-holocaust literature is written in the 'future anterior' (or the future perfect tense, as in the verb phrase 'will have'), a mode which assumes that some people will survive a nuclear war, and accuses such writers of presuming such an occurrence is inevitable. There are two problems with his thesis. The first is that he does not offer an alternative theory of how to achieve the impossible and represent post-holocaust 'nothingness' in a text (perhaps this is a legitimate example of 'impossibility fiction'). The second is that post-holocaust literature is not as reassuring and collusive as he suggests. It can constantly remind the reader of the annihilation that has occurred, and of his/her privileged pre-holocaust perspective. For example, in John Wyndham's novel *The Chrysalids*,[21] the defects of the mutants who scavenge the waste lands created by 'Tribulation' were inspired by accounts of the birth-defects caused by irradiation of foetuses, including microcephaly, myopia, liver cirrhosis, and tuberculosis.[22]

If, as I have so far argued, it is inadequate to represent the 1945 bombings and a projected nuclear holocaust with various linguistic silences, a form of language must be found which can successfully engage with them. This, I believe, can be located in the aesthetics of awkwardness I discussed in the last section. I shall use Masuji Ibuse's novel *Black Rain*[23] as an example of the style in this context, but first I would like to stress that linguistic awkwardness is not always the result of a deliberate strategy. For example, in a report on the bombing of Hiroshima, the *Daily Worker* adopted a heightened rhetoric reminiscent of some biblical passages:

> the fundamental power of the universe, the power manifested in the sunshine
> that has been recognised from the remotest ages as the sustaining force of
> earthly life, is entrusted at last to human hands.[24]

The tone is awkward because it is embarrassingly melodramatic. The grandiose diction hides the basic premise that humanity can now commit genocide instead of waiting for God to do so. The noun phrases pile up relentlessly to enforce the notion that nuclear power is a wonderful and natural entity: this denies the manufactured and dangerous nature of the substance. The rhetoric is inadequate because it actually glorifies the possibility of mass suicide, working in abstracts such as 'human hands' instead of stating who exactly possesses nuclear power.

In contrast to this example of linguistic awkwardness, which silences the vast destruction that atom bomb caused, in the novel *Black Rain* Masuji Ibuse forges a deliberate 'barbaric' style which attempts to represent the reality of the Hiroshima bombing. Religious rhetoric features prominently in the novel, but Ibuse subverts and recycles it to highlight its inefficacy in the face of the devastation. The following passage is representative of this process:

> The stones of the river bed gradually gave way to sand, then to running water with a slowly shelving bed. As I took my clothes off, I murmured to myself the 'Sermon on Mortality.' 'Sooner or later, on this day or the morrow, to me or my neighbour... So shall the rosy cheeks of morning yield to the skull of eventide. One breath from the wind of change, and the bright eyes shall be closed...' [25]

Awkwardness manifests itself here in the form of embarrassment. The language is excruciatingly sentimental, yet the narrator Shigematsu sees it as appropriate to the symbolic re-birth he undergoes by entering the water, and thereby purging himself of the holocaust. Awkwardness also arises in the form of the inappropriate in the slippage between images of life and death. The religious rhetoric traces a development from life to death, whereas the passage describes an opposite movement: Ibuse signals its failure to register this displacement. The rhetoric is deemed even more disconcerting by the likening of 'rosy cheeks' to youth, and 'the skull of eventide' to death. In the post-holocaust landscape he has just encountered, corpses - not babies - have burnt 'rosy cheeks'; Shigematsu wishes to symbolically strip his body to the bone in order to be re-born. Conventional images of mortality are thus reversed in a post-holocaust context.

In this chapter I have examined the limitations of the prevalent attitudes surrounding the impossibility of representations of the Jewish Holocaust, the bombing of Hiroshima and Nagasaki, and a projected nuclear holocaust, and suggested that the aesthetics of awkwardness, the embarrassing, struggling and sometimes tortured linguistics that Adorno recognises in post-Holocaust poetry are a means of avoiding this linguistic silence. According to my thesis, then, post/pre-H/holocaust literature is in desperate need of re-valuation.

Antony Rowland

NOTES

1. George Steiner, *Language and Silence*, Harmondsworth: Penguin, 1969, p.15.
2. *Ibid.*, p.70.
3. Theodor Adorno, 'Cultural Criticism and Society', p.34; Steiner, *op.cit.*, p.75; Alvin Rosenfeld, *A Double Dying*, Bloomington and Indianapolis: Indiana University Press, 1980, p.13; James Young, *Writing and Rewriting the Holocaust*, Bloomington and Indianapolis: Indiana University Press, 1988, p.62.
4. Tadeusz Borowski, *This Way for the Gas, Ladies and Gentlemen*, 1967, p.84.
5. Gershom Shaked, 'Facing the Nightmare: Israeli Literature on the Holocaust', in *The Nazi Concentration Camps*, Jerusalem: Yad Vasham, 1984, pp.683-96 (p.690). See also L. Dawidowicz, (ed), *A Holocaust Reader*, New York: Behrman House, 1976; S.D. Ezrahi, *By Words Alone: The Holocaust In Literature*, Chicago: University of Chicago Press, 1980; M. Gilbert, *Auschwitz And the Allies*, London: Michael Joseph. 1981; J. Harris, 'An Elegy for Myself: British Poetry and the Holocaust', *English*, 41, 1992, pp. 213-33; V.M. Patraka, 'Contemporary Drama, Fascism, and the Holocaust', *Theatre Journal* 39, 1987, pp.65-77; A. Rosenberg, 'The Genocidal Universe: a Framework for Understanding the Holocaust', in J.N. Porter (ed), *Genocide And Human Rights: A Global Anthology*, Washington: University of America Press, 1982.
6. In Rosenfeld, *op.cit.*, p.79.
7. Primo Levi, *If This is a Man* (trans. S. Woolf), London: Abacus, 1958, p.129, p.208.
8. Rosenfeld, *op.cit.*, pp.55-8.
9. *Ibid.*, p.8.
10. Young, *op.cit.*, p.66.
11. *Ibid.*, p.9.
12. See H. Langbein, 'Holocaust Themes: Their Expression in Poetry and in the Psychological Conflicts of Patients in Psychotherapy', in *The Nazi Concentration Camps*, Jerusalem: Yad Vasham, 1984, pp.273-88 (p.287).
13. Young, *op.cit.*, p.217.
14. Steiner, *op.cit.*, p.140.
15. Thomas Morrissey, 'Armageddon from Huxley to Hoban', *Extrapolation* 25(3), 1984, pp.197-213.
16. David Dowling, *Fictions of Nuclear Disaster*, London: Macmillan, 1986, p.196. See also his 'The Atomic Scientist: Machine or Moralist', *Science Fiction Studies*, 3(2), 1986, pp.139-47.
17. See R.J. Lifton and N. Humphreys (eds), *In A Dark Time*, Harvard: Harvard University Press, 1984, p.14. See also M. Abrash, 'Through Logic To Apocalypse: Science-Fiction Scenarios of Nuclear Deterrence Breakdown', *Science Fiction Studies* 3(2), 1986, pp.129-38; M. Bartter, 'Nuclear Holocaust as Urban Renewal', *Science Fiction Studies*, 3(2), 1986, pp.148-58; B.J. Bernstein, *The Atom Bomb: The Critical Issues*, Boston/ Toronto: Little, Brown & Co., 1976; J. Derrida, 'No Apocalypse, Not Now (full speed ahead, seven missiles, seven missives)', *Diacritics*, Summer 1984; B.H. Franklin, 'Strange Scenarios: Science Fiction, the Theory of Alienation, and the Nuclear Gods', *Science Fiction Studies* 3(2), 1986, pp.117-28; David Ketterer, 'The Apocalyptic Imagination, Science Fiction and American Literature', in M. Rose (ed), *Science Fiction*, Englewood Cliffs: Prentice Hall, 1976.
18. Michael Freeman, 'Speaking About the Unspeakable: Genocide and Philosophy', *Journal of Applied Philosophy* 8(1), 1991, p.15. See also: David Ketterer,'Myths of Re(-)creation: Mythology in the (Post-) Nuclear World', in J. Kleist and B.A. Butterfield (eds), *Mythology From The Ancient To The Post-Modern*, New York: Peter Lang, 1992, pp.185-194; Eric S. Rabkin, M.H. Greenberg

and J.D. Olander (eds), *The End Of The World*, Evanston, Ill: Southern Illinois University Press, 1983; P. Schwenger, 'Writing the Unthinkable', *Critical Enquiry*, Autumn 1986, pp.33-48; D.L. Zins, 'Rescuing Science From Technocracy: *Cats Cradle* and the Play of Apocalypse', *Science Fiction Studies* 3(2), 1986, pp.170-81.

19. Michihiko Hachiya, *Hiroshima Diary* (trans. W. Wells), London: Victor Gollancz, 1955, p.17.

20. Robert Lifton, *Death in Life*, New York: Basic Books, 1967.

21. John Wyndham, *The Chrysalids*, London: Penguin, 1955.

22. See J.J. Farrell, *The Nuclear Devil's Dictionary*, Minneapolis: Usonia Press, 1985, p.65.

23. Masuji Ibuse, *Black Rain*, Tokyo and New York: Kodansha Internationai Ltd., 1969.

24. In Lifton and Humphreys, *op.cit.*, p.14.

25. Ibuse, *op.cit.*, p.277.

7.

GEORGE S. SCHUYLER AND THE FATE
OF EARLY AFRICAN-AMERICAN SCIENCE FICTION

'What good is science fiction to Black people?' Before going on to explain how it can be very good, indeed, Octavia Butler - by her reckoning one of only four African-American science-fiction writers - mentions the pointed frequency of this question. 'I was usually asked this,' she continues, 'by a Black person'.[1] The query implies that any fiction should possess discernible, practical social value and ameliorative force and that the world of science fiction has been a white world or, perhaps, a world in which race plays little part. Fictionality of any sort would appear to weaken political statement. Science fiction, conceived as fantasy, escapism, mere entertainment, would seem simply no business of the responsible black writer whose degree of essentialized 'Africanness' and dependence on folk traditions separate her or him from the heritage of Western science and technology which science fiction has been said to celebrate. In this way of thinking, science fiction expresses the ethos and values of the West in a literary genre also Western. The author's choosing the genre becomes a choice, willy-nilly, to accent the American in 'African-American' and to denigrate pride in race. 'Because industrial society emerged first in Great Britain, Europe, and the United States, science fiction,' writes H. Bruce Franklin, 'has been until recently a `Western' literary form, that is, one practised exclusively by white Europeans and their American descendants, and one utilizing the literary and other cultural conventions of these people'.[2] How, then, have African-American writers managed to accommodate themselves to the formulas of science fiction? Or accommodate the formulas to themselves? Or to challenge and change the formulas?

The 'insidious problem' which Butler sees with science fiction is that it has 'always been nearly all white, just as until recently it's been nearly all male'.[3] Although it treated the extraterrestrial, older science fiction rarely made us think about 'women, blacks, Indians, Asians, Hispanics,' and then only as 'oddities' or 'stereotypes'.[4] Kathleen Spencer joined in an exchange of a few years ago in the pages of *Science-Fiction Studies* by mentioning that since science fiction 'has proved such a powerfully liberating genre for women, allowing writers to create and readers to experience alternatives to patriarchy' she 'would have expected it to prove equally liberating for Blacks'.[5] Why this conspicuous absence? Three related issues become relevant here: blacks as characters in fiction by whites ('science fiction as a genre has seldom evoked an authentic African setting or employed non-stereotypical blacks as characters'[6]), science fiction by blacks, and black science fiction. By 'African-American science fiction' I refer to the third: science fiction which is African-American in the sense that Arna Bontemps's *Black Thunder* is and Frank Yerby's *The Foxes of Harrow* is not, to mention two examples of another popular form, the historical novel, from the 1930s and 1940s. That is to say, race must figure importantly in the text itself, its content and/or language, albeit one among perhaps many concerns.[7]

Science fiction either by or about, or by *and* about, African-Americans was rare before the 1930s - not that it has been common since. Those drawn to racial themes found themselves having to adopt or adapt, if not altogether reject, a genre in which blacks figured little as subjects or authors. Clearly, almost no science fiction reflected black perspectives. Could it? Generally, rejection was the choice, and adaptation more usual than all-out adoption. Science fiction had developed little as progressive and enlightened political and social commentary about the realities of race. On the one hand, speculative cosmic scale, an orientation to the future, and the presence of unhuman races and robots make 'the differences between human races seem appropriately trivial'.[8] On the other hand, much science fiction was racist and preoccupied with race, either overtly or in the guise of confrontations with aliens and Others of various stripes and hues. The immensely popular Edgar Rice Burroughs was obsessed by the theme.[9] Utopian fiction and the future-war tale, related sub-genres delimited by science-fiction critics and forms written by George Schuyler, have an especially tawdry history of racist polemic.[10] The most well-known early British example of the story of future war is George T. Chesney's *The Battle of Dorking* (1871). (Also 1871 is Bulwer-Lytton's fantasy of a subterranean coming race, which owes as much to the two nations of Disraeli's *Sybil* as to strictly science-fictional sources - class and race were sometimes transmuted in the telling, as in the later *Time Machine*). The 'hallmark' of the many imitations spawned by *The Battle of Dorking* before World War I 'was crass Anglo-Saxon, Gallic, or Teutonic chauvinism'.[11] In William Delisle Hay's *Three Hundred Years Hence* (1881) unending Victorian progress takes the form of an applied science which fructifies the Sahara and routs all non-white races.[12] The 1880s also saw the initial significant development of the tale of the future in the United States. In one turn-of-the-century narrative, King Wallace's *The Next War* (1892), civil rebellion is portrayed in black/white terms, as a plot to poison their employers fails and African-Americans disappear into Southern swamps. J. Stewart Barney's *1915 L.P.M.; The End of the Great War* posits and validates racial separatism and white supremacy.[13] During the period from 1871 until 1939 'the future-war motif,' concludes Thomas D. Clareson, 'gave voice to some of the deepest anxieties and hatreds of the Western imagination'.[14] Apparently the sole exception to this strain, a book which anticipates Schuyler's *Black Empire*, is T. Shirby Hodge's *The White Man's Burden: A Satirical Forecast* (1915), which is 'pro-black, and ends with a utopia being founded by blacks in Africa, after they have overcome white Americans'.[15]

The 1930s were something of a watershed in science fiction's treatment of race. Although the future-war story now appeared more commonly in the pages of mass market pulp magazines, the occasional book still took up the old irrational images. Anti-Semitism and fears of the 'yellow peril' come together in the 'indiscriminate genocide' of Solomon Cruso's *The Last of the Japs and the Jews* (1933), a novel dedicated to 'the Rulers, Statesmen, Diplomats, and Militarists of the Caucasian Race, the white Aryans, who fell on the battlefields of Europe, Asia, Africa, America, and Australia in the period of 1980-1985, A.D.'[16] (Anti-Oriental rather than anti-black sentiment probably predominated in the future-war genre because the modern industrialized, thus potentially threatful, nation-state arose more conspicuously in the East - racism could be joined with militaristic chauvinism.) A *Wonder Stories* offering of the same year exults in its 'references to storm troopers tramping over Africa'.[17] In 1939 *Argosy* carried a trio of stories by Arthur Leo Zagat about 'black and yellow men' who 'have come out of the East to make this world a Hell'.[18] One of *Astounding Stories'* own contributors complained of the pulp writers' tendency to create stock characters who embodied ethnic and racial stereotypes. Readers of this magazine fiction seemed unwilling even during the 1930s to grapple seriously with social and political issues like racism and the Nazi question.[19] Then, again, perhaps international social and intellectual realities of the decade go a long way toward explaining this lack, this defensiveness or insecurity, this appeal of escapism and power fantasy. The Great Depression had followed hard upon the disillusionments of World War I. Future wars, real or imagined, simply *had* to have more positive - at least more definitive - outcomes in the wish-fulfilments of the chauvinistic (in the same sense that the Gulf War was the twenty-year belated residue and conclusion of the Vietnam War). And the war itself had been viewed by intellectuals like Oswald Spengler as a manifestation of the decline of the West.

Yet the decade also witnessed a spat of revisionist stories like Nat Schachner's 'Ancestral Voices' (*Astounding Stories*, 1933), a predecessor of stories of the 1940s and early 1950s like Lester del Rey's 'Nerves' (a sympathetic Japanese-American), Anthony Boucher's 'Q.U.R.' (a black man ruler of Earth's planetary government), Mark Reynolds's and Frederic Brown's 'Dark Interlude' (a one-race future in which the Southern belle has no choice but marry a 'colored' man). Post-World War II 'science fiction continued this trend away from the old caricatures'.[20] Critics have discerned other trends as well: 'the xenophobia that created alien races in the image of Bug-Eyed Monsters had already begun to yield in the thirties to more hospitable notions of foreignness'.[21] (One thinks of the kindly, gentle, eccentric Tweel of Stanley G. Weinbaum's 1934 'A Martian Odyssey.') If the skies, to paraphrase Wallace Stevens, were proving more friendly then than now, Earth's contentions were increasingly being viewed as monstrous. Instead of the future war functioning as just another extension of national or nationalistic policy, many science-fictional conflicts of the 1930s resulted in calamitous destruction and carnage.[22] If these pre-atomic bomb scenarios did not portray the utter obliteration of the planet, they did portray widespread devastation and wars which left no real winners. Apocalypse could be seen as an end, but perhaps no beginning.

How, then, could the African-American writer of the 1930s use science-fictional discourse for socially and politically responsible purposes? Limits on imagining possibilities of betterment were also imposed by the realities of history: the disenfranchisement resulting from continued racism, the Great Depression, Fascism, and the fallout from the Great War. If there existed an American faith in strong-minded people's and 'science and technology's power to change things,' in contemporary formula science fiction these changes existed between the boundaries of 'very traditional American political and economic values'.[23] Technology itself could run amuck. Perhaps Mark R. Hillegas is correct in saying that the genre 'provides an extraordinarily flexible instrument for social criticism' and 'is particularly able to deal with problems of life in a new age of science and technology' (though African-Americans had little sense of access to or control over advanced technology), but his comment that it is able to reach 'a much larger audience than does most mainstream literature'[24] must here be qualified by mentioning that this audience was predominantly young, male, and white.[25] The African-American writer hoping to lean on a significant black tradition in the genre would likewise be disappointed. Even anomalous classics to equal Charlotte Perkins Gilman's *Herland* were not to be found. Black language, including colloquial usages, seemed to have as little place as black ideology. If the formulas of pulp fiction could be variously blended, formulas nonetheless they remained.[26] No black writer made a living from science fiction. We have already surveyed the paucity of African-American characters as well as authors, and the persistence of racist stereotypes.

For George S. Schuyler to adopt this genre, therefore, meant a great deal of adapting, indeed. He had to reconcile himself to generic traditions and at the same time determine how to make them serve his own purposes. Given the history of science fiction and its associations with the white middle class, appropriating the genre was itself an assertion of an African-American self, an assertion paralleling Olaudah Equiano's eventual mastering of his master's theretofore silent book in the eighteenth century (the book itself being an artefact of Western technology). (Others, like Kenya's Ngugi wa Thiong'o, have countered that the author true to her or his Africanness would employ one of the tribal languages - to do otherwise being a selling out to French or English, alien cultural expressions. Similarly, many African-American critics insist on the use of a distinctively African-American idiom and the validity of a unique and discrete oral and literary heritage.) 'Schuyler found in science fiction an emancipatory vision of science that he used to work out his frustrated youthful ambitions. He used science fiction as a literary device for both satirical and allegorical purposes'.[27] This space for Schuyler's project is signalled by a comment of Robert M. Philmus *in Into the Unknown*: 'in many satiric science fantasies, a seemingly improbable social order (or chaos), sometimes the logical result of an imagined technological discovery, displaces what is commonly thought of as a social reality; and the consequent deformation reveals aspects of the true nature of the existing social order'.[28] Technological discoveries are central to Schuyler's science-fiction novels, *Black No More* and *Black Empire*, which clearly do critique the 'nature of the existing social order.' Applied science creates the possibility of the two books' 'answers' to the race question: eliminate blacks and eliminate whites. The former option is the choice to be black no more, the fantasy of a world beyond race; the latter a vision of racial confrontation and conflict. In these two approaches to the theme Schuyler unwittingly recapitulated the attitudes toward race expressed in (white) science fiction: acknowledgement of human kinship in the face of cosmic difference and the contemplation of Earth or star wars against the alien Other. But Schuyler was not simply one who revised the old; he was a true revisionist doing what had not been done before. His manipulations of the counters of the form place him near the beginnings of a science fiction which could also be African-American.

Technology and the future, not to mention sarcasm, figure in the title of Schuyler's first science-fictional venture: *Black No More: Being an Account of the Strange and Wonderful Workings of Science in the Land of the Free, A.D. 1933-1940.*[29] In this speculative, fanciful and funny novel of 1931, called in a review of a recent reprint at once one of America's best satires and best science fiction novels,[30] the science-fictional trappings serve the ends of the satire.

Racialism and racism are Schuyler's targets rather than whites or blacks *per se*. Improbable potion and improbable plot produce preposterous precedent: the book is a *Gedanken*-experiment extrapolating hypothetical results of blacks becoming white. The ploy allows Schuyler access to the additional sub-theme of the privileging of fairer skin color, a contemporary phenomenon of African-American society. He attacks any and all 'professional' race people, those who make a living from maintaining and promoting racial difference and contention, whether or not this is disguised as 'race pride.' In so doing Schuyler characteristically lumps together black and white groups which have racially exclusionary policies. The Marcus Garvey character, for example, on one occasion telephones the Imperial Grand Wizard - collect. Black 'racial integrity talks would click with the crackers' (p.117). Likewise, those who have a vested interest in erasing racial difference are ridiculed. The premise takes the form of Dr. Junius Crookman's process of 'electrical nutrition and glandular control' which can change even 'hair and features' in three days (p.27). Other traits, like behaviour and dialect, Crookman - trained in a Germany soon notorious for notions of 'racial' purity - attributes to environmental influences. Our Harlem hero, Max Disher, becomes the first candidate for the treatment, having been spurned by his pretentious 'high 'yallah' flapper' (p.17) and by a white woman. Contemplating the pleasures of being white, Disher calls on Crookman at the Phyllis Wheatley Hotel.[31]

The balance of *Black No More* follows Disher's career as a newly-white man and in broad strokes debunks individuals or groups who would be put out of business by a one-race society - the fictional counterparts of Madame C. J. Walker (the hair-straightening magnate who in the novel is elected for the fourth time as Vice-President of the American Race Pride League), Marcus Garvey (as Santop Licorice promoting the Back-to-Africa Society - though he has no intention of leaving his American women - until selfish interest leads even him to take the treatment), Walter White (who for two reasons titled his 1948 autobiography *A Man Called White*), Father Divine (or some Harlem notable like him, in the book pastor of the Ethiopian True Faith Wash Foot Methodist Church), James Weldon Johnson (as the pretentiously named Dr. Napoleon Wellington Jackson maintaining that the Garden of Eden was located in West Africa), the Ku Klux Klan (called the Knights of Nordica), and the N.A.A.C.P. (dubbed the National Social Equality League and headed by the snobbish Dr. Shakespeare Agamemnon Beard, the W.E.B. DuBois figure). Thousands, millions, become white as Black No More, Incorporated expands its operations to fifty sanatoriums in the United States and purchases four airplanes, a radio station, and several potentially hostile politicians. Crookman's thought that the country could now turn its attention to more constructive issues - 'evidence that he knew little about the human race' (p.55) - is not borne out by events. As Matthew Fisher and feeling for the first time like 'an American citizen' (p.48), Max travels to Atlanta in search of the Southern belle who had rejected him at the Honky Tonk Club in New York. Parading as a member of the New York Anthropological Society sympathetic with the goals of the Knights of Nordica, Max finds employment as orator and organizer for the Knights, 'all ready and eager to be organized for any purpose except improvement of their intellects and standard of living' (p.76). (An unsuspecting Klan had actually invited Walter White to infiltrate their group in 1923.) Speaking before a raucous meeting like 'the religious orgies of the more ignorant Negroes' (p.77) Max spots his long-sought love on the front row - the daughter of the Imperial Grand Wizard, the 'ignorant ex-evangelist' Henry Givins (p.76). Meanwhile, back in New York, a concerned N.S.E.L. meets: 'getting the Negro leaders together for any purpose except boasting of each other's accomplishments had previously been impossible' (p.89).

Complications arise because Black No More does not affect inherited traits: Black No More whites have black babies whose race can be disguised only by keeping parents and children separated in lying-in hospitals until the infants are transformed. Max becomes Grand Exalted Giraw of the Knights of Nordica and is joined in Atlanta by his now-white New York friend, but grows apprehensive upon the pregnancy of his wife, Helen Givins Fisher. He continues active in the Knights' projects: aiding a generous management in South Carolina by raising the spectre of race to preempt class consciousness, and forming an alliance with the rival and more elitist white supremacist Anglo-Saxon Association of Virginia (Arthur Snobbcraft, President). Givins and Snobbcraft become the national Democratic Party ticket to oppose Black No More's man, incumbent Republican President Goosie (Herbert Hoover). Snobbcraft's plot to defame the opposition by finding documentary evidence of miscegenation in old birth records backfires when his investigator - Dr. Samuel Buggerie - turns up proof of the mixed heritage of even Givins and Snobbcraft. When the Republicans steal and publicize this evidence, Snobbcraft and Buggerie must flee an angry white mob. A forced landing in rural Mississippi eventuates - although they had tried to disguise themselves with shoe polish - in their being lynched by the adherents of the racist and licentious Reverend McPhule's True Faith Christ Lover's Church (the hypocrisy of the 'Christ lovers' is matched by the absurdity of the victims' having to paint themselves black to hide the fact that they are the 'black' escapees). Both Max and Helen acknowledge and accept their own blackness, and conclude that with baby and love 'all talk of race and color was damned foolishness' (p.193). The arbitrariness of racial definition, its social rather than biological dimension, becomes Schuyler's point. Crookman is appointed Surgeon-General of the United

States and writes a monograph on variations and differences in skin tone between 'real' and Black No More whites, suggesting that on average the latter are lighter. Prejudice immediately springs up against those 'who were exceedingly pale' (p.219) and, thus, inferior; a renamed and now white Dr. Beard founds a league to combat this new racism; 'those of the upper class began to look around for ways to get darker' (p.221). The one-race society becomes no utopia, and humans are nefariously inventive in creating divergence. Many are disoriented and made insecure by no longer being able to define themselves by the extra-personal and by difference, by what they are *not* (since they are evidently uncertain of what they are, their intrinsic worth). Where all are of one race, all are of no race; self-conscious contrast is no longer available as a way to identify the self and assert superiority. Race must be recreated. Amusing fare were it not all too familiar: Schuyler titles this final section 'And So On And So On.'

Thus, in brief, *Black No More*: set in the future, extending the capabilities of present science, speculative - technically science fiction in the line of, say, David H. Keller's 1928 *Amazing Stories Quarterly* story on turning blacks white (a work which possibly influenced Schuyler[32]). Yet the book communicates no sense that its author's principal interest was science or science fictionality; Schuyler's message is all-important, his vehicle incidental. The satirical nature of the text overrides other generic considerations in the same sense *that Gulliver's Travels* does not come immediately to mind as pre-eminently a work of science fiction. This is and was the more true for the black intelligentsia and for any acquainted with African-American culture and cultural history, who understand the more clearly that *Black No More* is an African-American document full of allusions to contemporary life and traditions of black literature. Schuyler was not taking lightly the responsibilities of the black novelist by amusing himself with a white form which could communicate only 'white' meanings.[33] He was not used by the science-fiction format: he put his own stamp on it for his own ends. W. E. B. DuBois, Madame Walker, James Weldon Johnson, Walter White, Father Divine, Marcus Garvey and the rest do not step out of these pages to the uninitiated. Charles R. Larson goes too far - and speaks with the voice of 1971 - when he concludes in his introduction to the novel that Schuyler mounts his primary assault on the worth of black American life.[34] *Black No More* in fact opens with a dedication 'to all Caucasians in the great republic who can trace their ancestry back ten generations and confidently assert that there are no Black leaves, twigs, limbs or branches on their family trees.' The archival discoveries depicted in the novel, in effect, also render whites black. Madame Walker (as Sisseretta Blandish) is pilloried, as are 'blue-vein' societies. The developer of the transforming process is a Crook-man. Schuyler indiscriminately attacks racism and separatism whether they are promoted by blacks or whites, and the book's note of authenticity communicates to all.

Max Disher feels immense trepidation in choosing to be white: 'it was either the beginning or the end' (p.34). His uncertainties continue as he feels a 'momentary pang of mingled disgust, disillusionment and nostalgia' (p.40) and finds whites 'less courteous and less interesting' (p.63) than blacks. When he can stand forth as his own racial self at book's end he feels 'a great load lifting from his soul' (p.192). The Black No More technology has simply furnished Schuyler a convenient means of dealing with the psychological and social dynamics of the old African-American (and American) theme of the 'tragic mullato' and 'passing,' passing now artificially induced and on a massive scale. The motif is extended, but Schuyler did not need science fiction to accomplish his purposes. Mark Twain and Kate Chopin, among white writers, had created characters beset by the challenges of being 'black' but living 'white.' Perhaps the most celebrated turn-of-the-century African-American novel on the theme is Charles W. Chesnutt's *The House Behind the Cedars* (1900). Nella Larsen's novel entitled *Passing*, which 'treats the schizophrenia which results from racial dualism',[35] had appeared less than two years before Schuyler's book. 1927 had seen the republication of James Weldon Johnson's *Autobiography of an Ex-Coloured Man* (1912). 'Ex-coloured' carries the same weight as 'black no more': both titles communicate loss and absence (thus devaluating whiteness), and both protagonists define themselves by what they no longer are and express ambivalence about their choices. (In *Black No More*, Johnson's given names also suggest an internal battle - Napoleon and Wellington). Rather than 'white' (unnamed and absent), they are 'ex-coloured' or 'black no more.' Ironically (perhaps), Crookman is a 'race man,' a lover of his race who 'wanted to remove all obstacles in their path by depriving them of their racial characteristics' (p.55). The point, and Johnson's point, is that the price of surviving in a racist society can be not surviving: merging, surrendering a racial sense of self as significant and universal as that of a member of any other race. Johnson's nameless protagonist finally feels that he has sold his birthright. Schuyler did not surrender. Like Johnson, he assumed freedom to express African-American racial motifs in what Johnson called 'classic' (European) forms. Johnson's project, too, was 'to fuse the celebration of blackness with an essentially integrationist perspective on both society and literature'.[36] Just this option of naturalizing another (a white) sub-culture's literary traditions by combining elements of two traditions was an option not available to whites in exactly the same way, no more than being black was an option. Independent and non-conformist, never wholly defining himself by race in any case, Schuyler did not hesitate to take up the tools that had in practice been reserved for whites. In so

doing, in bringing together the (black) psychological and social with the (white)
science fictional, he created his own form and furnished the link that joins Wells's
invisible man with Ellison's.

   Black Empire, on the other hand, represents at once a complete surrender
to white generic conventions and, on the surface, an asserting of black militancy.[37]
(Schuyler's 1934 serial, 'Strange Valley,' had portrayed a central figure transitional
between those of *Black No More* and *Black Empire*.) Its science fictionality lies in
its being a near-future and future-war tale, replete with violence and futuristic
technology. Whereas *Black No More* speculated on the meaning of a world
without racial difference, *Black Empire* imagines the racial theme epitomized -
race warfare. This novel, as R. D. Mullen puts it, is 'of great interest for the ways
in which Schuyler, in order to write on psychological and sociological themes for a
black audience, inverts the modes of racist fiction intended for a white audience'.[38]
The book is 'an Afrocentrist's dream'; its Dr. Henry Belsidus a 'W. E. B. DuBois,
Booker T. Washington, George Washington Carver, and Marcus Garvey rolled into
one fascist superman'.[39] Had Schuyler drastically changed in five years? Not
really, for the book's ideology is deflected and defused by considerations of genre,
audience, and authorial intent. Read innocently, it is a black power fantasy which
'recreates an important moment in the history of African-American thought.' But
the mediating factors just mentioned preempt the possibility of the text's apparent
meanings, for it is also pulp fiction 'filled with an abundance of the science fiction
motifs of what has been dubbed 'that amazing decade,' 1926-1936'.[40] *Black
Empire* becomes ludicrous both because the formula was simplistic and because
African-Americans are implausibly forced into white roles.

   It is important to know that *Black Empire* - actually two stories, 'The Black
Internationale' and 'Black Empire' - appeared in weekly instalments between 1936
and 1938 in a black newspaper, the *Pittsburgh Courier*, and that its author used a
pseudonym, Samuel I. Brooks. Schuyler was 'greatly amused by the public
enthusiasm' for the book, 'which is hokum and hack work of the purest vein. I
deliberately set out to crowd as much race chauvinism and sheer improbability into
it as my fertile imagination could conjure. The result vindicates my low opinion of
the human race'.[41] The 'sheer improbability' of pulp formula science fiction,
'hack work of the purest vein,' could not be taken seriously; the 'race chauvinism'
was so self-evidently excessive as to deprive the narrative of the validity of milder
statement. Yet the book was, largely, taken as straightforward and sincere, if a
wish fulfilment. Those who might have taken it otherwise had little access to the
Pittsburgh Courier in 1936 (only in 1991 has *Black Empire* been published as a
book - a fact which itself helps to canonize texts and make them black no more). It

«»was«» genuine - the genuine expression of Schuyler's other self, Samuel I.
Brooks (whose name shares a word - Samuel - with Schuyler's and whose initials
begin the word 'sibling').   Since pseudonymity is tantamount to anonymity
Schuyler absolved himself of the need for sincerity, since 'Schuyler' took no
responsibility for the text.   We might say what in effect Schuyler's black
newspaper readers said - that he was subverting a Western and middle-class form
for African-American uses.   Real-world persecution and persecution complexes
made the content, as power fantasy and revenge, overwhelm distant elitist
intellectuals' possible considerations of formal elements, though the narrative's
melodramatic action and suspense made its entertainment value obvious to all. But
to Schuyler genre subverted meaning. To write a science-fictional racist diatribe
packed with 'displays of bravery and intelligence and romance that leap out of the
popular imagination of the day',[42] then simply to reverse the colors, was not to
domesticate an African-American form or make the characters convincing. Texts
yield answers only to the questions we ask of them. To the few non-white readers
of 1936, therefore, the futuristic format might co-opt other meaning and render it
innocuous by communicating altogether something else about African-American
culture: that a worthy and advanced black civilization can exist only as a
science-fictional fantasy.

The ruthless and megalomaniacal Dr. Belsidus masterminds a scheme to
employ the black talented tenth in developing economic and political power in the
United States (he has already employed himself in limiting white power and
population through performing illegal abortions). Belsidus's far-flung enterprises
include farms, factories, power plants, and airports; the dionysian 'Church of Love'
provides a propaganda which guarantees racial unity and psychological
commitment while Black Internationale operatives promote and exploit ethnic and
religious divisions in white America. Meanwhile - and secretly! - Belsidus trains
five thousand soldiers in Texas. This expeditionary force sails for Africa on the
Nat Turner, the *Fred Douglass*, the *Sojouner Truth*, the *Phyllis Wheatley*. With
prohibitive force Belsidus 'liberates' Liberia - that is, he simply annexes it and
appoints himself 'King of Kings' (p.111). From the capital safely inland at Kakata,
Belsidus embarks on his plan to consolidate all of Africa under one rule. (Africa's
permission is not sought; African cultures are not really depicted, nor do they
figure in the formula.) He sets about ridding the continent of whites, defeating
European imperialism (or replacing it with his own), and so sabotaging and
dividing the European powers as to render them little future threat. A late chapter
of 'The Black Internationale' is entitled 'European Nations Plunge into War as
Africa Is Redeemed' (p.130). Our young narrator hero, Carl Slater, whispers to his
glamorous aviatrix fiancee, "Tomorrow." 'She smiled and whispered back: `Yes,

love. Tomorrow we, like Africa, shall be united, after so long. United forever"
(p.142).[43]

In 'Black Empire' this uniting of Africa is achieved through the labours of
black genius (the subtitle of 'The Black Internationale' had been 'Story of Black
Genius Against the World'). An advanced Western-style civilization, what
science-fiction critics call a near-future utopia (it goes without saying that one
person's utopia is another's dystopia), develops from the application of technology
and its attendant gadgets: quick-freezing techniques and a perfect diet, the virtual
elimination of disease (though incurables, along with traitors, are simply put to
death), superior radio and television, the photo-electric eye door opener, a
precursor to the fax machine, a 'stratosphere plane.' The Empire, the 'greatest
revolutionary organization the world had ever seen' (p.145), seeks to defeat an
envious Europe by bombing the great cities with rats, 'a strange and deadly army'
(p.169) infected with the plaque, cholera, and spotted typhus. Terrorism
supplements bacterial warfare, as Black Internationale subversives cripple British
production capability by capitalizing on European fascination with the supposedly
primitive: gassing inexpendable machinists at a performance of Della Crambull
and her black dance troupe, staged as a West African village. (Josephine Baker
had been a Parisian celebrity for a decade.) Carl Slater and company manage to fly
off, lighting London skies with thermite incendiary bombs but being themselves
shot down by French aircraft over Africa. A subsequent forced landing results in
the Black Internationale group's falling prey to a band of cannibals who mistake
them for a French force. *Deus ex machina* takes the form of a squadron of Black
Empire flyers snatching their comrades to safety 'just as natives prepare to light
fire and roast them' (p.235).[44] Meanwhile Belsidus's experts perfect the Super
Weapon, a Doomsday Device, a 'death-ray' machine which generates a proton
disintegrating beam as well as a radio beam capable of disabling machines and
their power sources. 'Like huge prehistoric monsters' (p.248), Belsidus's Big Guns
roll into Monrovia and summarily annihilate the offshore navies of France and
England. No thought here, as in some progressive thirties' white science fiction, of
conciliation or technology's proving an enemy in disguise. The Black Empire
ousts remaining foreign armies from the continent and Belsidus delivers his final
inspiring speech on the new Africa's remaining independent, feared, and free.

In *Black Empire* Schuyler consciously took on the whole convention of a
certain sort of popular science fiction. Once the premise is allowed all else
follows. But the premise is absurd, the premise of a Samuel I. Brooks who
Schuyler knew existed only as a fantasy who created a fantasy in which
African-Americans monopolize all talents and possess open access to technology.

Belsidus organizes a war against whites, but otherwise his co-workers seem conspicuously like Charles Lindbergh or Amelia Earhart or Albert Einstein. In this fantasy Belsidus aborts white babies and employs sympathetic whites - especially love-lorn women like Martha Gaskins, alias the Countess Maritza Jerzi - only to reject them. But the fantasy form itself is a case of (white) genre using an author for its own 'purposes,' forcing him into simplistic racist paradigms which erase his actual thought. Hence, since Schuyler in the candour of the non-fictional essay considered all race fanatics as one, the characters of *Black Empire* are white no less than those of *Black No More*. For all its black militancy and asserting of supremacy and separation *Black Empire* is thus the 'whiter' book. The text itself enacts the pertinent literary war, that between its form and its content. Neither is discrete, no more than Schuyler thought the races or ethnic cultural traditions could be in the United States. But in this book the reader familiar with the author's corpus senses a real rending between the two. We join Schuyler in perceiving the preposterous and therefore declaring form victorious, but appreciate why a contemporary black readership would have chosen content and why Schuyler indulged the whim to imagine this alternate world. At the same time he recognized that the formula trivialized any significant message and that the book therefore served as parody of both pulp science fiction and of works about racial confrontation: this form could trivialize and this message could be trivialized. (Other than this parodic element, the sole unmediated textual assertion of black pride is thus the implied assertion that the black writer can write anything he or she pleases.) For these reasons, to salvage at least a bit of the socially responsible at book's end, Schuyler must pull back and force Belsidus out of character in the conclusion to his final speech: 'You must not make the mistake of the white man and try to enslave others, for that is the beginning of every people's fall. You must banish race hatred from your hearts' (p.257).

Paradoxically, then, Schuyler speaks with his own, an African-American, voice, in *Black No More* rather than in *Black Empire*. To take the latter at face value is to dwell with Samuel I. Brooks in the same fantasy as Henry Belsidus and to make the error of reductionist ideological critics who ignore science fiction's 'complex and changing system of formal conventions which mediate "content," of unique codes of reception, and, most importantly, of tensions of generic and ideological components within individual texts'.[45] The assimilationist point of *Black No More* evidences itself through a statement which assimilates a Western form with African-American uses but also says that George Schuyler may combine and create his own forms. 'African-American' is always already hyphenated. And, as we have seen, the novel is intrinsically more pro-black than some critics have made out. Its depicting the effects of being white, *per se*, does not make it the less

African-American, but rather enables its author the more clearly to define the fate of being black in America. Otherwise, the African-American literary canon would include *Black Like Me*. 'Personally,' Schuyler wrote in 1937, 'I am opposed to worship of things Nordic as I am of things Negroid'.[46] The effect of *Black Empire*, on the other hand, becomes something like the effect of expressing Ethiopia's perspectives on Mussolini's 1935 invasion in the form of an Italian opera. If one accepts, *in toto*, a convention, only she or he, not the convention, has adapted. If Schuyler is a case of a consciousness divided between American and African-American sensibilities, it is the all-American ('racial integrity talks would click with the crackers') which has created *Black Empire* as a tongue-in-cheek experiment in science fictionality. If this experiment pictured genocide against whites, its pulp science-fiction formula equals what we might call 'genrecide' against African-American modes of expression.[47]

George Schuyler defined options for future black science-fiction writers if he did not create those options. He inadvertently discovered how readers might take African-American science fiction, and certainly furthered the 'trend away from the old caricatures' (even the caricatures of *Black Empire* are not the *old* caricatures). No later African-American writer would be the first to indulge in these wild inventions of science fiction. If he or she felt conviction, not invention, were at stake, the writer had to be aware that her or his themes might not be taken seriously by audiences anticipating the pleasures of the usual fare of the utopia, the lost race yarn, or the future-war tale. Black audiences might be apt to take themes too seriously, though, certainly to the extent that the formulas of pulp science fiction were not generally well known to these readers in any case: the African-Americanness of the African-American science-fiction writer would be the salient point. (For the most part this remained the point, even to writers, through the civil rights movements of the 1950s and after, when 'by far the greatest volume of sf novels dealing with black-white relations'[48] was written, novels like William Melvin Kelley's *A Different Drummer*, Warren Miller's *The Seige of Harlem*, John A. Williams's *The Man Who Cried I Am*, and Sam Greenlee's *The Spook Who Sat by the Door*.) But Schuyler in *Black No More* also pointed the way to an integration of theme and formula, to a discourse at once science-fictional and African-American and the more truly ethnic for the circumstance. He had absorbed important motifs of science fiction but also knew traditional concerns of African-American literature. Schuyler showed that science fiction could be a viable and natural medium if it were refigured in substantive and stylistic terms meaningful to the individual who happened to be African-American and, perhaps, as idiosyncratic as George S. Schuyler. If science fiction remains by no means a genre of choice, it can now seem an organic medium for writers like Samuel R.

Delany and Octavia Butler who have much besides race on their agendas. Delany can focus on the ecological and technological concerns of the black humanoid narrator of *The Einstein Intersection* while Butler can portray a powerful African ancestress in *Wild Seed*. Dr. Junius Crookman, who changed blacks into whites but remained black and lived at the Phyllis Wheatley Hotel, had been instructed by his sociology teacher that there were three ways for blacks to solve the race problem in the United States: 'get out, get white, or get along' (p.27). *Black Empire* represents getting out; *Black No More*, getting white. But Schuyler himself 'got over' (the African-American term for obtaining advantage for one's own purposes); he got along as a writer by appropriating whatever he wanted. He anticipated Butler's answer to 'what good is science fiction to black people?' by half a century: it could promote alternate ways of thinking and doing, stimulate creativity and imagination, and even portray 'the possible effects of science and technology, of social organization and political direction'.[49]

Benjamin S. Lawson

NOTES

1. Octavia Butler, 'Birth of a Writer', *Essence*, May 1989, p.134.
2. H. Bruce Franklin, *Future Perfect: American Science Fiction of the Nineteenth Century* (Revised Edition). London: Oxford University Press, p.vii.
3. Quotes in Ruth Salvaggio, 'Octavia Butler and the Black Science-Fiction Heroine', *Black American Literature Forum* 18 (Summer 1984): 78.
4. Octavia Butler, 'Future Forum', *Future Life* 17 (1980): 60.
5. Kathleen S. Spencer, 'More on Black Writers of SF', *Science-Fiction Studies* 16 (July 1989): 247.
6. Sandra Y. Govan, 'Connections, Links and Extended Networks: Patterns in Octavia Butler's Science Fiction', *Black American Literature Forum* 18 (Summer 1984): 83.
7. To differentiate between science fiction by African-Americans and African-American science fiction is to posit the very simplistic images we challenge. But this critical strategy, besides being convenient, brings to the fore an apparent contrast which was also meaningful, relevant, and argued during the 1930s. Countee Cullen had complained that reader response had forced him to be a black poet whereas a white poet was free to be, simply, a poet. If the writer was not self-aware of race, the audience's expectations operated to make him or her so and to make literature 'black' merely by virtue of the author's identity. To these readers there could be no science fiction by African-Americans; inherently, it was African-American science fiction. Only whites did not have to be defined by race; the empowered always possess the luxury of mistaking their ethnicity for the universal. One of the failings of traditional science fiction, writes Butler in a later day, was its unwillingness to portray black characters unless their race was essential to the plot (this would not be true for white characters, of course). The presence of blacks 'drew attention away from the intended subject' (quoted in Govan, *op.cit.* p.84). White critics, says Samuel R. Delany, are all too prone to

express 'the troubling anxiety that, indeed, you may not really *be* black' (p.158). Yet to define and limit the present subject I propose an analogue to what Spencer calls 'alternatives to patriarchy' in her allusion to feminist utopian fiction. It would seem that only fiction of this sort could be any good to black people in the terms of Butler's questioners - short of the good for the handful of African-Americans whose living is made as a function of their writing, *per se*. And in the period considered here, ending in the 1930s of the Scottsboro Boys, perhaps the notion of 'racelessness' was not available to African-Americans in anything like more recent senses.

8.   Robert Scholes and Eric S. Rabkin, *Science Fiction: History, Science, Vision*, London: Oxford University Press, 1977, p.187.

9.   See Benjamin S. Lawson, 'The Time and Place of Edgar Rice Burroughs's Early Martian Trilogy', *Extrapolation* 27 (Fall 1986): 208-20. John Carter is a Virginia gentleman who eventually dominates the alien races of the planet as the 'warlord of Mars' and husband of the 'red' Dejah Thoris. Leslie Fiedler writes of the early twentieth-century American writer's depiction of Mars as a landscape transposed from the American West, in which encounters must be with transmuted Native Americans (*The Return of the Vanishing American*, New York: Stein and Day, 1968, p.27). Edgar Rice Burroughs's Mars books portray races of a rainbow of familiar and not so familiar colors: blue, green, black, red, white.

10.   The genres merge because, presumably, a new order--utopian, dystopian, or a mix--would eventually arise after the future war and be defined by altered circumstances. Thomas Jefferson, for instance, wrote of the need for the periodic reordering consequent on revolutionary violence, but in *Notes on the State of Virginia* commented on the slave economy: 'I tremble for my country when I reflect that God is just: that his justice cannot sleep forever: that considering numbers, nature and natural means only, a revolution of the wheel of fortune, an exchange of situation, is among possible events: that it may become probable by supernatural interference!' (George F. Horner and Robert A. Bain, *Colonial and Federalist American Writing*, New York: The Odyssey Press, 1966, p.347). Later hopes for a peaceful emancipating were slashed during the 1860s by God's 'terrible swift sword,' a blood-letting which to the hopeful seemed a blood of birthing. The Civil War was the violence which freed some of George Schuyler's forebears if it did not produce utopian conditions. This apocalyptic imagination, which David Ketterer finds so American, 'demands that the destructive chaos give way finally to a new order' and 'finds its purest outlet in science fiction' (*New Worlds for Old: The Apocalyptic Imagination, Science Fiction, and American* Literature, Garden City, New York: Anchor Press, 1974, pp.14-15).

11.   Darko Suvin, *Metamorphoses of Science Fiction: On the Poetics and History of a Literary Genre*, New Haven, Connecticut: Yale University Press, 1979, p.166.

12.   I.F. Clarke, *Voices Prophesying War: Future Wars 1763-3749* (Second Edition), Oxford: Oxford University Press, 1992, pp.54-5.

13.   Thomas D. Clareson, *Some Kind of Paradise: The Emergence of American Science Fiction*, Westport, Connecticut: Greenwood Press, 1985, p.42, pp.62-3.

14.   *Ibid.* It must also be borne in mind that, insofar as science fiction expresses scientific thought, racist ideology was unavoidable and too often unquestioned in this age of 'scientific racism.' Paul Broca in France, Cesare Lombroso in Italy, Samuel George Morton in the United States, Sir Cyril Burt in England - through the nineteenth century and well into the twentieth, the ideas of these and other physiologists, criminologists, statisticians and educators were appropriated to bolster and provide rationale for racist beliefs and policies. Stephen Jay Gould finds such legal enactments as the American Immigration Restriction Act of 1924 and the British Butler Education Act of 1944 (which gave official sanction to the so-called 11+ school placement examination) practical victories for hereditarians, victories with racist implications (*The Mismeasure of Man*, New York: W.W. Norton & Co., 1981, p.293).

15. *The Science Fiction Encylopedia* (ed. Peter Nicholls), Garden City, New York: Doubleday and Co., 1979, p.467.

16. Clareson, *op.cit.*, pp.73-4.

17. Paul A. Carter, *The Creation of Tomorrow: Fifty Years of Magazine Science Fiction*, New York: Columbia University Press, 1977, p.121.

18. Quotes by Clareson, *op.cit.*, p.77.

19. Carter, *op.cit.*, p.138, p.118.

20. *Ibid.*, p.118, p.139.

21. Scholes and Rabkin, *op.cit.*, pp.187-8.

22. Clarke, *op.cit.*, p.166.

23. Albert I Berger, 'Theories of History and Social Order in *Astounding Science Fiction*, 1934-55', *Science-Fiction Studies* 15 (March 1988): 12.

24. Mark R. Hillegas, 'Science Fiction as a Cultural Phenomenon: A Re-Evaluation', in *SF: The Other Side of Realism: Essays on Modern Fantasy and Science Fiction* (ed. Thomas D. Clareson), Bowling Green, Ohio: Bowling Green University Popular Press, 1971, p.280).

25. Lester del Rey, *The World of Science Fiction: 1926-1976: The History of a Subculture*, New York: Ballantine Books, 1979, p.73.

26. See Frank Cioffi, *Formula Fiction? An Anatomy of American Science Fiction, 1930-1940*, Westport, Connecticut: Greenwood Press, 1982.

27. Robert A. Hill and Kent Rasmussen, afterword to George S. Schuyler, *Black Empire*, Boston: Northeastern University Press, 1991, p.306.

28. Robert M. Philmus, *Into the Unknown: The Evolution of Science Fiction from Francis Godwin to H.G. Wells*, Berkeley: University of California Press, 1970, p.4.

29. George S. Schuyler, *Black No More*, New York: Collier Books, 1971, introduction by Charles R. Larson.

30. R.D. Mullen, ;The Black Mencken (and Black David H. Keller)' (review of Northeastern University Press' *Black No More* and *Black Empire*), *Science-Fiction Studies* 19 (July 1992): 268.

31. A self-reflexive touch this, if unconsciously so. Wheatley's poems have long been viewed as neo-classical overlays on African or African-American substance and modes of thought. Houston Baker in a 1993 essay reports of a black female undergraduate complaining quietly from the back corner of his classroom: 'You know, we have been going on and on about conventions and how Wheatley subverted them and everything. But I'm not so much interested in conventions as in what Phillis means to the black community *per se*' ('Local Pedagogy; or, How I Redeemed my Spring Semester', *PMLA* 108 (May 1993): 403). When Max's friend later hears of Max's marriage, he exclaims, ' Well, hush my mouth! This sounds like a novel' (p.114).

32. Mullen, *op.cit.*, p.268

33. Not that this would have troubled him. To Schuyler the African-American was ineluctably American and 'had no more recollection of, connection with, or interest in Africa than any other American' (*Black and Conservative: The Autobiography of George S. Schuyler*, New Rochelle, New York: Arlington House, 1966, p.157). Schuyler's controversial 1926 essay on African-American aesthetics, entitled 'The Negro-Art Hokum,' became an incitement to on-going arguments with other black intellectuals like, for example, Langston Hughes. While Hughes and several others praised the unique achievements of the 1920s 'Harlem' or 'New Negro' Renaissance, Schuyler excoriated it as the 'Sambo Era,' the 'Coon Age,' the 'Cult of the Negro,' and promoted what he felt were trans-racial and objective standards of artistic appraisal (afterword to *Black Empire*, p.297). On the one hand, racial labels denied the essential Americanness of art; on the other, they made it all too easy for non-blacks to trivialize what could be dismissed as the merely parochial and, therefore, irrelevant.

34. Introduction to *Black No More*, p.10.

35. Nathan Irvin Huggins, *Harlem Renaissance*, London: Oxford University Press, 1971, p.159.

36. Dickson D. Bruce, Jr., *Black American Writing from the Nadir: The Evolution of a Literary Tradition, 1877-1915*, Baton Rouge: Louisiana State University Press, 1989, p.233.

37. George S. Schuyler, *Black Empire* ('The Black Internationale' and 'Black Empire'), Boston: Northeastern University Press, 1991 (foreword by John A. Williams, afterword by Robert A. Hill and Kent Rasmussen).

38. Mullen, *op.cit.*, p.269.

39. Henry Loius Gates, Jr., 'A Fragmented Man: George S. Schuyler and the Claims of Race', *The New York Times Book Review*, 20th September, 1992, pp.42-3.

40. Hill and Rasmussen, *op.cit.*, p.310, p.307.

41. Quotes in afterword to *Black Empire*, p.260.

42. Williams, *Black Empire*, p.xi.

43. In non-fictional prose Schuyler inveighed against what he called the 'Separate State Hokum,' although he realized that doing so 'was treason at a time when there was so much talk about African heritage' (*Black and Conservative*, p.157). 'The independence of the Dark Continent was the sheerest wishful thinking of a few racist zealots.' (*Black and Conservative*, p.120). 'Surrender to segregation' could only be 'acceptable to every Klansman, Fascist, and Nazi.' Schuyler argued that nowhere else were black people so well off as in the United States (*Black and Conservative*, p.227, p.121). His view that calculated segregation was deplorable lead him to lump pan-Africanist Marcus Garvey with the Ku Klux Klan as a race fanatic; 'all Garvey ever freed Negroes from was their hard-earned cash' (quoted in *Black Empire*, afterword p.275). Garvey's Black Star Line suggests Belsidus's fleet. Schuyler's novel *Slaves Today: A Story of Liberia* (New York: AMS Press, 1969) published during the same year as *Black No More*, exposes the atrocities and corruptions of the black rulers of a black country, Liberia. Into the sixties and seventies he continued to insist that the third world needed guidance and aid from the West.

44. Condescending stereotypes like this furnish matter to those who view Schuyler as ironist and satirist. Here the actual inhabitants of Africa do not even recognize differences among the various earnest combatants--they are all interlopers on their lands. Such critics could marshall other examples: the black nationalist leader being portrayed as cold and unsympathetic, one who hypocritically espouses his political cause while recruiting whites for sexual as well as ideological reasons; the unasked imposing upon Africa of a foreign (French, perhaps, the cannibals thought), industrial, technological regime; Della Crambull's surname and her entertainers' satisfying white audiences' post-Freudian desire for the exotic with portrayals of pseudo-Africa; the Church of Love constructing armaments in its basements and preaching hate; crazed Africans in a ludicrous frenzy of revenge beheading white victims, their ' hands and feet cut off to be dried as charms, and their bodies thrown to crocodiles' (p.129).

45. H.-J. Schulz, 'Science Fiction and Ideology: Some Problems of Approach', *Science-Fiction Studies* 14 (July 1987): 173.

46. Quotes in afterword to *Black Empire*, p.300.

47. Form and content working at cross purposes in this way creates confusions endemic to teaching, as well. Emphasis on formula makes *Black Empire* a work of science fiction; emphasis on content makes it African-American literature (quite apart from any concern with authorial intent and tone) and skews this content to the black militant side. Were the book included on our syllabus for African-American literature it would be a different book, in the perceptions of our students, from the same text on our science fiction list. Criticism's and pedagogy's labels lack the precision which would preempt misapprehension of the complexities of unique discourse. The best that can be hoped is to restrain the persistent impulse to label.

48. Nicholls, *op.cit.*, p.467.
49. Butler, *op.cit.*, p.134.

8

ON THE SUBVERSION OF CHARACTER IN
THE LITERATURE OF IDENTITY ANXIETY

One

'Science fiction is a home for invisible men and women'.[1] There they nestle, shivering, fragile, naked, tiny, lost, weak, dissolving, always dissolving, into an unbearable simulacrum of fractured, fragmentary, dehumanised being. As a literary genre, science fiction is peculiar in its treatment of character in that it reacts against an attention to traditional forms of characterisation. There are two contradictory epistemologies regarding the management of character in the conventional novel. The first of these, captured exquisitely in Virginia Woolf's (1924) sentient formula 'Mr Bennett and Mrs Brown', maintains that character-construction not only constitutes both design and destiny of the novel, it also engenders the *sine qua non* of its existence.[2] One only needs to look at the titles of various popular nineteenth-century bourgeois novels to realise the centrality of character to the genre: *Jane Eyre, Tess of the D'Urbeville's, Oliver Twist,* and *Anna Karenin,* to name but a few, are novels which accord their central protagonists title roles in their own discourse, highlighting the extent to which character came to dominate and eventually overtake the bourgeois novel. Conversely, the stereotypical, diminished roles of science fiction's actors, (who rarely achieve title status other than as collective nouns - *The Day of the Triffids, The Midwich Cuckoos, The Invasion of the Body Snatchers*), has made it difficult to recall any outstanding protagonist in the history of the genre, in part because it contemplates the scope and magnitude of our species in its *generic condition,* rather than offering an insight into the complexities of a single personality.

In considering the polemics of characterisation in science fiction, critics have tended to look upon it for the most part as a weakness that is accepted as given, falling back upon the same logical dialectic: that the notable lack of resonant characters as heroes in their own fiction is the inevitable result of the increased technical and metaphysical ramifications of the genre. In this way, in science fiction narratives we encounter the second epistemology regarding the status of character in the novel. This holds that character is disregarded, mass produced, or inadvertently relegated to the peripheries of the dramatic action, because something other - scientific technology, futuristic visions, complicated plot - controls centre stage. Hence the paradox: whilst on the one hand character belongs centrally to science fiction, by virtue of the genre's exploration of our human condition, it is generally accorded a supplementary position. Joanna Russ notes this curious de-emphasis of characterisation when she says that 'the protagonists... are always collective, never individual persons (although individuals often appear as exemplary or representative figures)'.[3] In a similar vein Kingsley Amis argues the case of 'Idea as Hero', claiming that science fiction inevitably deals in bulk figures, in categories rather than individuals, because 'theme replaces character as the organising principle of the genre'.[4]

In her restatement of Woolf's article, appropriately entitled 'Science Fiction and Mrs Brown', Ursula Le Guin proposes that this consistent failure of characterisation in science fiction hinders the genre from attaining the prestige of a 'conventional novel', typically defined by its extensive attention to character-creation. But character in speculative fiction is not simply disregarded; on the contrary, it is subverted. In the visions of conformity, homogeneity, and uniformity; in the guise of aliens, androids, robots and monsters; in the semblance of social machines and totalitarian governments; and in the metamorphoses of humans into something horribly 'other' than themselves, we are presented with a distortion *ad infinitum* of our own fictional representatives.

Such radical treatment of character clearly warrants a more cogitative *raison d'etre* than its dismissal as the inevitable result of inward centralisation of outward thematics (universe, topography, spacio-temporal defamiliarization). The thrust of this chapter will propose that science fiction in the twentieth century is fundamentally about what Sanders[6] terms 'the disappearance of character', in the same sense that twentieth century sociology is about the anonymization and dehumanisation of the individual by the impact of scientific and technological change. Lack of detailed characterisation in science fiction is intentional rather than accidental in genesis; a facet of the genre's strength rather than its weakness, given that the dissolution of character constitutes both object and subject of the formal literary critique.

In its treatment of character, science fiction generates a form in which not character itself, but the scaffolding which shapes character is the point in question. And this scaffolding, though of defamiliarized contour, constitutes what we recognise as the contemporary social world. The protagonists of science fiction dissuade from attentive character-analysis or reader-identification precisely because they are not ends in themselves but means, through which we are encouraged to re-examine our own sociological, cosmological and ontological theories via a process of formal disruption. In this way, the impoverishment of character in science fiction is an artistic device which bespeaks the indispensable condition of the genre's central theme; namely the impoverishment of the social self, of the sense and expression of human identity, as an inevitable consequence of contemporary social experience.

In all the worn down, emptied out, alienated and mechanical figures struggling to become self-governing in their fight against socio-historic forces, technological and scientific fiction represents the central predicament of people in the modern world.

> While society grows more rationalised, the experience of living in it grows more alienated. We are pushed towards anonymity by bureaucracies and technology, by the scale of life in the cities, by the mass media, by the techniques of manipulation perfected in government and business. To borrow a term from Max Weber, these social phenomena are the bearers of certain structures of consciousness, chief among them being the fear of *anomie*, of external control, of invisibility.[7]

The contemporary fear of becoming invisible, of having one's self subordinated to system, is one which hounds the protagonists of this century's most critically acclaimed 'social' science fictions. Aldous Huxley's *Brave New World*, George Orwell's *Nineteen Eighty Four*, and Yevgeny Zamiatin's *We*[8] are anti-utopian narratives which transfer onto nebulous time many of the socio-historic experiences - repression, militarization, dictatorship, invasion, possession, genetic engineering - that are documented in the evidence of our recent historical experience, of which the holocaust is exemplum *par excellence*. If we look at *Schindler's List*, Spielberg's (1994) Oscar-winning documentary film, recounting the Jewish experience of Nazi Germany during the Second World War, we discover many of the spectacles which predominate the choreography of post-war speculative fiction: the totalitarian regimes and torture chambers (*Nineteen Eighty Four*), the numbered, state-programmed inmates (*We*), the dehumanised individuals (Kafka's *Metamorphosis*), the brainwashed collective subjects (*Brave New World*), and the visions of apocalypse (Clarke's *Childhood's End*, Wells' *The War of the Worlds*).[9]

In presenting these images, founded on actual historical experience, science fiction presents the logic of our world extended; a world where there is virtually no privacy, in which the all-powerful government has absolute control of the press, advertising and propaganda, where to challenge the state's rule is to incur imprisonment or institutionalisation, where the military hierarchy and multi-national corporations have reduced human beings to numbers, uniforms, lists, and where the family has suffered a steady decline. Above all ours is a civilization in which the individual has no fixed or stable subject position, a society where every aspect of autonomous life is subordinated to the state. Science fiction evidently comprises the *modus operandi* through which to channel contemporary sociological epistemology. Whilst the genre is ostensibly a perception of the future, it is in fact intended as an allegorical critique of the present. As Calder suggests, *Nineteen Eighty Four* is an extrapolation into the future of a present that involved Stalinism and a past that had observed the effects of Nazism, whilst *Brave New World* is presented as the inevitable result of a society dominated by consumerism and the all-powerful forces of the mass-media, where the means are scientific and the ends are commercial consumption.[10]

Behind science fiction's anti-utopian narratives lurks the metaphor of society as some sort of machine that has diminished humanity to the condition of mass automata. The vehicle of the metaphor imparts the formal method by which to dramatise the contemporary crisis of identity through forms of external manipulation and control, enforced by the various reductive systems which constitute modern society. The arresting feature of society in speculative dystopias is standardisation and lack of individualism. Separatism is a menace to the state and behaviour which threatens the corporate system cannot be tolerated for the sake of its survival. Citizens are classified and categorised, and within the subdivisions there is little to differentiate them. Conformity is the governing principle, strengthened by manipulated practices and a conditioning which serves the dual function of defeating self-awareness whilst reinforcing collective power. In this way, science fiction epitomises a kind of virtual reality that consciously replicates a state of social existence symptomatic of a cultural movement in which individualism has undergone a process of exhaustion.

By the scientific application of genetic manipulation and post-natal conditioning *Brave New World* State Controllers have succeeded in grouping people into larger and larger units until by controlled ectogenesis and the Bokanovsky Process an average of almost eleven thousand brothers and sisters in a hundred and fifty sets of monozygotic twins can be manufactured from a single ovary, as one of the leading mechanisms of social stability. The 'problem' of individuality has clearly been eradicated in the 'new' civilization, 'solved by standard Gammas, unvarying Deltas, uniform Epsilons. Millions of identical twins. The principle of mass production at last applied to biology.[11]

In Structuralist Marxist terms, science fiction's anti-utopian narratives explore and enact a contemporary social phenomenon defined by Althusser as the 'interpellation of the subject'.[12] Individuals in *Brave New World* and *Nineteen Eighty Four* are subjected beings who submit to the World Controllers' and Big Brother's higher authority and consequently lose all freedom except that of freely accepting their submission. The notion of free subjectivity in the ordinary sense of humans being authors of their actions is revealed as an incongruous, as a false ideology which represents the imaginary relationship of individuals to their real conditions of existence. This concept of the 'death of the subject', manifested in science fiction's 'invisible' characters, becomes an overriding authority of our contemporary social condition. The result is that human individuals no longer *create* societies; they are created *by* societies.[13]

This is certainly true of the creatures who populate *Brave New World*. The World Controllers create an extraordinarily stable, classifiable society by means of ectogenesis, which endorses the systematic application of eugenics and dysgenics at the same time:

> In one set of bottles biologically superior ova, fertilized by biologically superior sperm, were given the best possible pre-natal treatment and were finally decanted as Betas, Alphas, and even Alpha Pluses. In another much more numerous set of bottles, biologically inferior ova, fertilized by biologically inferior sperm, were subjected to the Bokanovsky process and treated pre-natally with alcohol and other protein poisons. The creatures finally decanted were almost sub-human but they were capable of performing unskilled work...
>
> Additionally, concentrated programmes of post-natal Behaviourist and hypnopaedic conditioning are exercised, predominantly engineered to make the subjects' minds accept the already predetermined status of their social destiny. As the Director of Hatcheries expounds, 'That is the secret of happiness and virtue - liking what you've got to do. All conditioning aims at that: making people like their inescapable social destiny'.[14]

It follows from this that anti-utopian social-science fictions like *Brave New World*, *Nineteen Eighty Four*, and *We* stand as perfect narrative examples of the assimilation of the individual into the social organism of society. The ideologies of these quasi-fictional worlds require subjects who are prepared to become willing workers in their social systems if they are to be maintained in a stable and operational state. Consequently people are not ends in themselves, but means to ends, expendable, renewable, co-ordinating a collective existence as components which perform specific functions for the greater social body. In *Brave New World* the intellectually sub-normal Delta and Epsilon castes are only valuable because they comprise a category of workers that will happily perform the obligatory menial tasks. Ensuring that subjects perform these functions depends on their knowing and agreeing about how to behave, thus indoctrination into the correct state ideology is the key. In *We* the necessary socialisation is achieved by computer programming, in *Nineteen Eighty Four* it occurs through brute physical and psychological force, and in *Brave New World,* as we have seen, the work is accomplished by genetic engineering and post-natal, Neo-Pavlovian conditioning, in 'elementary class consciousness' begun in infancy:

> Alpha children wear grey. They work much harder than we do because they're so frightfully clever. I'm really awfully glad I'm a Beta because I don't work so hard. And then we are much better than the Gammas and the Deltas. Delta children are stupid and wear khaki. Oh no I *don't* want to play with Delta children.[15]

In this way, the characters of science fiction stand as touchstones for this generation's existence. Their struggles against the powers that be - the party, the State, the World Controllers, Big Brother - parallel our own protests against the reigning institutions which define modern society (government, bureaucracy, mass media, education, religion), made manifest through the fictive system. Manipulated by revolutionary forces of industry, commercial advertising, psychological conditioning, scientific technology, and cybernetic dialogue, human beings are constructed as the products of obscure and collective discourses, and all sense and expression of individuality is dissolved.

Two

While the crisis of identity at the social level is presented as an inevitable consequence of society's ideological state apparatus, which indoctrinates the assimilation of the subject into the dominant structures of a particular cultural order, the crisis of identity at the individual level is manifested *vis à vis* the *alien encounter.* Using the category of 'alien' as cipher, science fiction does violence to identity, raids chaos upon sense of 'self', and wrestles with the disconcerting fragilities of 'subjectivity' as a fixed and meaningful construct from which to ground one's self-expression or lay claims to the 'I' of the discourse. Aliens in science fiction naturally embrace a metaphorical capacity. As Parrinder suggests, the tenor of the metaphor comprises a particular component of human existence which the author seeks to defamiliarize or reveal as fictitious, for example, the notion of the 'subject' as self-governing. The vehicle comprises a recognisable variation of the human norm, typically embodied in the various types of actual and imaginary alien beings: the monster, robot, android, super hero, spaceman.[16]

These types of alien figures are the skeletons of human beings, devoid of emotion and sensitivity, and confront us with grotesque personifications of humankind. They suggest what we might become if society is allowed to have its way with us; what we might be reduced to if we continue to be repressed and dominated by threatening alien forces. These fears have been defined as *invasion anxiety*: 'the self erased, hollowed out, filled with alien spirit',[17] and may be interpreted as an inevitable consequence of our twentieth century post-holocaust experience, in which threats of nuclear attack and mass invasion on every level and by all kinds of foreign bodies, are no longer the exception but the rule. Whatever label we give to the invading body - AIDS, Advertising, MTV, McDonalds, Nuclear War-Heads, Communism, Post-Modernism - the signified principle is the same: they communicate an awareness of being corrupted by external forces over which we are powerless to control, forces that are symbolised in science fiction by the alien encounter.

Novels like H.G. Wells' *The War of the Worlds*, and A.C. Clarke's *Childhood's End* are fables enacting precisely this type of symbolic encounter. In *Childhood's End* the world is invaded by an alien species of 'Overlord' who are themselves instruments of an 'Overmind'. At the climax of the novel an involuntary metamorphosis inflicts the entire population of the Earth's children. They become a grotesque, telepathically linked quiddity, their individuality dissolved, their autonomy destroyed, as they are assimilated into the collective body of the Overmind.

The War of the Worlds offers itself as a fictional allegory of external invasion, taking our twentieth century fears about war and disaster and effecting them symbolically in the attack made upon Earth by Martian invaders. These observing intellects - 'vast, cool and unsympathetic' - regard the planet with envious eyes, arriving on Earth from Mars with the intention of replacing Man as Earth's dominant species. It is exactly in light of this monstrous assault that the Martians appear so threatening; they do not simply aim to conquer the human race, they aim to eliminate all traces of its existence. By the time the Martians have finished wreaking their havoc, the only evidence of Man's presence on Earth is a fine ash. The world is no longer recognisable but the landscape 'weird and lurid of another planet'; an environment altogether overtaken by an ominous red weed which depletes atmospheric oxygen and suffocates flora and fauna.

The metaphors of this scenario are numerous: it echoes the current problem of ecological catastrophe, which poses a very real threat to the survival of our planet (home), and species (family); it plays upon society's hostile xenophobia towards any persons embodying any phenomena - homosexuality, schizophrenia, disability, AIDS, colour, race, religion - perceived to be in some sense 'alien'; and in the 'age of anxiety', it dramatises contemporary social fears of annihilation by means of mass global destruction.

The War of the Worlds, like many speculative fictions, may be defined as a war anticipation story, which renders one of humanity's predominant fears, that which Kermode has termed 'apocalyptic thought' or the 'sense of an ending'.[18] Every historical age is marked by the sense of apocalypse impending, typically characterised by the notion of the catastrophe finite, or the end of the world as it is known. According to Wolfgang Iser's phenomenological approach, readers seek to make their reading process relative to their own experience and transpose onto the text the contents of their social and cultural patterns of thought.[19] Subsequently the text is 'concretised' by the extra-literary norms and values of particular socio-cultural environments. In this way, *The War of the Worlds*, though written before the invention of nuclear power and the advent of Hiroshima, can be (re)-constructed as an allegory of total nuclear destruction, by means of post-event interpretive strategies.

Similarly the figures of the Martians may be (re)-defined as a metaphor for society's catastrophic nuclear weapons which anticipate the potential apocalypse and its holocaustic aftermath, seminal to an understanding of our contemporary, post-modernist anxiety. This is the beauty of science fiction's alien creatures: as figures with no articulation proper, other than suggestion or innuendo, they operate as artistic devices through which to explore the fantastic idea of 'non-signification'.[20] 'Alien' as signifier offers no real truths about 'alien' as signified. This deliberate gap between signifier and signified is a major defining characteristic of science fiction which aims above all to aspire beyond the arbitrary medium of language to something 'other', by extending the rule of the signifier and posing a more radical 'loss' of the signified.

In his excellent response to Woolf's and Le Guin's inter-connected character epistemologies, Parrinder points out that 'the word "alien", in the special sense appropriated to it by science-fiction writers and readers, shares the same stem as one of the most fashionable twentieth century metaphysical concepts, that of "alienation"'.[21]

Indeed 'alien', as defined in *The Concise Oxford Dictionary*, has both noun and adjective sense respectively. As noun, 'alien' is the physical 'other', typically a non-naturalised foreigner or extra-terrestrial being from another world; as adjective, 'alien' has the primarily descriptive function of naming the attributes which characterise the noun, and includes notions of being 'not of one's own', 'out of harmony' and 'repugnant'. The point is that the two senses of the word - 'alien' as *physical* being, and 'alien' as metaphysical *state* of being - are simply different manifestations of a single condition, that of alienation.

It follows that although physically 'distinguishable' from the human by means of its physiological 'otherness', the alien paradoxically represents the human by the very virtue of its 'alien-ness' in terms of feeling and sensibility. Only by understanding the alien can we come to understand the human condition which reflects the alien; which the alien is a reflection of. Viewed in this light, the concept of the alien mirrors the concept of the 'self' writ large, and the gist of science fiction can be inferred as a variant of the principle dichotomy through which we contrive our identity.

In *The War of the Worlds,* the recurrent opposition between human and alien generates a constant reinterpretation on the bases of similarity and difference. While the malevolent, foreign appearance of Martians provokes hatred and aversion earlier in the novel, their monstrous demeanour itself becomes a point of identification with humanity when a subsequent parallel is drawn between their behaviour and the behaviour of human characters. This 'martian-man' dichotomy is reinforced by the literary strategies of the narrator who juxtaposes descriptions of the Martians' treatment of humans with the way humans have treated certain races and religions within their own species, pointing out that Martians are only doing to humans what humans have already done to themselves:

> The Tasmanians, in spite of their human likeness, were entirely swept out of existence in a war of extermination waged by European immigrants, in a space of fifty years. Are we such apostles of mercy to complain if the Martians warred in the same spirit?[22]

The emotional focus of numerous science fiction narratives is that which Rose defines as 'the magical permeability of the boundary between the self and the other; the conscious ego in relation to the boundlessness of the cosmos that is not the self'.[23] It is no coincidence that this theme constitutes the primary focus of modern psychology. Three of the leading theorists of discipline, Freud, Piaget, and Lacan, structure their idiosyncratic theorems by means of the same basic principle: during infancy the child learns to construct an existence based on the distinction between 'self' and 'other', which occurs upon recognition of the self as object, as the means of self-definition and self-identification, during what Lacan has termed the *mirror stage* of human development. Yet this 'self-other' distinction, rather than being fixed, is dynamic, shifting and being re-established all the time.

Most speculative narratives entail the discovery of a repressed personality or alter-ego rendered in the device of the 'other'. It is through such figures the genre gives expression to our crisis of self, manifested through a dualism motif indicative of a basic socio-cultural desire for 'otherness'. This 'otherness' is conceptualised in the figure of the alien or monster, whose manifestation is symptomatic of a latent wish to be re-integrated with a 'lost self'. In science fiction this 'lost self' is typically one which is considered socially transgressive or disobedient - that which threatens the dominant socio-cultural order - and is consequently repressed or relegated to the hidden realms of the unconscious.

Mary Shelley's *Frankenstein* may be interpreted as a symbolic dramatisation of the disturbing relationship of 'self' set in diametric opposition to 'non-self' or 'other', effected by the relationship of Frankenstein and his self-created monster respectively.[24] Frankenstein embodies the 'I' or 'self' of the discourse, and the monster the 'not-I', which is paradoxically self-generated by Frankenstein through a scientific experiment which might be construed as the figurative manifestation of unconscious desire. The monster is the unconscious impulse, the *Das Heimlich* of the psyche, mediated existentially through Frankenstein's expression of the darker, more socially unacceptable part of his personality, which has become repressed by the forces of socialisation. In Freudian terms the creature Frankenstein 'births' is the *id* of the personality; that which constitutes the infantile part of the human psyche. He signifies what the human being is - what we all are - before the socio-ideological environment has begun to exert any influence over us; that is, he is the pre-socialised part of our make-up, from which our socialised part has become alienated and estranged.

In this sense *Frankenstein* voices the unseen as well as the unsaid of contemporary culture, personifying society's existential dis-quiet and dis-ease. The Creature may be seen to enact the metaphorical tenor of humanity's cultural and ideological limitations. The speculative genre employs alien encounters to reveal human beings as victims of ideology. Ideologies are self-perpetuating primarily because they operate habitually, functioning to indoctrinate humankind to endorse the particular socio-hierarchical structures of the society in which they live. Consequently these structures are perceived as 'normal' and 'healthy' processes of existence. Following the Russian Formalist movement, and its key notion of *defamiliarization*, twentieth-century literature has increasingly become the vehicle through which to cipher the artificiality of ideological systems by dehabituating automatized perception and undermining taken for granted beliefs. The literature of science fiction, as evidenced in the creature's bizarre ponderings on the nature of humanity, brings to bear a particular kind of defamiliarization, designed to enact the contemporary metaphysical phenomenon which Suvin has termed 'cognitive estrangement'.[25]

> Of my creation and my creator I was absolutely ignorant... My person was hideous and my stature gigantic. What did this mean? Who was I? Whence did I come? What was my destination?[26]

Since the task of envisaging the *entirely* alien is impossible (we can only conceptualise something as 'alien' by relating it to that which is already in some sense familiar), any feat of defamiliarization will only be relative rather than absolute. It follows that the Creature's metaphysical and ontological speculations serve to humanize him, and bring him within the circle of our own anthropomorphic vision. His crisis of identity parallels that of our own, leading us to view human beings as the unconscious puppets of an ideology-defined existence which constructs the individual as 'subject'.

We live in a society which, for its own survival, cannot allow us to give free expression to our *id* impulses. Our 'true' personalities are repressed by the socially constructed *ego* which develops as a direct result of our socialisation. In effect, the poetic *ostranenie* (defamiliarisation/estrangement) enacted *vis à vis* Frankenstein's monster, reveals both human and alien coming to an awareness that their alleged identity is nothing but a model of conditioning, a cultural imprisonment that operates to assimilate individuals into the dominant order of the status quo.

In this sense the story of *Frankenstein* combines two semantic levels: it uncovers what is hidden (the socially suppressed *id* of the psyche) and in so doing effects a disconcerting transformation of the familiar (Frankenstein) into the unfamiliar (Monster). Moreover, by giving expression to those desires and taboos which conventionally remain concealed (Frankenstein's production of his socially transgressive self), *Frankenstein* compensates for society's limitations by permitting vicarious gratification.

Such subject matter is not just the concern of the theorists, or even the writers, but is increasingly the concern of the men in suits. There is big money, big business and huge box office hits to be made from precisely this field of enquiry, and Spielberg's million dollar-grossing film *E.T.* stands as exemplar *par excellence*. Although structured around the alien figure of an extra-terrestrial being, the focus of *E.T.* is neither outside the Earth nor beyond its atmosphere; on the contrary, the 'alien' is much closer to home, embodied in the figure of an eight year old child.

Eliot, the boy-focaliser of the narrative, is the sensitive, middle child of a family in crisis: a family defined by its absent father-figure, its working, emotionally unavailable mother, and its structural instability. Eliot feels 'lost'. He misses his father, but must repress these emotions to keep from upsetting his mother and younger sister. Consequently his behaviour is 'false'; he has no scope or outlet for his feelings, no stable or cohesive subject position from which to ground his self-expression.

Eliot's crisis of identity provokes terrible ontological questions on the reality of his being - 'Who am I?', 'What am I?' - tempered for him by the unfathomable incongruities of his existence (personal and familial stability). Hence the arrival of E.T. - the 'extra-terrestrial' from outer-space, who is not really an extra-terrestrial in the literal sense of the word (alien body) at all, but rather the extra-(unconscious) personality of the young boy's mind, manifested as a signifier of his psychological distress. If we look at the names 'E.T.' and 'Eliot' we can see that E.T. is an abbreviated form of the name 'Eliot', with the notable absence of the 'I' denoting the loss of Eliot's sense of the 'I' of his discourse. It follows that E.T. may be interpreted as Eliot's 'lost' self made manifest through an alternative aspect of the same psyche. The psychic connection between Eliot and E.T. serves to reinforce this interpretation; Eliot 'thinks his thoughts', and 'feels his feelings'. Additionally, when questioned about E.T., Eliot provides the emphatic response, 'He came to me. I found him. He belongs to me. He's mine'. Experienced this way, E.T., the 'extra-personality' produced from the boy's unconscious mind, is revealed as a fundamental part of Eliot's - as well as our own - alienated *persona non grata*, symptomatic of twentieth-century intra-familial disruption and estrangement.

In this way, science fiction novels and films alike make use of the alien encounter to reflect contemporary anxieties about the condition of the individual human psyche. The fear of losing one's conscious self to the repressive mechanisms of one's unconscious mind - although displaced onto an alien 'it' -

represents a fundamental insecurity towards the modern world-structure which incites the individual to experience a type of self-alienation or estrangement.

Three

As Rose proposes, 'feelings of self-alienation typically express themselves as narratives of metamorphosis, stories of the transformation of man into something less or more human. Dehumanized man, man as either monster or superman, is in principle indistinguishable from any other kind of alien, and the figures of such stories are sometimes synonymous with aliens'.[27]

In this respect the narrative of transformation may be interpreted as analogous to the narrative of the alien encounter. The line distinguishing the two is exceptionally fine and depends on Lacan's 'self-other' dichotomy established during the formulation of the 'I' in the 'Mirror Stage' of human development. In lieu of confronting the alien as 'other', across a threshold of difference, the individual recognises his or her *self* to be in some way 'alien', and becomes the agent for his or her own transformation. This particular experience of self-alienation may be defined as a metaphor for the contemporary feeling of alienation from both internal consciousness (self), and external universe (other), made visible through the fictive system.

In Kafka's *Metamorphosis,* the central protagonist Gregor Samsa undergoes a physiological conversion from man to giant beetle, a shift from human to non-human which is the correlative of the transformation in *Frankenstein.* 'Self' becomes 'other' through a self-generated metamorphosis, as a direct result of the subject's alienation from himself. Gregor as an autonomous individual is transformed first to the coleopterous order, by means of the hierarchical, automatized, regimented social system, in which he is forced to be a willing worker, and secondly to the product of waste matter, by the artificiality and fragility of the entire human condition. Consequently Gregor perceives himself to be horribly alien, an experience rendered as he *becomes* alien. An 'it' not a 'he', Gregor as beetle loses all sense of his identity, and all recollection of his human background. He circles to a point of absolute zero, gradually losing the use of his species' isolating and identifying mechanisms (vision and discourse) which are contingent upon his human senses. He is finally obliged to become depersonalised; to cease to be. The story can be read as a movement from self to 'other' in protest against an oppressive social reality; his desires and instincts stifled by the greater body of the all-powerful social organism, Gregor enacts a physio-psychological return to the inorganic (freedom and death), increasingly withdrawing from society's 'humanizing' schemes.

The parallels in Kafka's novel with the modern human experience are here too obvious to be missed. As a character Gregor smacks of the powerlessness and loneliness of the individual who, when he discovers the artificiality of his existence, creates a barrier between himself and the outside world which manifests itself in the limited pseudo-self (alien figure) created for himself. The *Metamorphosis* expresses the contemporary anguish of the 'trapped consciousness', of the awareness that our conscious desires and feelings are closed to us and must be relegated to the hidden realms of the unconscious, as well the impulse to escape the limited physical body of the self, and merge with some other. This longing for undifferentiation is one of the central forces of psychological epistemology, and may be translated as an attempt to revert to a 'pre-Mirror Stage' which exists prior to socialisation and indicates a 'non-relationship of zero, where identity is meaningless'.[28]   Science fiction's transformation narratives are subsequently revealed as vehicles through which to channel some alternative reality of being.

In this way, metamorphoses in science fiction harbour an overt metaphysical significance. The realisation that we are governed almost entirely by the power of a corporal existence, is perhaps the most traumatic blow of all to our sense of independent identity. It negates our ultimate hope to give at least some sense to our existence. As Flores suggests, 'our corporiety makes the inhuman world our master. It mocks at our pretended autonomy. The fragility of the identity of our character when a radical metamorphosis occurs cruelly shows the fragility of our entire condition'.[29]

Since the transformations in science fiction are primarily physical, they become that much more symbolic of our bodily as well as our psychic self-estrangement; or, inversely, of the physical *manifestations* of our psychic self-estrangement, typically the largely Western dis-eases of anorexia nervosa and obesity. Both types of anxiety disorder involve obvious physical 'transformations' by either excessive weight loss or gain, which may be defined as outward expressions of inward psychological and physiological chaos. As with all species, our material body and our total physiognomy is persistently involved in the socio-evolutionary process of transformation. From the day we are born, we are subject to constant biological and physiological changes in our development, which manifest themselves particularly evident in the stages of adolescence (physical maturity), and old age (physical deterioration). Consequently the individual is no longer self-governing over his or her own body, which itself appears to have overstepped the bounds of reason and grown strange. The metamorphoses in science fiction, particularly like that of the film *The Fly*, which explore the transmutation of human anatomy, may be read as narratives which express the anxiety of losing control of our own physicality; documenting our fears about the inevitable stages of physio-psychological growth and change which transform us from dependent infants, to independent adults, and back to dependency again in the geriatric phase. Tales of metamorphosis thus bespeak our deep seated desire to escape the agony of change (which threatens our existing identity), and preserve our 'selves' from that ugly, mysterious, unavoidable passage to maturity and eventually death.

Finally, the tales of metamorphosis in post-war science fiction provide a vehicle through which to articulate the (post)-modernist experience of *fragmented subjectivity*.[30] Our contemporary social experience is characterised by an onslaught of isolated, disconnected, discontinuous events which fail to link up into any form of coherent sequence. Instead they are haphazardly strung together into a simulacrum of chaotic, free-floating stimuli. It follows that the individual in modern society is constructed as a product of intersecting discourses which produce a 'death' of the subject and subjectivity following its fragmentation into separate, conflicting, identities. Individuals are unable to 'place' themselves in relation to a 'coherent' reality, as that itself is seen to be disintegrating, characterised by its multiplicity of contradictory styles, images, and discourses. Subsequently, the individual becomes overwhelmed, exhausted, and subject to dispersal of parts.

Nowhere is this phenomenon more sharply evidenced than in contemporary science fiction films, comic strips and cartoons. In 'Superman', 'Super Ted', 'Batman', 'Wonderwoman', 'Banana Man' and countless other 'transformation' formulae, we bear witness to a condition that has coined the term *Menippea*: the juxtaposition of incompatible elements, the dissolving of philosophical ordering systems, the breakdown of unified notions of character.[31] The protagonists in science fiction's transformation narratives typically lead two completely separate lives, laying claim to two distinct personalities - as 'normal' people with ordinary feeling and sensibility, and following transformation as 'super' people with special powers.

It is clearly the genre's capacity to subject the category of 'self' as a coherent, known and successive unity to radical defamiliarization. The ideological concept of 'character' as a signifier of social unity is subverted in science fiction, by effecting the fragmentation of many of its central protagonists into polypsychic identities. The division of these protagonists into contradictory psyches - the 'boy next door' and the 'super hero' - provides the *modus operandi* through which to effect our unstable, fragmentary, cultural condition. To borrow a phrase from Bakhtin, people have ceased to 'coincide with themselves', failed to lay claims to the 'I' of the discourse, and consequently experience themselves as double, even multiple identities.[32]   Such conditions have commonly become labelled as 'schizophrenia' or 'multiple personality disorders' and are very much a reflection of our contemporary social experience.   These types of identity confusion or anxiety are precisely engineered in science fiction through the metaphor of the individual's production of other selves (aliens, androids, monsters, super heroes). The arbitrary grand narrative of the 'unified subject' as a signifier of social unity is dissolved at its very base through the character's own fragmented subjectivity, collapsing moral, social, and political parameters.

The narratives of these types of transformation stories are frequently heteroglossic, involving a plurality of confusing, contradictory, de-centred voices which deflect attention away from any predominantly consistent narrative voice to a multiplicity of dissonant, frequently interrupted voices. The effect is indicative of an attempt to create a fictional form characterised by fragmentation. As there is no single, integrated personality controlling them, more often than not the 'normal' and 'super' voices become fused and blended at the level of narrative discourse, highlighting the fact that the 'characters' are not separate entities at all, but rather confused and disparate manifestations of a single psyche. Using this formally disruptive literary technique, science fiction renders the schizophrenic mentality of the contemporary post-modernist consciousness, marked by its disconnection between thought, feeling, action, and place. Moreover, the effect of such diversity of discourses at play communicates the post-modernist scepticism about the claims of a single narrative authority to be rendering the truth about the contemporary social condition, or the official version of the world.

Evidently the treatment of character in science fiction, increasingly stereotyped, violent and subversive, fosters a socio-ontological model of knowledge which, however dismissed as a 'weakness' or 'fault' of the genre, has become one of the most revealing and comprehensive epistemologies of contemporary civilization.   The literary form functions primarily as a socio-psychological study of actual and hypothetical changes in environment and cosmology, documenting our emotional, metaphysical, and physiological reactions towards them, not only as one species among other species, but as individuals within a particular species.   As such science fiction may be seen to comprise a dialectical extension of many of this century's most influential epistemologies - biology, sociology, psychology, psychiatry, and philosophy - rendered by way of its revolutionary semiological and literary frames of meaning.

The genre projects its particular ideology regarding the status of the individual onto the situation of character transformation *vis à vis* the alien encounter, dramatising the profound crisis of identity located within the history of this century. By blaming alien signifiers for our loss of identity - Government, Ideological State Apparatus, scientific technology, foreign bodies, - we are able to explore and protest our dehumanizing social condition while appearing to maintain the status quo.

In the final analysis, in literary form as well as subject matter, science fiction operates as a means of descriptively analysing contemporary social and individual reality, as well as presenting a theoretical critique about that reality. The genre signifies an attempt to find an artistic form which will be in its own way defamiliarized and poetic, but will systematically express the confusion and chaos of the world it renders. Science fiction is thus a relatively new form; a form of such a type that it admits the chaos through ontological (character) and cosmological (fictional setting) distortion.

Invariably, the crisis of identity in science fiction, manifested via the subversion of characterisation, awaits a solution to the crisis of identity in modern society. Only when something is done to make society juster and more rewarding for the individual; when people can work together *as* individuals and not as the embodiment of specialised functions; when science is subjected to democratic control and humane purposes; when human beings are free to follow their *id* impulses - only then will science fiction find it possible to render detailed, recognisable characters who are heroes in their own fiction. Until then the writers must continue to project critical epistemologies onto alien figures and alien worlds, if they are to reproduce the identity crisis of both society and the self; if they are to find a shape in which to contain the mess; if they are to make their visions not simply 'escapist' but charged with significance.

Victoria Maule

NOTES

1. S. Sanders, 'The Disappearance of Character', in Patrick Parrinder (ed), *Science Fiction: A Critical Guide*, London: Longman, 1979, pp.131-47 (p.31).
2. Virginia Woolf, 'Mr. Bennett and Mrs. Brown', in *The Captain's Death-Bed and Other Essays*, London: Hogarth Press, 1950.
3. Joanna Russ, 'Towards an Aesthetic of Science Fiction', *Science Fiction Studies* 2, 1975, pp.112-129 (p.126).
4. Kingsley Amis, *New Maps of Hell*, London: New English Library, 1979, p.131.
5. Ursula K. Le Guin, 'Science Fiction and Mrs. Brown,' in Peter Nicholls (ed), *Science Fiction at Large*, London: Victor Gollancz, 1976.
6. Sanders, *op.cit.*, p.131.
7. *Ibid.*, p.145.
8. Aldous Huxley, *Brave New World*, London: Chatto & Windus, 1932; George Orwell, *Nineteen Eighty Four*, Secker & Warburg, 1948; Yevgeny Zamiatin, *We*, London: Penguin, 1924.
9. Franz Kafka, *Metamorphosis and Other Stories*, London: Penguin, 1933; Arthur C. Clarke, *Childhood's End*, London: Penguin, 1953; H.G. Wells, *The War of the Worlds*, London: Penguin, 1942.
10. J. Calder, *Brave New World and Nineteen Eighty Four*, London: Edward Arnold, 1976, pp.11-15.
11. Huxley, *op.cit.*, p.23.
12. Louis Althusser, 'Ideology and the State,' in P. Rice and P. Waugh (eds), *Modern Literary Theory: A Reader*, London: Routledge, 1989, p.58.
13. *Ibid.*, p.60.
14. Huxley, *op.cit.*, p.29.
15. *Ibid.*, p.33.
16. Patrick Parrinder, 'The Alien Encounter: Or Mrs. Brown and Mrs. Le Guin,' in *Science Fiction: A Critical Guide*, London: Longman, 1979, pp.149-161 (p.155).
17. Sanders, *op.cit.*, p.143.
18. Frank Kermode, *The Sense of an Ending*, Oxford: Oxford University Press, 1968.
19. Wolfgang Iser, *The Act of Reading*, New York: Johns Hopkins University Press, 1978.
20. Tzvetan Todorov, *The Fantastic: A Structural Approach to Literary Genre*, Press of Case Western University, 1970, p.51.
21. Parrinder,*op.cit.*, p.149.
22. Wells, *op.cit.*,
23. Mark Rose, *Alien Encounters: The Anatomy of Science Fiction*, Harvard: Harvard University Press, 1981, p.192.
24. Mary Shelley, *Frankenstein*, Harmondsworth; Penguin, 1992.
25. Darko Suvin, 'On the Poetics of the Science Fiction Genre', in Mark Rose (ed), *Science Fiction: A Collection of Critical Essays*, Englewood Cliffs, NJ: Prentice Hall, 1976.
26. Shelley, *op.cit.*, p.116.
27. Rose (1981), *op.cit.*, p.179.
28. Jacques Lacan, *The Language of the Self: The Function of Language in Psychoanalysis*, New York: Delta, 1968, p.88.
29. A. Flores, *The Kafka Problem*, London: Stratford Press, 1946, p.131.
30. Jacques Lacan, *Ecrits* (trans. Alan Sheridan), New York: Norton, 1981, pp.88-91.
31. Mikhail Bakhtin, *Problems of Dostoevsky's Poetics* (trans. R.W. Rotsel), Ann Arbor: Ardis), 1978.

32. Mikhail Bakhtin, *The Dialogic Imagination: Four Essays* (ed. M. Holquist, trans. M. Holquist and C. Emerson), Austin: University of Texas Press, 1987.

III. SPECULATION

9.

J.G. BALLARD: NEUROGRAPHER

In 1953, in *New Statesman and Nation* magazine, J.B.Priestley published 'They Come from Inner Space'. Priestley explained the phenomena of UFOs and science fiction as 'the myths and characteristic dreams of our age' and predicted that they might overwhelm modern humanity's soulless technocracy.

> We prefer to think of ourselves travelling to the other side of the sun rather than sitting quietly at home and then moving inward, exploring ourselves, the hidden life of the psyche. All this comes of trying to live a dimension short, with infinite length and breadth, from here to Sirius, but with no depth, without the spirit.[1]

In 1962 Ballard was invited by John Carnell, editor of *New Worlds* magazine to write a guest editorial. He produced an essay called 'Which Way To Inner Space?', in which he called for

> not science fact but more science fiction... more psycho-literary ideas, more metabiologicial and meta-chemical concepts, private time-systems, synthetic psychologies and space-times, more of the remote, sombre half-worlds one glimpses in the paintings of schizophrenics, all in all a complete speculative poetry and fantasy of science.[2]

This chapter will examine the stories and novels by Ballard immediately before and after this essay, analysing the development of the concept of inner space within Ballard's work. I will also examine how Ballard worked through the implications and possibilities of 'inner space' fiction within SF and other genres, and how he apparently came to the conclusion that inner space could be more profitably explored outside the confines of science fiction.

In order to examine how Ballard delineated the workings of the mind in his early work I will consider 'The Concentration City' (1957) and 'Billennium' (1961).[3] 'The Concentration City' (originally titled 'Build-Up') is set in a far future earth where the city, like Isaac Asimov's Trantor, covers the entire surface of the globe, and the idea of 'free space' is incognizable. 'Billennium' details the freak discovery of an empty room in a world where the living space allocation is constantly being reduced. These are among the most readily identifiable as genre SF among Ballard's stories, but a closer examination of them reveals underlying stresses in the science-fictional form.

'Billennium', a story of a vastly overpopulated city, is constructed through taking the contemporary world and packing it with humans; the urban architecture is, unlike in 'The Concentration City', largely that of the period in which the story was written. It differs from Ballard's later work in failing to integrate the external environment into the psychological profiles of the characters. 'Billennium' does not explore, in the usual exhaustive Ballard manner, the marginalised fragments of contemporary psychology that could be activated by a sociological alteration. It assumes, as does most genre or popular fiction, the existence of a certain type of psychological profile even when it is removed from the determinants that created it. Constructed largely according to the rules for the 'well-made' realist story 'Billennium' seems to be assembled from SF clichés, from well-worn images and plot elements. Similar 'collage' methods of producing a text appear in other Ballard works, but 'Billennium' is too much a part of the tradition it uses to present original Ballardian research into human psychology.

The protagonist of 'The Concentration City', Franz Matheson, has a vision of flying, of freeing himself from the constrictions of a regimented society. The society rations heat, and also the imaginative 'flights of fancy' that would arise from the study of pure science. It is another extrapolation of 1950s Britain, but unlike 'Billennium' the additional ramifications of the future world are fully integrated into the psychological profiles of the inhabitants, who are truly products of their context. The combination of Franz Kafka and Richard Matheson, signalled by the name of the protagonist, created a psychological science fiction-horror story, with a large element of absurdity. Whereas 'Billennium' ends ironically, the climax of 'The Concentration City' is that of a horror story, as Franz rides the Supersleeper trains in search of free space, only to return to the place he set out from, on the day he began.

'The Concentration City' is an interesting variation on the strict genre guidelines set up by Tzvetan Todorov for the delineation of fantasy as a genre. Todorov largely deals with late nineteenth-century works and insists on a narrow definition of the mode whereby

> (t)he fantastic is that hesitation experienced by a person who knows only the
> laws of nature, confronting an apparently supernatural event... If he decides

that the laws of reality remain intact and permit an explanation of the
phenomena described, we say that the work belongs to another genre: the
uncanny. If, on the contrary, he decides that new laws of nature must be
entertained to account for the phenomena, we enter the genre of the
marvellous.[4]

Science fiction, however, lays claim to the high-ground of literary realism.
Robert Heinlein claimed that the genre consists of 'realistic speculation about
possible future events'.[5] Marc Angenot's influential structuralist investigation of
science fiction's 'absent paradigm' is a variation of this:

While the realistic novel should lead the reader to believe in the events it
narrates, the SF novel must also have him believe in what it does not and can
not show: the complex universe within which such events are supposed to take
place... The reader engages in a conjectural reconstruction which 'materialises'
the fictional universe.[6]

Science fiction is held to be a branch of realist fiction (either late nineteenth
century social realism or modernist psychological realism) with changes in the
physical, social or technological environment.

If it is therefore accepted that science fiction is a special case of realism,
then 'The Concentration City' becomes an example of science fantasy. The story
avoids being placed in Todorov's class of the marvellous (see above) by the police
surgeon's statements near the end of the story about the 'curvature... built into the
system'.[7] Hesitation, the moment of the fantastic, is produced in the mind of the
reader as s/he wonders if the curvature of space is of greater significance than
simply the spherical structure of the planet (of which the inhabitants are unaware)
and if it can be applied to the operation of time in this different world. The story
subtly shifts from being a tale of a 'built-up' far future ('Build-Up' was the title
assigned to the story by the magazine's editor), to a story of the 'concentration city'
('The Concentration City' was Ballard's preferred title), an environment which
moulds the minds of those living within it, and in which mental and physical
entrapments interact.

Ballard had been exploring in neurological detail the workings of the brain
in a number of other stories. 'Manhole 69' (1957) features an experiment in which
three men undergo surgery removing the requirement, or the ability, to sleep. Lang,
one of the guinea pigs, muses on the purpose of sleep.

'Eliminate sleep... and you also eliminate all the fear and defence mechanisms
erected round it. Then, at last, the psyche has a chance to orientate towards
something more valid.'
'Such as?' Morley asked.
'I don't know. Perhaps... Self?'[8]

Shortly after this the three men experience a shrinking of their environment. The
vast gym that they are in becomes

the manhole: a narrow, vertical cubicle, a few feet wide, six deep... As if
crumbling under the impetus of their own momentum, the surface of the walls
had coarsened, the texture was that of stone, streaked and pitted...[9]

It is in this story that inner space first becomes an explicit theme in
Ballard's fiction. Whereas in 'The Concentration City' the labyrinthine, enclosed
city can be seen to alter the inhabitants' perception of physical laws (how society
can influence the perception of 'reality'), in 'Manhole 69' the state of mind of the
characters changes the way that the world appears to them. This is the first sign of
Ballard's technique of exploring psychology through the manipulation of
mindscape. In this early example the coincidences between state of mind and
external reality are given a neurological explanation. The dominant world view of
the early novels (*The Drowned World* (1962), *The Drought* (1965), and *The
Crystal World* (1966))[10] comes from the impressions of the central characters; the
question of objective perception becomes marginalised as psychological
exploration becomes more important.

Ballard explores variations of this in other short stories, the most important
of which is 'Zone of Terror' (1960). This is the story of Larsen, a psychologically
disturbed computer programmer who begins to spawn doubles of himself. At the
story's climax these 'simultaneous images'[11] have become concretely established
in the landscape (they can be seen by another person) and result in the death of the
protagonist in an attempt to shoot, and thus symbolically 'kill' the simulacra.
Larsen had before his breakdown been working on programming an electronic
'brain simulator... to construct models of dissociation states and withdrawal
syndromes - any psychic complex on demand'.[12] It seems, however, that Larsen is
also being manipulated by the psychologist, Bayliss, who has brought him to the
'desert site (which) had been chosen for its hypotensive virtues, its supposed
equivalence to psychic zero'.[13] Ballard combines the landscape with Larsen's
neurosis and drug-induced overstimulation so that

Suddenly the chalet seemed dark and cramped, a claustrophobic focus of
suppressed aggressions... (T)he chalets seemed to shrink towards the ground

> as he strolled to the rim of the concrete apron... The whole scene seemed suddenly unreal.[14]

And in fact the landscape of the story is unreal - it is the country of the mind.

Many of Ballard's stories are psychological constructs. 'Zone of Terror' features the literary idea of the 'double', as in Edgar Allen Poe's 'William Wilson', or E.T.A Hoffmann's *The Devil's Elixir*, discussed in Freud's essay on 'The Uncanny'.[15] But Ballard's story is post-psychoanalytical, and includes the analysis within the text. Thus there are self-conscious Freudian references (to, for example, Bayliss' 'number - 0, on the internal system - (which) was almost too inviting'. It is stated that the double 'isn't the shining hero of the super-ego or the haggard grey-beard of the death-wish' and there are Jungian allusions (the double throws light 'on one of the oldest archetypes of the human psyche - the ghost'. More significant, though, is the presence of a psychologist in the story. The express purpose of the characters in 'Zone of Terror' (and in a great deal of, but not necessarily all of, Ballard's other fiction) is to undergo psychological examination. This is signalled by the way in which Bayliss experiments with Larsen's treatment, and also by the fact that much of the conversation between the characters consists of reports on psychological states or theories. Larsen is even conducting an investigation into his own psyche, 'larding the case history with liberal doses of speculative commentary'.[16]

In legend and fable there is

> the belief that human beings have a detachable soul, which is an exact counterpart of themselves. This spiritual self could separate from the material self and wander abroad - the so-called *Doppelganger*. It was death to meet your own doppelganger.[17]

Freud's analysis of the 'double' states that it allows the ego to develop a critical awareness of itself - Ballard's story reclaims the theme for use in a psychologically aware horror fiction. In fact, the story suggests that it is psychoanalysis that has caused the formation of the doubles - Larsen has been working on creating psychoses in a computer and reading Kretschmer's *An Analysis of Psychotic Time*. The psychiatrist sees doubles 'not of himself but of Larsen, on whom his mind had been focusing for the past weeks.'[18] 'Zone of Terror' shows that Ballard was using psychological theories to provide a gloss on traditional fantasy themes, and also creating a new form of fiction based on these theories. Freud wrote that he

should not be surprised to hear that psychoanalysis, which is concerned with
laying bare... hidden forces, has itself become uncanny to many people for that
reason.[19]

Ballard's story shows how it is possible to use psychoanalysis to obtain the effects
of the fantastic, without making the theories uncanny in themselves.

The Drowned World, Ballard's first major novel, largely follows the
structure of the classic disaster story. It permutates the plot possibilities and
clichés of the traditional novel in a mechanical fashion, and it is clear that the
diegetic level is largely drawn from other sources, from Joseph Conrad, Graham
Greene and John Wyndham. The novel's real interest, however, lies in its
thorough exploration of inner space. *The Drowned World* is the culmination of
Ballard's early forays into the mindscape. The stories discussed above were only
partial and fragmented explorations of this dark realm - *The Drowned World* brings
together the distinctive mapping techniques used by the earlier texts in an attempt
to comprehensively plot the internal world.

The Drowned World is set in the twenty-first century after solar radiation
has melted the ice-caps and raised the sea levels and planetary temperature to such
an extent that only the polar regions are inhabitable. An expedition is recording the
biological changes in an unnamed city which is now a swamp. The climate
resembles that of the Triassic period, and giant reptiles have started to appear
again. All forms of plant and animal life are beginning to adapt to the new
conditions, and the biologist Bodkin asserts that

> Each one of us is as old as the entire biological kingdom, and our
> bloodstreams are tributaries of the great sea of its total memory... The further
> down the CNS (Central Nervous System) you move, from the hind-brain
> through the medulla into the spinal cord, you descend back into the neuronic
> past.[20]

The extreme alteration in the external world, and the concomitant change in the
human psyche, recall the central technique of 'The Concentration City'. Where it
differs from the earlier story, but resembles 'Manhole 69' and 'Zone of Terror', is
in the determination to place the scientific basis of the story firmly within the
bounds of psychology. The novel features detailed, if (as above) rather fanciful,
discussions of neuro-psychology.

However, what distinguishes *The Drowned World* as a new approach for
Ballard, other than the multiplicity of entrances to the psychological maze, is the

dedication with which the novel emphasises the landmarks that had already been labelled by a previous traveller. *The Drowned World* is a rigorous exposition of Jungian psychology. By this I mean more than just that the novel uses Carl Gustav Jung's theories of analytical psychology; it is actually structured according to the model of the brain conceived by Jung. Congruences between Ballard and Jung, both fundamental and insignificant, are remarkably prevalent. The dramatic dreams of Kerans, the chief protagonist, begin during the 'mid-life crisis' period. The classification schemata of Kerans and Bodkins, the expedition's biologists, reflect the obsessional neuroses characteristic of pathological introverts. The further emotional isolation experienced by Kerans, Bodkins and Hardman leads to the paranoid-schizoid position which (Freudian) psychoanalysts postulate as the condition of early infancy, and Jung would claim as exposing the near-naked collective unconscious. The dreams related by the characters are based upon archetypal situations stored in the nervous system, and also on the (novel's) current situation, in opposition to 'Freudian' dreams rooted in childhood sexuality; these dreams have a teleological function, promoting adaptation for a new world. With *The Drowned World* and *The Drought* in particular, inner space is not simply the exploration of a mind; it is the portrayal of landscape and consciousness as inseparable. At its simplest level it can be seen in *The Drowned World* where the dreams of the characters start to come true. Kerans dreams of,

> (stepping) out into the lake, whose waters now seemed an extension of his own bloodstream. As the dull pounding rose, he felt the barriers which divided his own cells from the surrounding medium dissolving, and he swam forwards, spreading outwards across the black thudding water...[21]

Some time later, during a dangerous diving mission, we find Kerans again.

> Far above him, as his consciousness faded, he could see the ancient nebulae and galaxies shining through the uterine night, but eventually even their light was dimmed and he was only aware of the faint glimmer of identity within the deepest recesses of his mind. Quietly he began to move towards it... like a blind fish in an endless forgotten sea, driven by an impulse whose identity he would never comprehend...[22]

Most of the characters could be claimed to be representations of the Jungian dissociated ego, with its aspects packaged into discreet personalities, which cluster around the archetypes proposed by Jung. These are the *anima* or the *animus*, which are respectively a man's internal idea of the female and a woman's internal idea of the male; the *shadow*, which is the negative aspect of the individual's personality, similar but opposite to the individual; and the *wise old man*, who is the source of wisdom and generally older than the individual. The major characters in *The Drowned World* correspond exactly with these archetypes; Kerans is the central character, Beatrice is the anima, Strangman is the shadow and Dr Bodkins is the wise old man. It can be seen that Ballard does not even attempt to draw his protagonists as three-dimensional characters - they are no more or no less than aspects of the internal landscape. And so the world that they move through is evidently there primarily to provide the impetus for the exploration of an individual's consciousness. But which individual? I would suggest that the consciousness explored is that of the book rather than of any particular character. This consciousness is literally an inner landscape, populated by aspects of the disassociated ego. The creation of this consciousness is still in progress, however. There still exist characters such as Riggs who do not belong in the drowned world. The power of the lagoon to awaken collective unconscious fails to affect this extrovert (in the Jungian, technical sense) who continually characterises himself according to his social persona, and has a stable, uncommitted relationship to the landscape, which thus has little influence on his psychology.

Following this argument I would identify *The Drowned World* as a narratorially complex Jungian fiction on the process of individuation. This implies the acceptance by the novel's consciousness of a deeper power than the conventional ego, and the integration of the disparate and conflicting elements within the consciousness and unconsciousness. This is the journey towards the (unachievable) archetypal Self, and explains why what I have claimed as the process of individuation 'by which a person becomes a psychological "individual", that is, a separate, indivisible unity or "whole"'[23] climaxes in apparent dissolution of Keran's personality (or what little he ever possessed). Jung claims that 'The self is our life's goal, for it is the completest expression of that fateful combination we call individuality'[24] and also that it is the archetype of the 'God-image'. Attainment of the supposedly indefinable totality of consciousness and unconsciousness results in the retention of individual characteristics only as a manifestation of the archetype's conscious element. That is, Kerans loses identity within the psychic sea, except for those aspects within the conscious psyche that had anticipated the eventual union of consciousness and unconsciousness, inner and outer worlds, ego and shadow. In effect, Kerans (the character) is no longer of interest to us (and Ballard concludes the novel) when a commitment to the 'neurotic odyssey' has been made, and the conscious residue of his character is merely going through the necessary physical motions.

> So he left the lagoon and entered the jungle again, within a few days was completely lost, following the lagoons southward through the increasing rain

and heat, attacked by alligators and giant bats, a second Adam searching for
the forgotten paradises of the reborn sun.[25]

Despite the frequent allegations of pessimism, *The Drowned World* is often
felt to be the most satisfyingly complete of Ballard's books. Its rigorous allegiance
to Jungian logic leads the predetermined plot to its inevitable conclusion, and its
sense of wholeness. This was plainly too good to be true, and Ballard's attempt to
retrace his steps with *The Drought* resulted, according to the author, in 'something
rather too arid'.[26] Ballard identifies several important elements of the novel:

> quantified image, isolated object, and emotion detached from any human
> context - (ideas) that I began to develop in *The Atrocity Exhibition* and in
> *Crash.*[27]

These important elements of the inner landscape will be discussed below when I
address the organising principles behind *The Atrocity Exhibition* (1970).[28]
However, *The Drought* reads more like a failed attempt to reproduce the psychic
wholeness of *The Drowned World* than a journey into wholly uncharted territory.

> Although it was not yet noon, the sun seemed to be receding into the sky, and
> the air was becoming colder. To... (Ransome's) surprise he noticed that he
> no longer cast any shadow on to the sand, as if he had at last completed his
> journey across the margins of the inner landscape he had carried in his mind for
> so many years.[29]

This climax differs fundamentally from the conclusion of *The Drowned World*.
Although Ransome is said to have completed his inner trek, he has not achieved
wholeness - he has not found 'self' by turning entirely within himself. I have
claimed that *The Drowned World* is the most 'complete' of Ballard's fictions -
however, this narrative pleasure is achieved by suspending judgement on the
success or otherwise of Keran's neuronic odyssey. At the end of the novel Kerans
is still 'searching for the forgotten paradises of the reborn sun'. The sun, which
throughout *The Drought* has been a less benign force, has abandoned Ransome,
and his psychological journey has ended in failure. Annihilation does not
necessarily result in satisfaction; it might bring only loss.

In a fundamental misreading (or perhaps too incisive a reading) of
Ballard's work, Brian Aldiss has stated that Ballard's 'central problem... (is)
writing a novel without having the characters pursue any purposeful course of
action'.[30] Ballard had already addressed that problem in his revisions of earlier
work that resulted in *The Crystal World*. An examination of the genesis of this

story published in 1964 called 'The Illuminated Man'[31] takes an area of indeterminate status and forces it into stasis by the introduction of the effect of crystallisation. The area of the Hubble Effect in the original version, and briefly mentioned in *The Crystal World* as a site of the phenomena, is Florida. Miami and the Everglades, humans and alligators are all forced into permanence. The uneasy boundaries between land and water in the Everglade, between exploding capitalism and small communities, between the wild and the pastoral countryside, between teeming life (human and animal) and concretised solidity are all made negligible by the new opposition between crystal and non-crystal. The crystal, like a viral cancer (a comparison made in the story), attacks the fundamentals of matter, effectively freezing the atom while reproducing its basic structure.

Much criticism of Ballard's work has rejected the importance of the characters in the fiction and emphasised the significance of the landscape. It is true that Ballard is a writer who is apparently more comfortable with descriptive passages than with social interaction. As Ballard said in an interview, 'I've always wanted really to be a painter... I've said... that all my fiction consists of paintings.'[32] However, 'The Illuminated Man' becomes *The Crystal World* not through a massive extension of the descriptions of the jewelled forest (now located in Africa), but by the addition of other major characters, and the construction of two triangular relationships parallel to the one in the earlier version.

It could, of course, have been tedious to read a 'novel' consisting of nothing other than metaphysical ponderings on the imminent stasis-death of the universe, and detailed delineations of its effect on an area barely touched by humanity. But, by Ballard's own account, the expansion of the character/action element of the story is not mere novelistic padding to bring the tale up to the required length.

> I felt that the short version was incomplete. It was too much of a science
> fiction fantasy. I wanted to develop more of the serious implications of the
> idea.[33]

In order to do this Ballard multiplies the human reactions to the phenomenon. The origins for this were present in the original story, with the varying perceptions of, and responses to, the crystallising process. But *The Crystal World* expands not only on 'The Illuminated Man', but also on *The Drowned World* and *The Drought* in developing the complexity of reactions to biospheric disaster. The earlier novels include the response of characters such as Riggs in *The Drowned World* and Reverend Johnstone in *The Drought* - characters who are psychologically untouched by the disaster, and respond to it with military ruthlessness and logic. *The Crystal World* largely removes such reactions from its frame of reference; the remnants exist only in the off-stage Russian team 'under the leadership of some Lysenkoist'[34] and other barely met experts. Radek is probably the nearest equivalent to Riggs among the named characters, but he meets a very different fate from the colonel. Unlike Riggs, Radek comes to accept the new world order. He is last seen struggling on into the affected area,

> his face lit by the jewelled light from the forest... One lurching stride after another, his pace quickening as the prismatic light of the forest mingled again with his blood.[35]

Even those who in previous Ballard novels would have resisted the encroaching crystallisation succumb to it or welcome it in *The Crystal World*. This would seem to contradict my assertion that the novel multiplies reactions to the phenomenon, as it in fact restricts the element of choice. But, as should be clear from other Ballard texts, the rejection of the future order is not a valid option. The world will change, is changing, and the individual must adapt to the alteration, or be overwhelmed by it.

What is evident in *The Crystal World* is the splintering of positive reactions to the biospheric disaster, and the multiplication of motives. In *The Drowned World* Kerans' motives (the search for the Triassic Sun, and thus the origin of the past, present and future of everything on earth) are relatively clear, and the different motivations of Bodkins and Beatrice are marginalised. With *The Crystal World* we encounter a plethora of characters acting out, and exploring, private obsessions in, and over the top of the crystallising background.

Sanders is identifiably the Kerans character, just discovering the changed world, and examining in detail his reactions to it, and his psychological state. Even early in the novel, 'His sharp reaction to the arrival of the priest made him realize how far he already identified with the forest'.[36] Most of the other major characters have already largely adapted to the crystal forest and are living on the borders of observation and integration. Through these characters Ballard exposes the different motivations that can lead to an acceptance of static eternity. Ventress had already attempted to impose such a state on Serena, his child bride who '(a)pparently he saw... in a sort of pre-Raphaelite dream, caged within his house like the lost spirit of his imagination.'[37] Thorenson rescues Serena from this entrapment, and supplies her with jewels which inhibit the crystallisation, but insists that, 'I've been in this forest a long time. The only chance she has is here'.[38]

Suzzane is developing leprosy, and aside from any motivations she ascribes to herself, it can be held that she is attracted to the forest because it is the external reality corresponding to the altered perception created by the disease ('in maculoanaesthetic leprosy there was an involvement of the nervous tissue'[39]). Alternatively, Suzzane could be fleeing the infection, by insisting that it is only the outer landscape that is changing, and not her neural tissue. She says, 'To be frank, I prefer the night. One can see the forest better'.[40]

With the introduction of human interaction, of 'society' in a very basic form, Ballard complicates the relatively simple relationship of progressive humanity to progressing environment seen in the earlier works. The triangular relationship used by Ballard is one of the 'classic' structures of Western fiction. It presumes a type of eternal relevance, in keeping with the linking of the crystal symbol with eternity. Even the relationships replicate according to the predicates of the forest, with the entry of Sanders to create another 'eternal triangle'. It could even be alleged that 'The Illuminated Man' is not just the precursor of *The Crystal World* but is the telling of a near identical story from one of the other affected areas of the globe. The crystal world is reproducing narratives of relationships, having a specific social effect on the human race, as well as the individual one evinced in *The Drowned World*.

The principle ordinance of the texts that I have discussed is the attempt to use various generic types and fictional tropes to represent the mindscape. Ballard was experimenting with different techniques in an attempt to capture internal reality. With each text he varied the ingredients, in order to analyse the efficiency of the constituent parts. Demonstrating an early acceptance of the postmodern condition, Ballard was unwilling to accept as given the traditional uses to which literary techniques, philosophical notions and scientific theories were put. *The Drowned World* blends Jungian analytical psychology and the English disaster story; *The Crystal World* sets a strange romance, populated by characters from a Graham Greene novel, within an exploration of Buddhist self-enlightenment and relativistic theory.

I have traced how Ballard has adopted strategies from various sources in order to delineate his map of the inner landscape. Before turning to the fragmented texts that make up *The Atrocity Exhibition* I intend to examine a more traditional story. 'The Gioconda of the Twilight Noon' (1964) tells the story of Richard Maitland, temporarily blinded by the bandages left on after an eye operation. He begins to see images of landscapes that become gradually more concrete. Exploring them, he finds a large house and encounters a green-robed woman.

When the bandages are removed he tears his eyes out in order to return to the inner world. This short story combines the ancient myth of Oedipus with elements from Freudian psychology, renaissance art and religion. The landscape that Maitland explores in simultaneously a wish-fulfilment world ('some image deep within Maitland's mind'. 'Gozo - ....Calypso's island' where his mother is on holiday and the 'blue rocks and spectral grottoes... (of) Leonardo's *Virgin of the Rocks'*. Maitland spends one night in his mother's bedroom which he had

> glimpsed only occasionally during the years since his marriage. The high bed, the deep rustle of silks and the echoes of forgotten scents carried him back to his earliest childhood.[41]

Initially, Maitland is not consciously controlling his movements within the imaginary world; he seems to be simply drifting. Soon he is being '(i)mpelled forward' and by the end of the story he is 'willing himself through the enveloping sea-mists, searching for the lost estuary'. It is intimated that the female figure that Maitland both fears and desires is his mother; although this is not explicitly stated. The assumption comes from references throughout the story to Madonnas, to Maitland's mother 'whose bland smile always seemed to conceal some potent private world', the visions reflecting 'some image deep within Maitland's mind', and, finally, Maitland's self-mutilation with which he becomes 'an eager, unrepentant Oedipus'.[42]

Ballard's story can perhaps most usefully be seen as an exploration of the great theme of Western art and thought, in a self-consciously post-Freudian mode. Whereas Freud's analyses of myth, legend and literature worked towards drawing out stages of psychological development, Ballard's story uses the insights given by Freud, and allusions to a wide range of artistic works, to create a form of fiction that is simultaneously an analysis of Freud's model of the mind and mental development, and also the manifestations of it in artistic production. It is also, though, a drawing together of Ballard's own early themes, and places them centrally in the tradition of Western culture, both artistic and scientific. It could be alleged that with this story in 1964 (and also, in a different manner, with 'The Terminal Beach' and 'The Illuminated Man' from the same year) Ballard is clearing the decks of his imagination - removing the elements of the past and expunging artistry - in order to depict faithfully and honestly the 'new reality', the confusing, existential, self-conscious and violent world that was the late 1960s.

In his early work Ballard had exhausted the traditional routes into inner space, and had discovered that they produced only a partial representation. The progression from *The Drowned World* to *The Crystal World* is one of dissatisfaction with the narrative conventions that insist on a sense of closure within a work. Ballard gradually added elements to the standard fictional cocktail in a form of literary experiment. *The Atrocity Exhibition* is a truly experimental work, being Ballard's final and most extreme attempt to intersect fiction and mental images. The conclusion of this paper will examine various elements of the stories that make up *The Atrocity Exhibition*, and judge the representation of reality contained within.

Central to the project of *The Atrocity Exhibition* is the depiction of public spaces. It is plain that the topography in which Ballard's psycho-dramas occur has significance beyond the simple provision of a realistic canvas. A recurring place of authority and conflict is the 'Institute', which is also variously a hospital and a university. This could be said to be a research and teaching psychiatric hospital, connected to a university. The conjunction of elements is revealing - psychiatric hospitals and universities should both be institutions in which progress is made towards some greater understanding of reality and of oneself. It is also instructive to note the use of the indeterminate term 'Institute', which is defined as 'an organization founded for particular work, such as education, promotion of the arts, or scientific research' (*Collins English Dictionary*) and in effect covers all the possible assumptions that might be made about its role in the stories, including the suggestions that it is connected with the security services. There is a collapsing of distinctions between supposedly discreet institutions - hospitals and universities put on art exhibitions and film shows, cinemas and planetariums occupy the same mental and similar physical spaces, psychological research is carried out on members of all segments of society.

The stories tend to begin with Traven leaving the Institute (resigning or being discharged) in order to begin his psychological exploration. If the definition of 'institute' used as a verb (to establish or initiate) is considered, then a link can be established between various levels of discourse pertaining to the text. The Institute is a part of the landscape within the world of the story; it is a diegetic component, a place in which events occur. It is also a psychological space, an area which is described only in terms of the psycho-dramas, atrocity exhibitions and psycho-sexual studies which are initiated there. Its place within the consciousness of Traven and the text is as a matrix or womb from which an escape must be made in order to explore the possibility of self-fulfilment. In the Institute violence, sex and art are created and controlled; and therefore castrated, rendered ineffectual and transient. They can provide only the seed for what is to follow, both in the narrative and in Traven's consciousness. But it is in the combination of the functions of the Institute, a place of treatment and study, of secrecy and explication, that Traven and Ballard conceive the possibility of a rearrangement of the standard discourse of society to create a new and more valid synthesis of the psyche.

The central character of *The Atrocity Exhibition* goes under a different name in each narrative section; Ballard has stated that the 'core identity is Traven'. Traven is variously a member of staff at the Institute, or an ex-patient; in 'The Assassination Weapon' it is unclear which of these roles he occupies. He takes on all of these roles, and several others in 'You and Me and the Continuum'. Ballard has written

> Throughout *The Atrocity Exhibition* its central character has appeared in a succession of roles, ranging across a spectrum of possibilities available to each of us in our interior lives.[43]

It is thus apparent that on a textual level Traven's changes of persona are internal fantasies; they are attempts to fulfil his deepest desires and to achieve his psychic destiny.

The Atrocity Exhibition tends towards the state proposed by Barthes, whereby 'What is obsolescent in today's novel is not the novelistic, it is the character, what can no longer be written is the Proper Name'.[44] The unself-conscious creation of 'fully-rounded' characters in the nineteenth-century tradition has been negated by the postmodern text. Structuralist and post-structuralist criticism has textualised the character constructs of realist fiction, while postmodern writers have applied these theories to the production of self-aware texts. The dissolution of Traven is partially legitimised by Joel Weinsheimer's claim that: 'As segments of a closed text, characters at most are patterns of recurrence, motifs which are continually recontextualised in other motifs'.[45]

Traven is continually recreated in different journeys of psychic exploration; for him the world has become a series of motifs, of geometric shapes and already-written psycho-dramas. Seymour Chatman suggests that character should be considered as a paradigm of traits, a collection of relatively stable qualities that can be seen 'metaphorically, as a vertical assemblage intersecting the syntagmatic chain of events that comprise the plot'.[46] In an attempt to achieve the same level of reality as the mindscape produced by the media Traven continually features himself in tableaux representing the summations of various psycho-dramas. Even this splintered character becomes part of a fossilised landscape of the mind.

The most immediately noticeable characteristic of *The Atrocity Exhibition* is that every paragraph bears a title. Ballard's thematic obsessions have occasionally been compared to those of Roland Barthes' *Mythologies*. The technique of detailed internal labelling recalls Barthes' *S/Z*, which also names every paragraph. In both texts these titles have an uncertain status. Sometimes they are directly referential to the fragment of text that they are the heading to; on other occasions they have a more general significance, referring to the process of reading encouraged by the work. What is clear is that breaking up the text in this way questions the supposedly logical flow of an organic piece of writing, either of fiction or of classical literary criticism. The frequent titles tend to crystallise the textual events, splitting the stories into individual significant cells.

Two of the named paragraphs in *The Atrocity Exhibition* bear the titles of novels by Raymond Roussel. These are "Locus Solus" (*Locus Solus* 1914) in 'The Summer Cannibals' and "Impressions of Africa" (*Impressions d'Afrique* 1910) in 'You: Coma: Marilyn Monroe'. The latter is also the title of a painting from 1938 by Salvador Dali, and the paragraph by Ballard exhibits some concurrences with it, though transmuted by modern technology. According to Brian McHale, Roussel's method of writing

> involved taking a standard French idiom or expression, or a line of verse by a
> 'classic' author, and manipulating it in such a way as to preserve homonymy
> (more or less) while radically altering the meaning... Next he constructs a
> fragment of a world in which the state of affairs projected by this reinterpreted
> line could occur.[47]

McHale goes on to claim that this works 'to expose the dependency of the reconstructed world on the text continuum'.

I would claim that Roussel's methodology can be considered as analogous to the technique used by Ballard to assemble *The Atrocity Exhibition*. David Pringle claims that 'Ballard is a writer who is drawn to visible symbols, an author with a painter's eye rather than a poet's tongue'.[48] With this in mind, it could be claimed that as the unit of Roussel's work is not the word but the phoneme, around which he then constructs an imaginative variation on the real world, Ballard's primary signifier is the visual image. It would thus be apparent that the tableaux constructed by Ballard, the frequent references to paintings, X-ray plates and architecture (among other identifiable extratextual items), and the apparently motiveless and non-sequential flashes of action result from random trawlings of images from his mind or his library. The book is thus revealed as an authentic exhibition. After attempting various methods of representing the mindscape, Ballard has arrived at a theory of mental images. Telelogical, dynamic and numinous models of the mind were tested and subsequently rejected in the texts that I have discussed previously. With *The Atrocity Exhibition* Ballard has stripped the detritus of literature and myth from the operation of the human mind, and arrived at a form of neurological fiction. *The Atrocity Exhibition* is assembled from mental images, some unique to Ballard, some (for example, the assassination of John Fitzgerald Kennedy) shared by all. Jean-Pierre Changeux argues that

> (t)he human brain contains representations of the outside world in the
> anatomical organisation of its cortex, and it is also capable of building
> representations of its own and using them in its computations.[49]

Neurobiologists have demonstrated experimentally the existence of mental objects, and the manipulation of them by subjects. In addition, Changeux claims that conceptual thought is constructed from images of reality. Inner space is therefore a form of virtual reality. The model for it is indeed spatial, but it is a space wallpapered with images of surrealist paintings, and stacked with banks of television screens repeating presidential assassinations and napalm bombings. *The Atrocity Exhibition* is a snapshot of the historical point at which inner space became conjunctive with public and media space. Ballard claimed in 1971 that

> It seems to me that the main points of reality are those points at which the
> various levels of public fantasy - Vietnam, the Congo, the assassination of
> public figures, and so on - cross the level of our own private fantasies and the
> third level of our private lives. Where these three levels intersect you find the
> only valid points of reality, the new reality which we all inhabit.[50]

Ballard has established that the inner landscape exists in a dynamic and complex relationship with other versions of reality. It cannot finally be reduced to a biological or psychological model, and the world outside the head cannot be considered apart from it. A dual process in which consciousness is mechanised, and externality is psychoanalysed, is the only valid route towards an explanation of existence.

Mark Jones

NOTES

1. See C. Greenland, *The Entropy Exhibition: Michael Moorcock and the British 'New Wave' in Science Fiction*, London: Routledge & Kegan Paul, 1983, p.52.

2. J.G. Ballard, 'Which Way to Inner Space?' *New Worlds* 118, 1962a, pp.2-3, 116-8 (pp.117-8).

3. J.G. Ballard, 'The Concentration City', in *The Disaster Area*, London: Panther, 1969a edition, pp.31-54; and 'Billennium', in *The Terminal Beach*, Harmondsworth: Penguin, 1966a edition, pp.177-93.

4. T. Todorov, *The Fantastic: A Structural Approach to Literary Genre*, Press of Case Western Reserve University, 1970, pp.25, 41.

5. According to Patrick Parrinder, *Science Fiction: Its Criticism and Teaching*, London: Methuen, 1980, p.16.

6. Marc Angenot, 'The Absent Paradigm: An Introduction to the Semiotics of Science Fiction', *Science Fiction Studies* 6(1), 1979, pp.9-19 (p.15).

7. Ballard (1969a), *op.cit.*, p.51.

8. J.G. Ballard, 'Manhole 69', in *The Disaster Area*, London: Panther, 1969b edition, pp.143-69 (pp. 156-7).

9. *Ibid.*, p.163.

10. J.G. Ballard, *The Drowned World*, London: Victor Gollancz, 1962b; *The Drought*, London: Triad/Panther, 1978a edition; *The Crystal World*, London: Triad/Panther, 1978b edition.

11. J.G. Ballard, 'Zone of Terror', in *The Diasaster Area*, London: Panther, 1969c edition, p.141.

12. *Ibid.*, p.126.

13. *Ibid.*, p.123.

14. *Ibid.*, p.129.

15. Sigmund Freud, 'The Uncanny', in *The Standard Edition of the Complete Psychological Works of Sigmund Freud: vol. 17* (ed. J. Strachey), London: Hogarth Press, 1919.

16. Ballard (1969c), *op.cit.*, p.123, p.131, p.133 and p.124 respectively.

17. S. Gooch, *Total Man: Notes Towards an Evolutionary Theory of Personality*, London: Abacus, 1975, p.23.

18. Ballard (1969c), *op.cit.*, p.141.

19. Freud, *op.cit.*, p.366.

20. Ballard (1962b), *op.cit.*, p.44.

21. *Ibid.*, p.71.

22. *Ibid.*, p.110.

23. C.G. Jung, 'Conscious, Unconscious, and Individuation', in *Jung: Selected Writing* (ed. A. Storr), London: Fontana, 1983, p.212.

24. *Ibid.*, p.422.

25. Ballard (1962b), *op.cit.*, p.175.

26. Quoted in J. Goddard and D. Pringle, 'An Interview with J.G. Ballard', in *J.G. Ballard: The First Twenty Years*, London: Bran's Head, 1976, pp.8-35 (p.23).

27. *Ibid.*, p.23.

28. J.G. Ballard, *The Atrocity Exhibition*, London: Re/Search (expanded 1990 edition of 1970 original).

29. Ballard (1978a), *op.cit.*, p.188.

30. Brian Aldiss and David Wingrove, *Trillion Year Spree: The History of Science Fiction*, London: Victor Gollancz, p.301.

31. J.G. Ballard, 'The Illuminated Man', in *The Terminal Beach*, Harmondsworth: Penguin, 1966b edition, pp.75-106.

32. In Goddard and Pringle, *op.cit.*, p.9.

33. *Ibid.*, p.21.

34. Ballard (1978b), *op.cit.*, p.65.

35. *Ibid.*, p.118.

36. *Ibid.*, p.63.

37. *Ibid.*, p.110.

38. *Ibid.*, p.111.

39. *Ibid.*, p.19.

40. *Ibid.*, p.125.

41. J.G. Ballard, 'The Gioconda of the Twilight Noon', in *The Terminal Beach*, Harmondsworth: Penguin, 1966c edition, pp.197, 199, 199 and 202 respectively.

42. *Ibid.*, pp.200, 201, 196, 197 and 203 respectively.

43. Ballard (1990), *op.cit.*, pp.19 and 81.

44. Roland Barthes, *S/Z* (trans. Richard Miller), New York: Hill and Wang, 1974, p.95.

45. Joel Weinsheimer, 'Theory of Character: *Emma*', *Poetics Today* 1, pp.1-2, 185-211 (p.195).

46. Seymour Chatman, *Story and Discourse*, Ithaca: Cornell University Press, 1978, p.127.

47. Brian McHale, *Postmodernist Fiction*, London: Methuen, 1987, pp.159-60.

48. David Pringle, *Earth is the Alien Planet: J.G. Ballard's Four Dimensional Nightmare*, London: Borgo Press, 1979, p.6.

49. Jean-Pierre Changeux, *Neuronal Man* (trans. Laurence Garey), Oxford: Oxford University Press, 1986, p.127.

50. In B. Hennessey, 'Interview with J.G. Ballard', *Translatlantic Review* 39, 1971, pp.60-4 (pp.62-3).

10.

LOST IN SPACE:
EXPLORING IMPOSSIBLE GEOGRAPHIES

*...there is a love for the marvellous, a belief in the marvellous, intertwined in all
my projects, which hurries me out of the common pathways of men, even to
the wild sea and unvisited regions I am about to explore.*[1]

The writing and reading of impossibility fiction opens up doorways into other
worlds, strange and unfamiliar places. Impossibility fiction - a suitably nebulous
term for a kind of cultural expression which attempts to escape definition -
contains elements of the unreal which lead us like Walton, Shelley's explorer,
away from 'the common pathways of men'. The strange and unfamiliar places of
impossibility fiction form a set of alternative geographies lying outside the known
world of realist fiction and everyday experience, a fascinating challenge to readers
and critics. Can these places be described, let alone 'mapped', by the academic
explorer and cartographer ?

I would argue that any attempt to literally map these impossible places is
missing the point; the fantastic, as we will see, resists classification. However, in
my tentative investigation of the impossible places of cyberpunk science fiction I
have discovered that readers find it relatively easy to orient themselves, create
'maps of meaning', and intuitively understand these fantastic landscapes. How
these explorers avoid becoming 'lost in space' is the subject of this chapter. I set
out to show this by examining two acts of transformation. Firstly how do readers
actively make sense of descriptions of places in literature, away from the visual
cues of the filmic or televisual *mise en scéne?* The transformation of the written
word into an experience of place is, I would argue, an integral part of the discipline
of geography ('writing about the earth').

The second theme rests on a distinction between science fiction and the
fantastic which draws upon the work of Rosemary Jackson and Carl Malmgren.[2]
The fantastic, as Jackson defines it, can generate impossible meanings which act to
subvert commonsense understanding. This potential can also be found in science
fiction, but is often denied by its writers and readers, who work to rehabilitate the
radical otherness of fantasy. I would like to stress that this generic difference is

arbitrary but nonetheless important. Generic conventions - in this case the tension between fantasy and rationality - are mutually constituted by authors and readers as a set of shared assumptions: a contract between producers and consumers. They are therefore fixed, at any one time, in writing and reading strategies, and visible in the text.

Tracing the act of transformation by which the fantastic is explained away in the act of reading allows us to understand something of the ideology of SF. I would like to argue that illustrating the workings of this 'reading strategy' through a focus on impossible places is a useful contribution to studies of the audience, to cultural geography, and of course to research into impossibility fiction.

I would like to begin with an introduction to cultural geography which will serve to situate my research within the discipline. Following this I would like to present the two main theoretical foundations of this study. The first is concerned with the fantastic and science fiction as genres, modes, or narratives, using the ideas of Rosemary Jackson and Carl Malmgren; the second provides a theory of the relationship between texts and readers. I argue that to understand the nature of impossibility fiction, or indeed of any cultural form, we need to look *beyond* the text as a site for the production of meaning. The chapter therefore concludes with an examination of the empirical work I have used to develop my argument. This involved in-depth groups interviews of science fiction readers, and I will use some material from these groups to show how the meanings of SF places are constructed in relation to the work of William Gibson.[3]

Cultural Geography

The 'new' cultural geography can be seen as part of a wider cultural turn in the social sciences.[4] Rejecting positivist and structural marxist views of culture as either epiphenomenal or determined, geographers have argued that

> Culture is not a residual category, the surface variation left unaccounted for by more powerful economic analyses; it is the very medium through which social change is experienced, contested and constituted.[5]

Representations and experiences of place enter the sphere of cultural politics, as meanings are contested by social groups.[6] There is therefore a *plurality* of cultures, constituted through the discourses of race, gender, sexuality, class and other forms of power.[7] Recent debates within geography have seen a shift towards post-structuralist and postmodernist approaches, linked to an increasing concern

for reflexivity and a critique of the project of geography.[8] Much of the 'new'
cultural geography takes the form of attempts to re-theorise the relationships
between identity, culture and space. The experience of place is considered to play
an integral part in the constitution of identity, but both must be seen as contingent
and socially constructed. Geographers have begun to investigate the cultural
politics of the experience of places, their representation in various media, and the
ways in which these meanings are regulated by dominant forms of culture.

Having discussed the framework in which I am working, I want to draw
upon the work of Rosemary Jackson and Carl Malmgren to examine the problems
inherent in studying impossibility fiction, problems which extend to the
description of impossible places. Having introduced this material, I will move on
to describe some of the common strategies employed in 'reading for place',
returning to the thorny question of 'managing the impossible' to show how readers
of William Gibson's cyberpunk science fiction are far from lost in space, and how
their transformative readings of impossible places have important ideological
consequences.

Theorising the Impossible

In this chapter, I use 'impossibility fiction' as an umbrella term for non- or
anti-realist fictions including SF, horror, and various forms of the fantastic. I want
to suggest that all these fictions contain varying degrees of impossibility, and that
the fantastic represents its most extreme form: it is fantasy that creates the
impossible. For this reason I will concentrate on the nature of the fantastic when
discussing impossibility. Rosemary Jackson writes that the discourse of the
fantastic *attempts* to discuss true otherness; it lies beyond language and is therefore
beyond description and understanding:

> Structured upon contradiction and ambivalence, the fantastic traces in that
> which cannot be said, that which evades articulation or that which is
> represented as 'untrue' and 'unreal'.[9]

As a result, the fantastic can only be theorised as an *absence*. I will use Jackson's
description of spaces and places in the fantastic to illustrate this point.

Her description of the 'topography of the modern fantastic' (pp.42-48) can
be read as an examination of three kinds of impossible places, although this

inevitably involves an act of rationalisation. The first kind of impossible geography is *the empty place*, '...with relatively bleak, empty, indeterminate landscapes, which are less definable as places than as spaces, as white, grey, or shady blanknesses' (p.42). Both space and time have been emptied of meaning, disorienting the traveller; here there is no other, only the self - or, following Jackson's development of this theme, only self-*become*-other (p.58). A second common location is the *place of fog and mirrors*: here meanings are obscured, shifting, or turned back upon themselves, so that stable meanings and understandings are denied. This 'preoccupation with problems of vision and visibility' (p.43) is central to the fantastic; vision is associated with the constitution of the unified self, with knowledge, and control (p.43-45). The third site is the *labyrinth*, an apt topographical metaphor for non-signification. Jackson agrees with Sartre that 'the labyrinth of corridors, doors and stairways that lead to nothing, the signposts that lead to nothing, the innumerable signs that line the road and that mean nothing' are all representative of the meaninglessness of signs in the fantastic.[10] The traveller never arrives at a final meaning, and the journey from signifier to signified can never be completed.

This would seem to present a problem to the mapper of impossible or fantastic places. However, science fictional places, while still impossible compared to locations in the 'real world', are qualitatively different from those listed above; the topography of the fantastic is *transformed* in SF. The key to this can be found in the hoary old film cliche: 'there must be a rational explanation to all this'. In fantastic fiction, and the horror film, there often *is no* rational explanation for impossibility, and this is the source of their power to disturb and subvert the world of the everyday. However, rationality in its broadest sense is the controlling discourse of science fiction.[11] It is this foundation that makes the impossible understandable in SF.[12]

Science fiction places, as a part of this general discourse, are generally *plausible* rather than fantastic, and their form is consistent with scientific principles. Carl Malmgren's work on SF[13] is enormously useful in developing this insight. The central premise of *Self and Other in SF* (1993) is taken from SF author Gregory Benford's acute observation that 'rendering the alien, making the reader experience it, is the crucial contribution of SF'. What Benford calls 'effing the ineffable' represents the chief strategy employed by authors and readers in the transformation of the impossible into the plausible. Malmgren divides SF into two types, *extrapolative* and *speculative*, explaining that the author may proceed either by extrapolation, creating a fictional novum by logical projection or extension from existing actualities, or by speculation, making a quantum leap of the imagination toward an *other* state of affairs.[14]

This distinction is very useful in discussing the relationship between the subversive fantastic and the rational science fictional. SF, I would argue, is *generally* extrapolated 'from existing actualities', and thus unable or unwilling to reach the subversive potential of the fantastic, while more speculative SF is able to promote the disruption of the reader's commonsense understandings. However, since SF must contain some element of impossibility, the fantastic always threatens to disrupt even the most carefully extrapolated description.[15]

I will illustrate the ways in which this is worked out in reading later, but two science fictional places can serve as illustrations for the moment. In Brian Aldiss's *Helliconia* trilogy,[16] the planet of Helliconia is so different from 'ours' that its nature is, at first glance, virtually unthinkable. However, by accepting the principles of astronomy, and applying them to the situation that Aldiss presents us with, we can begin to accept that the existence of Helliconia is possible after all. In this way the impossible becomes manageable through scientific rationality. I would argue that Helliconia is an extrapolated location. Malmgren supplies us with 'an extreme example of speculative Otherness'[17] in the form of Stanislaw Lem's *Solaris*,[18] a planet which proves to be unmanageable to the scientists who investigate it. Solaris, with its wilful and disorienting refusal to be understood, is indeed an excellent example of an impossible place.

I wish to sound a warning here, as I feel that Malmgren's opposition between extrapolated and speculative fictions, like Rosemary Jackson's distinction between the 'modern fantastic' and other, less subversive forms of fantasy, could be seen as a way of attributing value to some literary forms at the expense of others.[19] Jackson, in particular, goes to great lengths to define her preferred form of the fantastic, creating what can only be described as a canon of subversion. Both critics have valuably illustrated the central strategies of the fantastic and science fiction, but their emphasis on *whole texts* blinds them to the more subtle way in which these acts of subversion and rehabilitation operate.

Authors and readers create *moments* of impossibility in the act of writing or reading across a much wider range of texts than either Jackson's or Malmgren's typologies would allow. In particular, readers can 'misread' the plausibility of SF, refusing to follow the author's strategy of managing impossibility and creating fantasy in the midst of rationality. Similarly, readers of the fantastic can refuse to suspend their disbelief, applying a rational explanation to a situation intended to deny this strategy. The creation of rational meaning is a very delicate operation, and as such cannot be analyzed in such a reductive way.

However, for the sake of this argument, I will assume that the fantastic is *generally* written and read to create impossible situations, while SF is *generally* written and read to 'manage' impossibility. These generic characteristics are written into texts as conventions shared by authors and readers. To ascribe values to either form at this level of definition, is, however, meaningless. Instead, the critic must develop a more flexible understanding of the ways in which meanings are transformed from author to reader, so that we can start to trace *common strategies* of reading for and managing impossibility. Our claims must be made from particular instances, so we can see how readers follow or reject textual clues; Helliconia, for example, could be read as a fantastic place by readers with no desire to accept the strictures of astronomy, and Solaris could be 'understood' by other readers who despaired of the inadequacies of the scientists sent to investigate the planet. I will give some examples of this 'misreading' later, but the fact that Helliconia and Solaris are generally read as plausible and impossible respectively suggests that there *are* strongly established ways of writing and reading which either promote or deny impossibility. This emphasis on more localised analysis leads me on to the next of my theoretical foundations.

The Text-Reader Relationship: Exploring Impossibility

Audience research and reader-response literature has suggested many ways to conceptualise the experience of reading, which is now widely accepted to be an active and creative process, rather than something which is determined by the author or text.[20] However, in retreating from theories of textual power we risk over-estimating the power of the reader. For example, an increasing amount of critical attention is being focused on science fiction audiences, as forms of fan culture.[21] Valuable though this work is, it sometimes reaches the point where 'the text is simply dissolved into its readings'.[22] As a result the power of the text to set 'preferred readings' has been overcome by the endlessly resourceful reader as a kind of 'poacher'.[23]

Instead we must keep text and reader together, examining the ways that texts attempt to fix meanings and the strategies readers deploy to 'unfix' them. Martin Barker[24] suggests that we see this relationship as a dialogical one, and I feel that this is a fruitful approach.[25] Subjects in dialogue do not simply 'affect' each other; meaning is generated by the interaction of two people in conversation, or by a reader and a magazine. This conversation is not, however, always one of equals, and the resultant meanings often reflect the asymmetries of power. A complete definition of dialogism would take too much time to give here but I would like to argue that this approach allows us to situate the meaning of science fiction texts within their wider social and cultural contexts.[26] There are three levels of dialogue which I feel are interesting in terms of my research; to properly evaluate the meanings of SF, we must be able to assess the role each plays in constituting meaning for the reader.

The encounter between text and reader serves to create textual meanings, but this relationship is informed by other dialogical relationships. Within what I call the SF dialogues', the text is evaluated in regard to other texts in SF and related genres, which is how generic conventions and canons are formed and changed; similarly the reader is immersed in a network of other readings, informed by readers and critics. All these relationships are nested within more general dialogues, relating to the constitution of meaning and value within particular cultural situations. So a reader might evaluate Gibson's novels (the first level of dialogue) in the light of his or her reading of other cyberpunk texts and conversation with other readers (the second level), and any response to the social and cultural issues that Gibson raises in the text (the third level).

One useful way of situating particular understandings within these dialogues involves conducting discussion groups with readers. My own research is built around three such groups of readers, all interested in the work of cyberpunk author William Gibson, who discussed ideas of technology, future societies and SF places with me in a format designed to recover not just their 'responses' to texts but also the wider context of their reading. I would like to demonstrate the value of the dialogical approach in interrogating the material gained in these discussions by illustrating *how we read for place* and the ways in which impossibility is *managed* in the construction of science fictional places.

I will trace these reading strategies using excerpts from the third meeting of the first discussion group.[27] The first two pages of transcripts (reproduced below) will be used to show how readers create an experience of place in science fiction. Once these strategies have been introduced, I will go on to talk in more detail about the key places of William Gibson's fiction, cyberspace and the Sprawl, using the last set of transcripts.

Reading For Place in Science Fiction

The first excerpt concerns Peter's response to the setting of C. J. Cherryh's *Downbelow Station* (1983).[28]

Peter: ...its discussing this planet, and it's wet, soggy and miserable. Now I grew up in Lincolnshire *[laughter]*, and this place reminds me of - like the salt marsh, sort of estuarine, boggy, peaty *[laughter from Jeff]*, it could actually be the top of Kinderscout, mainly it's the Wash, only a whole fucking planet covered with this rivery grassland *[laughs]* *[laughter]*, around King's Lynn - so that was one place that actually hit it bang on the, er, nail... Unless an author actually puts some effort into describing his, er, background, I often find that I don't actually have to have my mind invent too much scenery in which the thing happens, I mean - unless he actually describes it in some detail, I find myself thinking of a very sort of minimalist stage set, you know, barren plains, maybe a bit of grass, windswept slaty sky and you've got... whatever building construction nearby described in detail, but I don't actually flesh out my landscapes that much without the author giving me key references...

That particular book she did make it quite clear, and fitting it in with her alien lifeforms, and er.. so the weather conditions and what it was like - and the ground, it was very important to the actual plot, the conflict between the - the Downbelow station, the people that were actually on the planet and station, that was actually the meeting point for a large interstellar trading operation, and it - it was actually a very complex story, so yes, it's not surprising that I had a picture of that planet.

The second excerpt starts with John's experience of reading Ursula Le Guin's *The Dispossessed*,[29] and then goes on to talk more generally about the setting for *Blade Runner*.[30]

John: Yeah, I did read *The Dispossessed* just recently, I re-read it,
             Ursula Le Guin, and she did a very good job - not... or not
             too obviously by saying this was here, this was there, but
             doing it through the story and the way the characters were
             interacting, you got a very vivid image of what the planet
             was like, more than usual, and... I think very often I'm in a
             similar thing, unless it's brought out to me, I'll leave large
             parts of the background blank, I haven't particularly
             fleshed it out... I'm following particular areas, but er... you
             know, unlike film, I won't fill in all the, all the holes.
             There's lots of holes there, I'm just sort of filling in the
             right particular area I'm generally - if it's left [out], it'll be
             references which I see every day, so an office block is an
             office block...

Peter: I think the *Blade Runner* thing's got a lot to answer for
             [agreement from Bob and Margaret] in our perceptions
             nowadays of cityscapes in er, in science fiction.

John: I had that idea though, before I ever saw *Blade Runner*.

Peter: Yeah, but now it's very hard to get out of it.

I feel that these transcripts can be interpreted to reveal two overlapping themes -
the ways in which we read for place, and the ways in which we read the
impossible. Both sets of strategies represent the reader's part in a dialogue
between text and reader. The fact that these strategies are relatively common
reflects the degree to which conventions, both generic (science fictional) and
novelistic (spatial description), are accepted by readers.

     Creating images of place, Peter starts with 'a very sort of minimalist stage
set', and John also leaves the background 'blank'. Unlike film, literature cannot
provide a constant reminder of the setting. The idea of place must be created by
more explicit textual strategies or by the actions of the reader, or 'filling in the
holes' as Peter puts it. The transcripts demonstrate three ways of doing this.
Firstly, Peter is able to conjure up memories of the area in which he grew up,
which he sees as similar to the setting of Cherryh's book. Similarly, John says that
he fills in 'holes' in his idea of place by adding *'references which I see every day'*.
If an office block is mentioned but not described, he will fill in the gap with an

office block that he knows or perhaps with a general idea of 'office block-ness'. The second way in which we fill in the background is through the workings of the text. Peter mentions that the complexity of the story, and the action in the foreground, helped bring the background into clearer view. John says that Le Guin achieved the same effect 'through the story and the way the characters were interacting'. This is a strategy employed by the author to create a convincing description of place. Lastly, the relationship between the city in *Blade Runner* and those in other SF texts depends upon his knowledge of the genre as a whole. In this way we can see that 'the *Blade Runner* thing's got a lot to answer for', as it helped to 'set' a powerful idea of the cyberpunk city within SF texts and in readers' expectations.

The most powerful literary experiences of place, therefore, are a combination of three strategies: the reader's use of personal experience; the author's deliberate descriptions of novelistic space; and intertextual links with other represented spaces, often within the same genre. However, this constitution of place is problematised in impossibility fiction, simply because readers cannot imagine the experience of the fantastic; authors cannot capture it in language; and links to other fantastic texts provide only more mystification. So how do these strategies of reading for place work in science fiction, a mixture of the possible and the unimaginable?

Much of the discourse of SF, as I argued earlier, acts to close off the subversive potential of the impossible, 'managing' fantastic elements of texts through recourse to scientific rationality. This can be seen in Peter's comments. Describing Cherryh's planet, he says that she made the setting 'quite clear' by 'fitting it in with her alien lifeforms', and 'the weather conditions'. I would like to argue that Peter is here suggesting that there is an *ecology* to Cherryh's world: that all these fictional elements are made to fit together in a coherent whole. When fantastic elements are 'fitted in' in this way, they lose their impossible nature. The metaphor of ecology is an important one in this strategy of scientifically managing impossible places in science fiction. Frank Herbert's Arrakis, the setting for the *Dune* series, is the most obvious example. An impossibly arid planet, complete with unthinkable sandworms, is carefully structured as a coherent ecological unit, moving from fantastic to plausible.[31] I would argue that Peter, who asserted that the mark of good SF was 'internal consistency' in an earlier discussion, is reading Cherryh's planet in the same way, and that this is a strategy commonly accepted by authors and readers.

This does not necessarily strip the text of its sense of impossibility; the reader using this strategy can still experience a sense of wonder. I would like to show this with an excerpt from the second group. Mark is discussing the setting of Helliconia's main sun, which will not return in the watcher's lifetime:

Mark: That idea, and the whole idea of the whole planet - of the ecology of the planet shifting to far greater extent than we experience here, would be the Great Year in a binary system... it just made me shiver to think of the sun going down and not seeing it again, even though you have a sort of other sun to keep you busy.

It is significant that Mark has a degree in astronomy and physics, and can see Helliconia's binary system as a plausible construction. However, the strangeness of experiencing such a world is still capable of making him shiver. Managing the impossible does not have to be a complete denial of impossibility.

Taken together, these strategies of reading for place and managing the impossible show us how meaningful ideas of place can be created in science fiction.

Gibson's Places: Cyberspace and the Sprawl

In this last section I would like to illustrate some of the ways in which managing the impossible allows readers to respond to fantastic places, and to show the ideological situation of these moves. I would like to look at cyberspace and the Sprawl, the settings of William Gibson's fiction, through the constructions of the three groups of readers I interviewed.

Reading cyberspace in the light of my discussion of the topography of the fantastic allows me to demonstrate the gap between the potential meanings of cyberspace and the readings that my group members made. Cyberspace can be read as a kind of virtual reality, and I would like to contrast the two to show how the fantastic is *ordered* in SF. VR is often represented as a playground, a place where all meanings are relative, where signs cease to signify. VR places do not have to possess dimensions, to be subject to linear time, or to respect the border between the self (the user) and the other (everything else). I would like to argue that in this form it is the contemporary equivalent of the fantastic *empty place*. The subversive implications of this are, I think, partly responsible for some of the fledgling 'moral panics' surrounding the introduction of VR technology.

Cyberspace, on the other hand, is an *ordered space*, with directions, linear pathways, beginnings and ends. Instead of an empty place it is a labyrinth, but one in which the heroic console cowboys (Gibson's hackers) can find a path and reach a goal. Gibson's cowboys impose their will upon cyberspace, and I would like to argue that in this way cyberspace is closer to Gibson's Sprawl than it is to a fantastic place.[32] Even when the fantastic irrupts into cyberspace in the form of voodoo in *Count Zero* (1986) and *Mona Lisa Overdrive* (1988),[33] it is quickly emptied of its subversive potential and contained. In the text, this otherness is resolutely racialized and sexualized, suggesting only reactionary meanings. Readers have their own strategies for dealing with the fantastic: the members of group three saw the voodoo material as evidence that Gibson's characters had been left behind by the pace of technological development, and were no longer able to make rational sense of it. The strangeness of Virek's end in *Count Zero*, killed by a voodoo *loa* in a computer-generated environment, is, to these readers, merely a function of the plausible sophistication of an artificial intelligence. Once again, potentially fantastic elements are rationalized away.[34]

The dystopian nightmarishness of Gibson's Sprawl (and urban locations in general) was generally read by my discussants as a simple extrapolation of contemporary cities.[35] This is a plausible future, rationally predicted; my groups expected it, but did not seem to think that it could, or should, be avoided. The following transcripts show that there are differing responses to Gibson's descriptions of urban settings.

Peter: I certainly wouldn't want to go - to go into Gibson's cities, er... I - well -

John: *[laughing]* It's not my idea of a holiday! *[laughter]*

Peter: No, no - I'll probably land up living in one of the bloody things! *[laughs]*

John: You are!

Peter: Yes, exactly! *[laughter]* But er... there's plenty of holiday resorts are often being described in some of these books,

it's the kind of place that I wouldn't mind going
[laughter]...

Peter: Quite often I think I'd actually prefer to steer well clear of
            it and go to some of these backward fantasies when the
            world was nice and green and fresh, and er plenty of
            space...

Bob: I wouldn't mind going to the *Blade Runner* city - for a
            week.

Peter: [...] - make sure you'd get back again.

Bob: Yeah - oh, with plenty of cash, and a nice hotel room.

Peter: But it's fairly rare that they end up describing... nice, laid-
            back *[laughter from Jeff]* relaxing places, with relaxing
            things happening in them, er...

Steve: Be a boring story, really, wouldn't it ?

These conversations reveal an interesting mixture of curiosity and fear. Peter
seems to want to avoid the Sprawl altogether, preferring 'nice, laid-back relaxing
places', but most of my other respondents attempt to reconcile their desires and
fears through strategies of *control*. There are two common forms in which they
imagine 'controlling' their experience of such a place: either they seek to control
the Sprawl through *force*, or they desire to *know* it in such a way as to be able to
avoid danger. Some of the most interesting strategies mentioned in my discussions
revolved around becoming a cyborg with body modifications like radar or some
kind of 'sixth sense', increased reflexes and speed, implanted weapons, or grafted
muscle. These choices, along with other comments, suggest to me that some of
my interviewees would attempt to control the Sprawl through being able to clearly
'read' it, in the same way that *noir* detectives know their way through the mean
streets, or through improved options for flight or attack. Both strategies seek to
manage what could otherwise be experienced as an impossible place.

I would like to argue that Gibson's Sprawl is an ordered labyrinth, and that
my group members seek to turn this maze into a knowable city. If they can impose
order on the labyrinth by force, or by 'reading' its apparently meaningless signs,

then they can negotiate it safely. This desire is similar to the way in which the console cowboy operates in cyberspace.

This conclusion must consider the key role that masculinity plays in these experiences of Gibson's cities, and the similarities between this and common masculine strategies for negotiating real urban landscapes. I feel that my groups statements correspond to Andrew Ross's interpretation of the cyberpunk aesthetic as a way of dealing with the experience of the city.[36] Ross argues that during the 1980s the image of the 'inner city' changed from a racialized place of danger to a masculinized place of *risk*. The traveller, often a male gentrifier, seeks to confront and control urban dangers. This transformation of the figure of the gumshoe still places great emphasis on the ability to read the codes of a hostile city, and to physically overcome its obstacles. Obviously, this is not the only way in which readers of cyberpunk read the future city, but it has been a common enough theme in our discussions that I feel it warrants discussion. I feel that these strategies are strongly (though not essentially) gendered, and that they do tie into common narratives of urban exploration, but there is insufficient space to cover these themes in this chapter.

Conclusions

The discussions I have carried out with readers of science fiction have illustrated two important themes: the ways in which we read for place in literature generally; and the ways in which we seek to order the fantastic through recourse to rationality in the case of science fiction in particular. Reading strategies like those described above prevent explorers from losing their way in the fantastic places of impossibility fiction, but their value as navigational aids is open to question. Readers may happily lose themselves in the impossibility of cyberspace, against the 'assumed reading' I have discussed above; other readers may find that their reliance on such mechanisms leads them to ignore other experiences, other forms of explanation.

James Kneale

NOTES

1. Mary Shelley, *Frankenstein, or, The Modern Prometheus*, Ware: Wordsworth, 1993 (1818), p.10.

2. Rosemary Jackson, *Fantasy: the literature of subversion*, London and New York: Routledge, 1981, and Carl Malmgren, 'Self and Other in SF: Alien Encounters'. *Science Fiction Studies*, 20: 15-33 (1993).

3. William Gibson, *Neuromancer*, 1984; *Burning Chrome*, 1986; *Count Zero*, 1987; *Mona Lisa Overdrive*, 1988, all published London: Grafton.

4. David Chaney, *The Cultural Turn: scene-setting essays on contemporary cultural history*. London and New York: Routledge, 1994.

5. Denis Cosgrove and Peter Jackson, 'New Directions in Cultural Geography', *Area* 19, 1987, pp.95-101.

6. Linda McDowell, 'The Transformation of Cultural Geography' in Gregory, Martin and Smith (eds), *Human Geography: society, space and social science*, Basingstoke and London: Macmillan, 1994, pp.146-173.

7. Peter Jackson, *Maps of Meaning*. London: Unwin Hyman, 1989.

8. Gillian Rose, *Feminism and Geography: The limits of geographical knowledge*. Cambridge: Polity Press, 1993.

9. R. Jackson, *op.cit.*, p.37.

10. Carl Malmgren, *Worlds Apart: Narratology of Science Fiction*. Bloomington and Indianapolis: Indiana University Press, 1991, and *op.cit.*, p.15.

11. For some excellent examples of the problems of creating and maintaining this scientific rationality in SF, see John Huntingdon, *Rationalizing Genius: Ideological Strategies in the Classic American Science Fiction Short Story*, New Brunswick and London: Rutgers University Press, 1989; David Samuelson, 'Modes of Extrapolation: The Formulas of Hard SF', *Science Fiction Studies* 20, 1993, pp.191-232; and Gary Westfahl, '"The Closely Reasoned Technological Story": The Critical History of Hard Science Fiction', *Science Fiction Studies* 20, 1993, pp.157-175.

12. In horror, the fantastic *may* be contained by the structures of science, religion, or myth.

13. Malmgren, 1993, *op.cit.*, p.42.

14. *Ibid.*, p.17.

15. I am thinking here of the fantastic as a form of Carnival (Mikhail Bakhtin, *Problems of Dostoevsky's Poetics*, (ed. and trans. by Caryl Emerson, with an introduction by Wayne C. Booth), Manchester: Manchester University Press, 1984a) or of science fictional rationality as a monological discourse which suppresses, but can never entirely contain, the voice of fantasy as otherness (Mikhail Bakhtin, *Rabelais and his World*, (trans. by Hélène Iswolsky), Bloomington: Indiana University Press, 1984b).

16. Brian Aldiss, *Helliconia Spring, Helliconia Summer, Helliconia Winter*, all published London: Triad Grafton, 1983.

17. Malmgren, 1993, *op.cit.*, p.42.

18. Stanislaw Lem, Stanislaw, *Solaris*, (trans. Joanna Kilmartin and Steve Cox), San Diego, New York and London: Harcourt Brace Jovanovich, 1970.

19. See Roger Luckhurst's study of the drawing of boundaries between 'good' and 'bad' SF for further illustrations of this critical strategy ('Border Policing', *Science Fiction Studies* 18, 1991, pp.358-366.

20. See for example Jane Tompkins (ed), *Reader-Response Criticism: from Formalism to Post-Structuralism*. Baltimore and London: John Hopkins University Press, 1980; Stanley Fish, *Is There a Text in This Class? The authority of interpretive communities*. Cambridge, Massachusetts: Harvard University Press, 1980; and Wolfgang Iser, *Prospecting: from reader response to literary anthropology*, Baltimore: John Hopkins University Press, 1989, for reader-response. See also John Fiske, *Television Culture*, London and New York: Methuen, 1987; Ellen Seiter, Hans Borchers,

Gabriele Kreutzner, and Eva-Marie Warth (eds), *Remote Control: television, audiences, and cultural power*, London: Routledge, 1989; Shaun Moores, 'Texts, readers and contexts of reading: developments in the study of media audiences', *Media, Culture and Society* 12, 1990, pp.9-29; and especially David Morley, *Television, Audiences and Cultural Studies*, London and New York: Routledge, 1992, for discussion of the 'new' audience paradigm in media studies.

21. For example Henry Jenkins, *Textual Poachers: Television Fans and Participatory Culture*, New York and London: Routledge, 1992, and John Tulloch and Henry Jenkins, *Science Fiction Audiences: Watching Star Trek and Dr Who*, London and New York: Routledge, 1995.

22. Morley, *op.cit.*, p.27.

23. Michel De Certeau, *The Practice of Everyday Life*, Berkeley, Los Angeles and London: University of California Press, 1984.

24. Martin Barker, *Comics, Ideology, Power and the Critics*, Manchester and New York: Manchester University Press, 1989.

25. See Barker's chapter 12 for his discussion of this.

26. See Robert Stam ('Mikhail Bakhtin and Left Cultural Critique', in E. Ann Kaplan (ed), *Postmodernism and its Discontents: theories, practices*, London and New York: Verso, 1988, pp.116-145) and Michael Holquist, *Dialogism: Bakhtin and his World*, London and New York: Routledge, (1990) for more information on the value of the dialogical method.

27. All names are pseudonyms to ensure anonymity.

28. C.J. Cherryh, *Downbelow Station*, London: Grafton, 1983.

29. Ursula Le Guin, *The Dispossessed*, London: Granada, 1974.

30. Ridley Scott (director), *Blade Runner*, 1982.

31. There is an eight-page appendix entitled *The Ecology of Dune* in the 1984 New England Library reprint of *Dune* (1965).

32. The members of my second group emphasised the distinction between VR and cyberspace in Gibson's novels. One discussant said that the key difference was that where VR modelled our reality, cyberspace was modelled on the 'world of the computer' - thus recognising the rational nature of Gibson's artificial environment.

33. Gibson, 1987, 1988, *op.cit.*

34. This idea parallels Arthur C. Clarke's famous maxim, 'any sufficiently advanced technology is indistinguishable from magic'. The popularity of this idea with my groups does, I think, demonstrate the power of rational explanation to deny other forms of understanding and other ways of seeing.

35. The term 'sprawl', though not a Gibsonian invention, is an apt description of the confusing spaces of the postmodern city.

36. Andrew Ross, *Strange Weather: Culture, Science and Technology in the Age of Limits*, London and New York: Verso, 1991.

11.

MARY SHELLEY'S LAST MAN
(THE END OF THE WORLD AS WE KNOW IT)

The literary end of the world is rarely the very end. Ends become new beginnings, and new worlds are born in depite of the death-throes of our particular self-absorbed universe. Time, which we had expected to be linear and final, proves at last, cyclic, provisional, and greater.

Within the genre of end-of-the-world narratives, there may be said to be the distinct sub-genres; the end of the world with and without survivors. And prominent among those with survivors is the narrative of the last man. Literature of the fate of the last man is fantasy; it is both an impossibility, and a vehicle for the consideration of impossibility fiction; it is both a nightmare, and the final egocentric wish-fulfilment. These narratives have been written for a long time; they are being written still. This is the story of one nexus of ancestry through which the last man is transmitted to us, one route by which he developed from a fiction into a myth.

In 1805 a rather extraordinary book was published in Paris, a romance describing the anguished and violent end of the world, entitled *Le Dernier Homme*, by Jean-Baptiste Cousin de Grainville, sometime Catholic priest, sometime polemical philosopher. In 1806 the English version was published in London, anonymously translated as a two-volume novel, *The Last Man, or Omegarus and Syderia, A Romance in Futurity*. It enjoyed considerable popularity, for a time, in the circulating libraries. *Omegarus and Syderia* became the prototype for a whole series of publications in the years that followed, devoted to the sole human survivor of a general catastrophe, making the last man a striking minor theme of Romantic literature. I propose to discuss the last man narratives and poems, first outlining them individually, and then considering some broader issues raised by the theme.

Cousin de Grainville's vision of the last days of the earth was published in 1805, ironically at the very height of the regeneration of strength and purpose in France under Napoleon. As early as 1756 a teenage Grainville was planning *Le Dernier Homme*, originally intending it as an epic poem. Grainville drew on a prevailing taste for gloom and pessimism in French literature, in which private confessions of despair were projected into fantasies of general destruction. Grainville became one of many to derive from visions of the past in chaos a chaotic, disintegrating future. While Mary Shelley's treatment of the last man theme was to be conspicuous for its secular, non-supernatural view of catastrophe, Grainville's novel is populated by all manner of spirits; its august cast-list includes, among others, the Celestial Spirit of Futurity, the Genius of the Earth, Nature, Time, Death, and indeed a brief cameo by God. The plot centres on the struggle of Omegarus, heir to the French empire, and the American Syderia, the last two mortals capable of reproduction in a sterile and and dying world. In a compellingly circular structure, Adam, the first man, is released from his torments to approach Omegarus, the last of his progeny, and persuade him to commit an act of supreme obedience to God that will undo his original transgression, allowing the fallen world to die and precipitating the Last Judgement. Omegarus is to desert his wife and abandon their prized fertility; the race of men begotten by their union is prophesied to be a foul species of murderers and cannibals, perverting yet further the seed of Adam. Yet Omegarus and Syderia's love is innocent, and has an emblematic force that tends towards consummation; the last man seeks the last woman, the urge to reproduce becomes the urge to create a new world.

Set against Adam, and the will of God, is the the Genius of the Earth, a personification of the world who needs the perpetuation of mankind for his own survival, and attempts to bring the couple back together, using false prophecy and guile. The novel ends in a combination of Christian eschatology and Grainville's own science fiction, the final battle between Death and the Genius of the Earth exploding the entire planet, as human souls are reborn and judged. Creation comes to a merciful full-stop, and the narrator's vision of the future closes with the instruction that he spread the word and celebrate the unsung achievements of Omegarus, last man and last hero. Or, in other words, give him readers.

The first English treatment of the last man motif was by Lord Byron, in his blank verse dream poem 'Darkness', penned in a melancholy mood in exile from London society in Geneva, in 1816. 'Darkness' depicts the extinction of the sun and the subsequent degeneration of mankind into barbarity, each individual crazed in a struggle for light, warmth and food, until the last two survivors face each other and die 'of their mutual hideousness' (1. 67).[1] Darkness is personified as female, incidentally, as are both Night and Darkness in *Omegarus and Syderia*, and as the Plague was to be in Mary Shelley's novel. Byron's line in 'Darkness' has a rolling Scriptural power to it. ('And they did live by the watchfires', 1. 10 ... 'Happy were those who dwelt within the eye / Of the volcanoes', ll. 16-17 ... 'Morn came and went - and came, and brought no day', 1. 6 ...). There is clearly a Biblical echo in the extinction of the sun, and the howling and gnashing of teeth recalls a verse from Matthew. A sense of desolation is achieved by ironic means; Byron makes use of some imagery from the Christian apocalypse, and yet robs it of its fortunate outcome. There is no point at which destruction gives way to 'a new heaven and a new earth', as in the Book of Revelation;[2] the nature of destruction in the poem is associated with chiliasm and the millenium, era of perfect godly rule on earth; but no millenium appears. Mary Shelley was to follow Byron in her treatment of the theme, in raising false millenial hopes. These texts, then, although 'revelatory' in some ways, cannot be said to be *apocalyptic* in the strictest sense, as a catastrophe does not give rise to a heavenly kingdom on earth. 'Darkness' was much praised, and likened to Dante by *The Literary Gazette*, which called it 'the finest specimen we have hitherto had of his Lordship's abilities'.[3]   It prompted two direct imitations.

Far from the majestic despair of Byron's poem, Thomas Campbell's 'The Last Man' of 1823 is lyrical, and displays a sanguine Christianity. Campbell, a popular rhymer of his day, was the auther of *The Pleasures of Hope*, and possessed of a rather more sociable muse than some of his rivals to last man fame. Campbell's 'The Last Man' has a prophet-like hero defying the fading sun to weaken his religious conviction; the wholesomeness of his Evangelical angle on the motif made Campbell's poem the most widely known version, being parodied as late as the 1850s. However, in his determination to associate his own name with the supposed invention of the genre, Campbell started a quarrel in the literary press that made the last man eventually a joke figure as well as a cult figure of the time. In a more than generous appraisal of Campbell's latest collection, *The Edinburgh Review* in 1825 suggested his owing a debt to Byron for his subject matter:

> There is a very striking little poem called 'The Last Man', the idea of which has probably been borrowed from a very powerful sketch of Lord Byron's, to which he gave, we think, the title of 'Darkness', and the manner in which the awful subject is treated by those two great authors is very characteristic of the different turns of their genius. Lord Byron's has more variety of topics, more gloom and terror, and far more daring and misanthropy. Mr. Campbell's has more sweetness, more reflection, more considerate loftiness, and more of the spirit of religion.[4]

Campbell replied in a letter to *The Times*:

> Now the truth is, that fifteen or it may be more years ago, I called on Lord Byron [...] and we had a long, and to me, very memorable conversation, from which I have not a doubt, that his Lordship imbibed those few ideas in the poem, 'Darkness', which have any resemblances to mine in The Last Man. I

remember my saying to him, that I thought the idea of a being witnessing the
extinction of his species and of the Creation [...] would make a striking subject
for a poem.[...] I abandoned, for a great many years, the idea of fulfilling my
sketch. But I was provoked to change my mind, when my friend Barry
Cornwall informed me that an acquaintance of his intended to write a long
poem, entitled The Last Man. I thought this hard! The conception of the Last
Man had been mine fifteen years ago; even Lord Byron had spared the title to
me: I therefore wrote my poem so called, and sent it to the press.[5]

Campbell's indignation was either uninformed or misplaced; it was pointed
with not little amusement that *Omegarus and Syderia* had a prior claim on the
theme. It was further suggested that the theme was a trite one, and needed no
amplification, original or otherwise. The popularity of Campbell's poem
notwithstanding, the last man was considered a ridiculous theme by the time Mary
Shelley's novel of the same was published in 1826; it received only antagonistic
attention in the periodicals, which, nevertheless, raised some interesting questions,
as we will see.

In January 1826 Mary Shelley published her three-volume novel *The Last
Man*, narrated by Lionel Verney, the eventual sole survivor of a pestilence that
spreads from Egypt to engulf the entire planet. The plot, although less grand than
earlier versions - of the death of the sun, and breakdown of the laws of the natural
universe - was more potentially disturbing in 1826 due to its immediacy. Mary's
unspecified but grisly plague corresponds to a frightening, incurable cholera
spreading westwards from its first appearance in Asia in 1817.

The Last Man pictures a republican England between the years 2073 and
2100. Verney marries into the family of the abdicated king, and witnesses the
affairs of state before and after the plague lays waste to the nations of Europe,
welling up in the besieged city of Constantinople before claiming every human life
save his own. The dwindling group of English survivors, having lived through the
onslaught of marauding bands of invaders and outbreaks of religious fanaticism,
leave their homes and begin a trek across mainland Europe, seeking an idyllic
climate that will stop the progress of the disease. Mary's picture of the 21st century
is recognisably a projection of certain elements of her own age; the Greek wars
against the Turkish oppressor continue, occasioning the death of the Byronic
character Lord Raymond. At times there is a specific indication that the events of
the projected future have derived directly from the novelist's day, seed grown to
maturity, as in this symbolic description of Windsor Forest:

> The ruins of majestic oaks which had grown, flourished, and decayed during the
> progress of centuries, marked where the limits of the forest once reached, while
> the shattered palings and neglected underwood shewed that this part was
> deserted for the younger plantations, which owed their birth to the beginning of
> the nineteenth century, and now stood in the pride of maturity.[6]

The novel exhibits both forthright commentary on its own time, and aso every age's belief that it stands in unique and meaningful relation to the age of apocalypse, in a state of dialogue with the end.

1826 was also the year of Thomas Hood's spirited poem, 'The Last Man', the jocular and macabre narration of a hangman who finds himself the lone survivor, also of a plague. Hood uses an extended ballad stanza, which combines to good effect a tone of cheerful burlesque with some undeniable horror in a bleak end-game. In 1826 also John Martin completed the first of his three paintings of the last man theme. These are the principal last men. There were others: the fragmentary drama of Thomas Lovell Beddoes (the presumptuous friend of Barry Cornwall mentioned by Campbell), the bombastic poem of Thomas John Ouseley, the exercises in Byronic imitation of Reade and Pollok, and innumerable satires loosely based on Campbell and Mary Shelley. More recently, much more recently, the title was revived by Thom Gunn in his fine sequence of poems. But I will focus in the main on Mary Shelley, and attempt to open up some of the richness of the motif.

I believe a last man narrative is of a distinct genre, and raises issues not necessarily present in any end-of-the-world narrative. The figure of the last man alive, alone in the world, stands in special proximity to the author, even if he is not a narrator; he is a figure outside of time, a scale-figure, perhaps, in a grand landscape like John Martin's; not only is he the *only* speaker, the quintessential speaker, and therefore author-like, but he is fast becoming equivalent to his own text - marooned in a vast landscape that no longer yields meaning save by his say-so, he is both writer and reader. The once-textual world is emptied of signs until the only functional sign is himself, his own dynamic body the only locus of experience.

In the first place, there is the problem of lastness, something Mary Shelley's critics were quick to point out. *The Monthly Magazine* pounced on the apparent paradox of a 'last' narrative having any readers, the fact that it had readers negating its putative lastness; this is hardly a profound point in itself, but underlines the general unimaginability of last things, and concomitant anxieties in writers and readers of the genre. In an essay entitled 'The Last Book: with a Dissertation on Last Things in General', the reviewer wittily complains:

> A term should be invented comprehensive enough to include those superlatively late comers that usually follow the last. [...] But, as words are at present, last things are generally the last things in the world that are last. [...] In short, there is no getting at the last of our never-ending, still-beginning language.[7]

Subsequent articles laboured the point with decreasing imagination, yet the quibble revealed sure enough a certain disquiet inherent in the subject matter, if not, perhaps, laughable self-contradiction. The answer to the question 'Well, if you're supposed to be the last man, who do you think you're talking to, and how can I be reading your story?' is clearly 'Don't be absurd. This is a novel'. Yet the fact that authors have felt the need pre-emptively to answer the charge attests to its nagging insistence. The *poet* of lastness has somewhat less of a problem, writing - and being seen to write - in a visionary rather than documentary vein. Byron and Campbell did in fact use the statement of dreaming to introduce the piece (respectively: 'I had a dream, which was not all a dream', l. 1; and 'I saw a vision in my sleep, / That gave my spirit strength to sweep / Adown the gulf of time!', ll. 5-7). Byron's 'I had a dream, which was not all a dream' is a strong opening line, in which the qualification serves to render more haunting the picture of the End that follows. Yet I would suggest that it is Hood's blatant opening that seems the most assured and secure in this respect, totally wanting any note of explanation or apology. ('Twas in the year two thousand and one, / A pleasant morning of May...'[9]).

The anxiety that prompts an explanation of readership is dealt with by the two novelists in comparable ways, except that for Grainville the story transmitted from the future is held to be definitive and immutable, whereas for Mary Shelley it is more apocryphal and relative. Grainville's 'I' is given a direct cinematic revelation of the future, but the narrator of Mary Shelley's introduction pieces together a fragmentary narrative from Sibylline leaves, herself partaking of the process of creation or authorship. Verney's story is found in the cave of the Cumaean Sibyl, near Naples, in a chaos of many languages - some living and some dead. This is the first of Mary's indications that this *last* experience has come completely outside of chronological time to reach, mysteriously, our eyes.

There are many instances in which the characters of the novel express a vertiginous sensation of having come outside of time, observing their circumstances from a great a detachment, in an infinite present. Lord Raymond, on hearing a prophecy of his death:

> Earth is to me a tomb, the firmament a vault, shrouding mere corruption. Time is no more, for I have stepped within the threshold of eternity; each man I meet appears a corse, which will soon be deserted of its animating spark, on the eve of decay and corruption.[10]

Mary Shelley is also accomplished at employing prolepsis in the novel; in her narrative, in direct speech, and in her ironic choice of quotations. In terms of its distortion of perception of time, *The Last Man* makes a perfect model for applying some of the arguments of Frank Kermode's *The Sense of an Ending*. Kermode suggests that we as readers and writers feel a need for intelligible endings, and project ourselves on to the supposed End of all things so as to consider the completed structure, which we are unable to do in our limited state of present, or middle. Thus the articulation of apocalypse, as of endings in general, is one way in which literature attempts to order and make sense of life. He goes on to develop a key distinction between *chronos* normal, passing time, the linear succession of events, and *kairos*, the point in time charged with significance that derives from its relation to the end; the fulfilling of the time, the coming of God's time.[11] *Kairos* transforms past and future, establishing a crisis that puts us in touch with origins. In her efforts to solve the problem of lastness and readership, Mary Shelley intensifies the vertigo of *kairos* in a way that is perfectly apt for a tale of the End.

In Mary Shelley's case, the portrayal of lastness draws on her personal feelings of isolation and despair at the time she was writing the novel. She records in her journal the misery of retreating into uninterrupted monologue since the death of her husband:

> To read and to communicate your reflections to none - to write and be cheered by none [...] Such is the alpha & omega of my tale - I can speak to none - writing this is useless - it does not even soothe me - on the contrary it irritates me by showing me the pityful expedient to which I am reduced.[12]

When a particularly malicious reviewer of *The Last Man* referred to the frustration of the 'last woman'[13] having no-one on whom to inflict her garrulity, he ignorantly identified a crux of the last man genre - its self-reflexive tendency, in the portrayal of the very literary nightmare of a world devoid of readers. The pain expressed in Verney's narrative at times centres on this very point; who is there left to witness his suffering? Not only that, but what is to become of the rest of Creation (since the author leaves it not only intact, but ironically vernal and flourishing) when man is extinct:

> Will the mountains remain unmoved, and streams still keep a downward course
> towards the vast abyss; will the tides rise and fall, and the winds fan universal
> nature; will beasts pasture, birds fly, and fishes swim, when man, the lord,
> possessor, perceiver, and recorder of these things, has passed away, as though
> he had never been?[14]

This passage evokes a major theme in Romantic philosophies, that of creation of the external world through perception. In addition, it could be said to recall the role of Adam, lord of the young world, of enumerating and naming all the various animals. Verney, like Omegarus, is an anti-Adam.

The Adamic, with its associations of kingship, is a prevalent theme. The symmetry of Adam and Omegarus, Adam and Verney, is irresistible, giving rise to some of the crueller ironies in the fortunes of the last man. Mary Shelley's Verney grows up an ignoble savage, as poacher and local ruffian, with resentful feelings of displaced nobility that point back to his father's exile from Court. Each major character in *The Last Man* is at times described in royal or noble terms. Wherever the migrant survivors travel, they lodge in the deserted palaces of plague-ridden Europe. There is a description of the introverted Adrian as absorbed 'in the little kingdom of [his] own mortality'.[15] Verney and Adrian even play a light-hearted game with the young girl Clara in their final days together, pretending she is the queen of the world, and attending to her royal whims. Returning briefly to Hood, it is the jealousy of the hangman as self-styled monarch that causes him to condemn and execute the penultimate man in order to confer lastness upon himself:

> An' if it were not for that beggar man
> I'd be the King of the earth... (ll. 69-70)

The beggar entertains similar fantasies; both men adopt regal attire when they explore the deserted city. The earth 'ain't big enough for the both of them':

> So there he hung, and there I stood,
> The LAST MAN left alive,
> To have my will of all the earth:
> Quoth I, 'Now I shall thrive!' (ll. 169-72)

Fantasies of kingship and ownership are linked with the themes of survival and of being last, in that to survive another's death entails a feeling of victory over the inevitability of death; to survive many others' deaths by fictively killing them off entails an ever-greater egotistical fulfilment. An empty world is a new world, to be inhabited, laid claim to, and made into one's *own* world, in one's own image. Such unlovely elements of the psychology of survival are certainly present in the later behaviour of Lionel Verney; wandering, quintessentially alone, in the city of Rome, vast museum of the ruins of time, and man as time's fool, Verney imaginatively populates the landscape, first with ancient Romans, then with the hierophants of the Catholic church, until a great array of characters are gathered around - around *him*, that is. Alone in the world, he is fulfilling a need to become the cynosure of his surroundings, a fantasy latent since childhood. Again, there is an intriguing tendency among last men to want to mark the landscape: Omegarus does it, inscribing on a stone 'Omegarus is not guilty',[16] in the hope that Syderia will know she has been abandoned for noble reasons. Verney does it twice, once announcing his presence in the hope of companionship; 'Verney, / the last of the race of Englishmen, has taken up his abode in Rome [...] Friend, come! I wait for thee!',[17] and he later announces to nobody the coming of the new century, by inscribing 2100 AD atop St Peter's. Also, in the last man short story of 1968, 'Mother to the World,' Richard Wilson has his hero write a notice reserving his favourite tree, an ironic statement of his peculiar need for privacy from his last woman.

Such inscriptions have a symbolic resonance that is threefold, I think; firstly, they represent a fulfilled fantasy of ownership, a laying claim to the landscape; then they are of the nature of memorial or epitaph, leaving one's mark on a world of death; finally, it is possible to understand them as impositions of meaning on to the world, even impositions of a particular reading. It is interesting to note that in the violent earthquakes of the Last Days in *Omegarus and Syderia* Syderia's footsteps are erased by the earth, almost as if deliberately rejected and thrown off.

If Omegarus writes his own epitaph, the Spirit of Futurity is also anxious to for him not to be unknown and uncelebrated. The Spirit explains to Grainville's narrator the purpose of unfolding the future to him:

> 'Think not that I intend by this spectacle merely to gratify thy curiosity; - a nobler design actuates me. The last man will not have any posterity to know and admire him. I wish before his birth that he may live in memory: I desire to celebrate his struggles and victories over himself... '[18]

In the 1950s a very similar device appears in the science fiction of Brian Aldiss, in *Galaxies like Grains of Sand*; at the death of the old universe, a

superhuman being emerges to recommence evolution. He pays tribute to his human forbears, and is in turn celebrated by a godlike race of the future, who have already superseded him and are telling his story. The end of the world is a time for commemoration. So with Mary Shelley's Verney, attempting to unpack his heart with words and write a memorial for his friends and for himself to send into the void: 'Learn the deeds and sufferings of thy predecessors'.[19] For Mary Shelley, these notes of epitaph and elegy have a strong personal dimenson, as *The Last Man* is partly biographically conceived. Sir Timothy Shelley, the poet's father, put a condition on his continued allowance to Mary and her son that she engage 'not to bring - Shelley's name before the public again'[20] during his lifetime. Instead, Percy Bysshe Shelley is commemorated in fictional form in the character of Arian in this novel - slight of frame, nobly born republican, fiery idealist and philanthropist.
The novel contains several portraits, some explicit, some submerged, of several of Mary's circle of a few years before; Byron, Claire Claremont, the child Allegra, and herself as Verney. She refers openly to her portrait of Shelley in a letter, and this is how she sees herself as she is writing the novel in 1824:

> The last man! Yes - I may well describe that solitary being's feelings, feeling myself as the last relic of a beloved race, my companions, extinct before me.[21]

Another feature which unites several last man narratives is the description of unfolding space. This is so, because the world is large as it is spacious, the relative world has size inasmuch as it has population. So it expands as never before. The revelaton of infinity can be alternatively exhilarating, or tantalising and delusory, full of false promise. *Omegarus and Syderia* has moments of sheer religious exhilaration. In Mary Shelley there is a feeling of an expanding universe, as the population inexorably diminishes - 'inexorably', since a last man narrative has its own generic expectation; the reader fully expects mankind to be killed off with a single exception and, sure enough, the bodies pile up chapter by chapter.
The climax of a startling passage in *The Last Man* describing the apparition of three anarchic suns ascending the sky reveals the desolation of space, but also an enlarged perspective for (disappearing) man:

> It appeared as if suddenly the motion of the earth was revealed to us - as if no longer we were ruled by ancient laws, but were turned adrift in an unknown region of space.[22]

One character to sing of the ampler, expanded perception of the universe is the astronomer Merrival, convinced that in 100,000 years or so 'The pole of the earth will coincide with the pole of the ecliptic, [...] an universal spring will be produced, and earth become a paradise'.[23] Pointedly, Merrival goes mad before joining the novel's catalogue of corpses. The dreamer Merrival, cheered by thoughts of coming paradise while all around people are dropping dead, is one example of Mary Shelley's ironic emphasis on false hopes of the millenium that precede and even accompany the catastrophe. Adrian's rapturous soliloquies on the perfection of man and earth are wholly without foundation. Raymond has similarly grandiose hopes as Lord Protector, of banishing disease and poverty. The pain caused by Mary's continual airing of millenial optimism as prelude to unrelieved disaster, and building up to a secular, dead-end eschatology, has about it an element of recantation, or at least bringing into rigorous question the idealism of her father and husband.

Disease and plague had been used as metaphors for revolution, not only by conservatives like Burke, but also by their political adversaries - Mary Wollstonecraft for one; and Percy Bysshe Shelley uses images of plague to threaten the forces of tyranny and reaction in *Laon and Cythna* and *Hellas*. In turning the metaphor into fictional reality, Mary Shelley's vision is one of despair. In disease metaphors of the past there was generally an abiding hope that mankind could survive the fever of revolutionary ardour, and order reassert itself; in *The Last Man* the plague is a blank absolute, permitting of no redemption or consolation. Nor is it a force of progress, overthrowing tyranny. The novel's use of the word 'Necessity' has a harsh, anti-millennial edge. For Mary Shelley to make Necessity a destructive power has an irony of deliberate rejection; for William Godwin, Necessity was allied to the perfectibility of man, and the progress towards his anarchist utopia. When Verney hears an inner voice warning him that man's fated destruction is bound to this hour by Necessity, he is hearing the language of Godwinian and Shelleyan idealism used in the service of a grand pessimism.

And all the while Verney and his tribe of survivors are trekking across Europe they are irrationally hopeful of finding a new paradise:

> We had not fixed on any precise spot as the termination of our wanderings; but a vague picture of perpetual spring, fragrant groves, and sparkling streams, floated in our imagination to entice us on.[24]

The reader is likewise enticed by the pleasing design of a full-circle, a return to Paradise in the last days of man.

Omegarus and Syderia and *The Last Man* have in common an impression of the inadequacy of prophecy and of art. Grainville matches each true and divine prophecy with an opposing corrupt fabrication by the powers determined to thwart providence. Mary Shelley takes as her motto for *The Last Man* some lines spoken by Adam in *Paradise Lost* rejecting the impulse to see into the future, after his vision of future suffering that he can do nothing to prevent; predictions of a new earthly paradise directly precede both the death of Verney's wife and the Shelleyan drowning of Adrian. As the wilderness encroaches upon the monuments of Verney's Rome, nature, he says, seems lovelier and more powerful for the contrast.

Denial of faith in outward and received wisdom results for Verney in a withdrawal into a profound solipsism that characterises the very condition of the last man. After his unique recovery from the plague he experiences an envigorating increase of power and insight, and a simultaneous withdrawal into a vertiginous state of expanded awareness and *deja vu*. He becomes convinced that he is the Oedipus who has solved the Sphinx's riddle of the plague; only that its meaning is a blank absence of meaning, a refusal to yield an intelligible answer. Verney experiences a sense of disjunction between his inner life and an outer universe of departed meaning. Having kept a record of the *chronos* of passing days, counted in notches on a willow wand, he abandons chronologically measured time and gives himself up to inner meaning, his personal *kairos*. He discards the wand in an action not dissimilar in kind to Ahab's breaking of the quadrant in *Moby Dick*, rejecting the empirical, resolving to navigate and understand by intuition alone.

Verney's bizarre and sad attempts at dialogue with the inanimate, in addressing the mocking statues of Rome, illustrates the extreme of solipsism and monologue that he has become. The writer's nightmare of a world without readers, that is the healthy aversion to monologue, has created monologue personified, in the fantasy of last man narratives; in the bombast of Campbell's prophet, the petulance of Hood's hangman. Mary Shelley's Verney is the most solipsistic of them all, and his final claim exposes him as thoroughly misled by his inner light. Mary Shelley's final irony is to have him echo Genesis, in 'I shall read fair augury in the rainbow',[25] the symbol of God's covenant with the earth that was revealed to Noah - Noah, the begetter of a renewed race, exactly what Verney is not. He is still reading the landscape wrongly, still misreading signs, determined not to be last.

If every fictive world can be seen as a world-picture, and every fictive end of the world as the breaking up of a point of view, the world still has not quite ended for the last man, nor the prison of his solipsism been broken. He is right back where he started - an author trying to communicate, driven to write by his fear of isolation, finding in the act of writing only monologue and lastness, weeping and gnashing of teeth.

Michael Bradshaw

NOTES

1. Byron, *Poetical Works* (ed. Frederick Page, new edn. corrected by John Jump, Oxford: Oxford University Press, 1970.

2. *Authorised Version of The Bible*, Revelation 21. 1.

3. Quoted in A.J. Sambrook, 'A Romantic Theme: The Last Man', *Forum for Modern Language Studies*, Vol. II, 1966, pp.29-30.

4. *The Edinburgh Review* Vol. XLI, No. 82, Jan. 1825, p.284.

5. *The Times*, 24 March 1825, quoted in Sambrook, *op.cit.*, pp.29-30.

6. Mary Shelley, *The Last Man* (3 vols), London, 1826, Vol. 1, p.75.

7. *The Monthly Magazine or British Register of Literature, Sciences and the Belles Lettres*, New Series, Vol. II, 1826, p.143.

8. *The Poetical Works of Thomas Campbell* (ed. Rev. Alfred Hill, MA), London: George Bell and Sons, 1908.

9. *The Complete Poetical Works of Thomas Hood* (ed. with notes by Walter Jerrold), London: Henry Frowde, 1906.

10. Shelley, *op.cit.*, Vol. II, p.47.

11. Frank Kermode, *The Sense of an Ending: Studies in the Theory of Fiction*, London: Oxford University Press, 1968.

12. *The Journals of Mary Shelley, 1814-1844* (ed. Paula R. Feldman and Diana Scott-Kilvert) (2 vols), Oxford: Oxford University Press, 1987, Vol. II, p.485.

13. In *The Literary Gazette*; also , a mock announcement in *The Wasp*. See Morton D. Paley, 'Mary Shelley's *The Last Man*: Apocalypse without Millenium', *Keats-Shelley Review* 4, 1989, p.3.

14. Shelley, *op.cit.*, Vol. III, p.224.

15. *Ibid.*, Vol. I, p.198.

16. *Omegarus and Syderia, A Romance in Futurity in Two Volumes*, London, 1806, Vol. II, p.89.

17. Shelley, *op.cit.*, Vol. III, pp.320-21.

18. *Omegarus and Syderia*, Vol. I, p.7.

19. Shelley, *op.cit.*, Vol. III, p.193.

20. Quoted in Walter Edwin Peck, 'The Biographical Element in the Novels of Mary Wollstonecraft Shelley', *PMLA*, Vol. XXXVIII, 1923, p.199.

21. *Journals*, Vol. II, pp.476-77.

22. Shelley, *op.cit.*, Vol. III, p.129.

23. *Ibid.*, Vol. II, p. 121.

24. *Ibid.*, Vol. III, p.156.

25. *Ibid.*, Vol. III, p.351.

12.

JURASSIC PARK AND THE GENERIC PARADOX IN
SCIENCE FICTION FILM

So ingrained is the assumption that science fiction is about special effects, space travel and futuristic gadgetry that many British critics seem quite ill at ease with the genre, and rarely capable of seeing what its creative writers and producers are showing them. You can frequently spot the floundering critic by the use of the abbreviation 'sci-fi' in the title or first paragraph of their copy. Reviews of Steven Spielberg's *Jurassic Park* were no exception.

In this article, I want to point the blame for this atrophying of critical faculties squarely where it belongs: with the paradox inherent in the genre. Although my focus is on the film, the issues have relevance to science fiction as a concept, whatever medium is used to convey the narrative. The paradox in science fiction is that an axiological discourse which by definition questions the values of scientific development and contributes to the development of alternative myth is itself dependent upon retention of the myth of technological progress and scientific certitude among the audience. In order for the story to work, it is essential that the audience accept a number of ideas and propositions within the text that conflict with their own experience of 'reality'. This acceptance depends upon the simulation of scientific credibility, built up by a number of carefully constructed ploys within the narrative, and itself reflecting popular faith in science. But at the same time, the plot-line of the story seems to be constructed to undermine that faith on which its acceptability depends. At first sight, we could simply say that the paradox is so integral to the genre of science fiction generally that it is both invisible and unworthy of remark. *Jurassic Park*, by this reckoning, is just the latest in a long tradition of technophobic films, the understanding of which is adequately covered by existing academic literature.[1]

But if we begin to make the paradox visible, we can see how it has developed and find some interesting implications which are not adequately dealt with by the concept of technophobia. In order to do so, I will show how the paradox arises implicitly through the imperatives which govern the genre of science fiction, and how there is a need for reassessment of the technophobic discourse to take into account the predominant myths of science in contemporary post-modern culture.

As a first step, we need to reconsider the notion of *genre* in relation to film. There is a justifiable view that the whole notion of genre is little more than a labelling device for selling a media product.[2] Without such labels, the assumption goes, the audience may have little idea as to whether the media product - be it book, film, musical recording or whatever - will be to their taste. With such labelling, more importantly, the production company is able to convince its financial backers of the commercial viability of the product. In the cinema and on television, the fluctuating availability of science fiction reflects not so much the fluctuating interest in the genre by the audience as the fluctuating assessment of its economic risk by producers. Awareness of this function of genre has been used with less justification to excuse the sloppy thinking which typifies the use of the label in application to film. Just because confusion currently exists, we do not have to suspend our search for clarity and retreat into the comforting mindlessness of convention.[3] When we use the term *genre* to refer to such diverse elements as *film noir*, Romance or Western, we are using concepts which are inherently incompatible. *Jurassic Park*, for instance, has claims to be labelled in at least three generic camps. It is a thriller, it is a classic realist film and it is science fiction. The way to resolve these apparent difficulties in labelling of filmic genre is to recognise that we are referring to three different methods of classification when we use the term. These are the *affective genre*, the *stylistic genre*, and the *discursive genre*.

The *affective* genre is when we use the term to classify the emotional response or affect which a film arouses. When we refer to genres such as Horror, Comedy, Thriller, Romance or Tragedy, we are classifying according to affect. Relatively recent classifications such as the Action movie, the Family film or the Feelgood romance are all variants of affective categorisation, where the audience's desired gratification is paramount. The second use of the term 'genre' in film relates to the style or technique in which the director has expressed the narrative. Use of this *stylistic* genre for classifying film as, for example, *film noir*, Soviet Montage, Classic Realism or Expressionism, has a narrow circulation, mostly confined to academic film students. A third form of classification is by reference to what might popularly be called the subject-matter or narrative emphasis of the film. It is the issues which are addressed within the film's story-line and the context within which they are framed which constitute the popular classification of Western, Crime story, Historical drama, or, of course, Science Fiction. This is the *discursive* genre.

By separating out the types of genre in this way, we can explain why there is often confusion in film criticism when allocating genre. *Alien*, for instance, is often seen as a cross between science fiction and horror. It is, of course, both sf in discourse and Horror in affect, and we may argue as to whether it is also a Classic Realist Text in style. But there is no inherent contradiction which makes any one of these labels superior to the others.

Many who have started have given up trying to define science fiction. Some are simply opposed to the attempt to classify, while others are seemingly confused by the enormity of the task, or perhaps by the variation in usage of the term genre as we have been discussing it.[4] The postmodernist cop-out that definitions are inadequate and therefore not worth attempting would ultimately render all interchange of ideas impossible, so I will attempt to clarify a simple working definition of sf here, so that we are agreed about what it is we are discussing.

Definitions of Science Fiction should relate only to what I have called the discursive genre. We need not trouble ourselves with the affective purpose or the style of presentation. A film is science fiction if it contains three defining ingredients of science fiction.[5] These are, firstly that the narrative is fictional. The story is not presented to the reader as factual documentary, but as imaginative invention. Although self-evident, this reminder does ensure that we rule out pretentious claims for books by the likes of Erich von Daniken.[6] It also enables us to appreciate the narrational device, used occasionally in science fiction by such as Orson Welles, Whitley Streiber and Daniel Keyes, of pretending that a work of fiction is a factual report.[7] Secondly, the narrative must be plausible at the level of current scientific knowledge.[8] In *Jurassic Park*, Crichton and Spielberg have gone to apparently inordinate lengths to maintain the film's credibility against overwhelming messages from past experience that the whole idea of humans meeting dinosaurs is impossible. By a mixture of skilful techniques, the film, like the book before it, utilises the audience's vague awareness of scientific developments as a tool for convincing them that what is described is able to happen. The main focus in this justification is, of course, the scientific credibility achieved by adept use of abstruse terminology and superficially technological gadgetry. Thirdly, the narrative must involve some speculation beyond what is currently considered to be scientific knowledge. This may be referred to as extrapolation based on developments known to the story-teller, or it could be the postulation of a development currently unknown - provided it remains plausible. In *Jurassic Park*, speculative ideas about gathering dinosaur DNA from traces left in mosquitoes preserved in amber have to be presented as extrapolation from current developments in order to enable the plausibility to be sufficient for ordinary viewers to suspend their natural disbelief.[9] These three ingredients are present in all science fiction, regardless of the medium. They are properties of the science fiction genre, and none can be dispensed with if the discourse is to be considered science fiction. Affective and stylistic qualities, which are classified in their own generic terms and which I have separated from the discursive genre, do not have any bearing on the sf qualities of a film. Woody Allen's *Sleeper* is as much science fiction as Michael Crichton's *Westworld* or George Lucas's *Star Wars*, even though all three belong to different affective genres.

In film, however, there are peculiarities of science fiction which are not all shared by literature, theatre or radio drama. In particular, there are three overwhelming imperatives of the genre, which apply more strongly to film than any other medium, and which I refer to as the three tyrannies. The first is the **Tyranny of the Narrative**. It is essential in successful science fiction for a crisis to occur as a result of the science involved or its application by human beings. If nothing went wrong with the set-up of *Jurassic Park*, the story would be about as exciting as a John W. Campbell short story. There would be virtually no plot development and the film would have been as dull as those 1950's films about trips to the moon which relied upon the supposedly witty interchanges between the handsome hero and the comic side-kick with a pet monkey. Or it would have to depend upon some other plot-line, such as a murder occurring within the theme park - this is the tried and tested formula which has failed its trials and tests so often before. So the crisis is required in order to keep the narrative flowing, and to craft a story worth the telling. Without a crisis, there can be no resolution; without a resolution there can be no plot development; without plot development there can be no fiction.

The second imperative is unlike the first, in that it almost exclusively applies to film and television. This is the **Tyranny of the Narration**. A verbal story allows the reader to imagine the effects described. A filmed story requires its leaps of imagination to be translated into visually acceptable objects and artefacts. There are well known anecdotes which illustrate the point, such as the need to change elements from the radio to other media in *The Hitch-hiker's Guide to the Galaxy*. The two-headed Zaphod Beeblebrox was a clever idea in radio, but an encumbrance on television. Nowadays in film the search for verisimilitude has resulted in spectacular special effects, and none more so than the dinosaurs in *Jurassic Park*. We have had monster movies before. We have had dinosaur movies before. But none of the previous attempts to recreate the prehistoric creatures passed our second defining test, that of plausibility. We all knew the monstrous creatures in *One Million Years BC* or *The Lost World* were lizards in fancy dress. Likewise, the robots in 1950's sf films looked like men in rubber suits - simply because they *were* men in rubber suits. Even Ray Harryhausen's spectacular monsters for *Jason and the Argonauts* or the *Sinbad* films looked like cleverly animated models, because that's exactly what they were.

But the dinosaurs in *Jurassic Park* are convincing both within the context of the story and in terms of the way they move on screen. They are products of painstaking attention to detail combined with the very latest gadgetry, and they convince because of the wealth of research that was put into making them convincing.[10] The tyranny of the narration in sf is that the special effects have to withstand the most critical inspection, well beyond the demands of verisimilitude. Inevitably, there are errors and flaws in *Jurassic Park* which slightly mar the illusion of reality, such as the continuity error when the Tyrannosaurus Rex approaches the children's vehicle after the adult has fled leaving the door wide open. The long shot from the second vehicle shows the door closed, and a few moments later the camera is showing one of the children leaning across to shut the open door. But although there are flaws in the verisimilitude at the point of continuity or post-production editing, we do not reject the scientific plausibility of the story because of this. The use of rather simple computers to run a supposedly ultra-sophisticated outfit like John Hammond's island ought to be more of a problem, and will no doubt be the flaw which future generations will find most noticeable, but because of the strength of the narrative and direction, it is only a minor irritation. There is more than enough apparent evidence of scientific and technological competence on the island to enable viewers to suspend their disbelief with alacrity. The turning-point of the narrative in *Jurassic Park* is the unpredicted development of mutated male dinosaurs to enable breeding to take place in the wild. By this point, the audience has to be totally convinced of the possibility of cloning from prehistoric DNA miraculously preserved in amber. It has to have accepted the model dinosaurs as real, and it has to have engaged with the heroes' dilemmas. Any blemish in the plausibility of the story-line or in that of the scientific explanations would be punished severely by the audience.

Both the **Tyranny of the Narrative** and the **Tyranny of the Narration** can be readily seen as relating to the first two properties of sf - those of fiction

and scientific plausibility.   The third imperative is virtually inseparable from
the genre of sf. This is the **Tyranny of the Myth**. By its very nature of
being speculative, science fiction cannot avoid confrontation with the
hidden assumptions within our 'common sense' view of 'reality'. Even at its
simplest level, perhaps, of *Metropolis*, the postulated future forced into the
open ideas about social organisation, albeit in a very simplistic way.   The
capacity of sf to handle myth so overtly may account for its relative popularity
as a subject of scholarship among feminist academics.[11] This is not to say that
science fiction deals fully or successfully with ideological issues. On the whole,
sf tends to be unidirectional, focusing its attention on one particular
speculative development, and often ignoring implications not directly related
to the myth which is being consciously addressed.   Although it may be
presented as evidence of hegemonic presumption, the unidirectional focus is
largely a consequence of the origination of science fiction stories as a response
to the question 'What if...?', together with the predominance of the short story
as the major vehicle for science fiction through its formative years in the first
half of the twentieth century.[12]   It is for the same reason that characters in
science fiction tend to lack conviction as rounded human beings, since they
serve the function of cyphers through which the narrative and the myth can be
expressed.

In *Jurassic Park* the narrational qualities of the film are so well crafted
that it is the characterisation which carries the weight of the myth.[13]   Grant,
Sattler and the two children are stereotypical heroes to which each member of a
family audience can relate. They are pitted against forces which are the result
of scientific hubris. The other characters symbolise other values which bear on
science. Because sf postulates change, it must deal with the difference between
the postulated changes and the reality which the audience perceives. In so
doing, conventional assumptions and attitudes are of necessity identified,
usually articulated, and then either challenged or reinforced. In essence this is
the basic course of the Classic Realist Text, once the initial sf scenario has been
established. So we can see that all three of these tyrannies are products of the
genre of science fiction film which we identified earlier. They are the generic
imperatives which govern both the classification and the discourses available.
But although, like most tyrants, they dictate, they are not omnipotent.

There are also certain production imperatives for film is a business, and
one with enormous costs. Film companies are not usually motivated by the
drives of artistic creativity or philosophical satisfaction which might
stimulate the writer or director. The generic imperatives which we have

just considered are subordinate to much more powerful influences. If a proposed sf film is not considered a sound investment by the people who hold the purse-strings, there will be no finance forthcoming for its making, however brilliant the director's ideas.   This financial consideration is probably the most important production imperative, and anecdotes which illustrate its influence can be found in many accounts of the making of science fiction film and television.[1] Other production imperatives include the vagaries of fashion which determine whether or not a product in a particular discursive genre or style is likely to become a 'box-office hit' and thus gain financial backers. The recent association, however accurate or misguided, of violent films with violent crimes in society , will have made it almost impossible for some projected films in the affective genre of horror to be made.[15]   In any conflict between generic and production imperatives, production imperatives always win. It is Spielberg's genius that he is able to work within the limits of these production imperatives in order to present a seamless narrative which is both artistically and philosophically of interest.

Generic imperatives and production imperatives affect the range of discourses which are available in any film. Although the audience brings an unquantifiable variety of interpretations to any filmic text, we can still talk about the principal or dominant discourse as the key to the ideological resolution of a film.

In *Jurassic Park* it is not a feminist discourse, even though there are conscious elements which reflect the success of feminist politics in influencing the production imperatives behind the film. The switching of the ages of Tim and Lex for the film, rather than maintain the book's primogeniture is a clear case of text being subordinate to studio decision. Sattler is a post-Star Wars heroine, still feminine but with a heroic role within the plot. And, of course, the whole notion of the female dinosaurs being able to breed without the aid of males could be seen as an archetypal feminist story-line, if only it had not been encumbered with the need for male mutations. The latter demonstrates the pre-eminence of scientific plausibility within the genre: it is more important to give the audience a seemingly satisfactory scientific explanation than it is to pander to the feminist academic searching to support her thesis on poststructuralism. The central or dominant discourse of *Jurassic Park* is inevitably subject to all those influences which we have looked at so far. Yet it remains clear that there is a very strong thread of edification within the story. At the end of the film, John Hammond is a chastened man, Nedry and Gennarro have paid the price of their folly, and Arnold has sacrificed his life as heroically as only a sympathetic black character in a white movie can. The sympathetic white characters, of course, escape unscathed, illustrating again the unidirectional nature of the tyranny of the myth in sf. All this sacrifice cannot be in vain. We can draw the lesson that the ruthless pursuit of science for the sake of financial gain, however exciting it may seem, is doomed to failure. It was Hammond's cost-cutting and Nedry's greed, combined with the superhuman forces of nature in the shape of a tropical storm, that led to the ultimate destruction of the dream that science had made possible.

It is a pessimistic view of science which undermines the credibility of scientific claims, yet it is based on a presupposition of respect for scientific credibility. We, the audience, need to see men in white coats in Hammond's laboratory, we need to see the structure of DNA dancing before us in cartoon animation, and we need to see Grant and Sattler painstakingly working on an excavation, to reinforce our respect for science, before we can accept the disastrous consequences of scientific enterprise. The paradox, therefore, is inevitable. As we have seen, the tyranny of the narrative forces the plot to develop in certain ways, and in this case, something must go wrong with the science and technology on which the theme park itself is based. At the level of discourse, this means that science and/or technology are inherently flawed. The tyranny of the narration requires believable monsters for the heroes to overcome. At the level of discourse, this reinforces the idea that human values will win through against inhuman odds. The tyranny of the myth postulates a change that identifies an assumption taken for granted in our culture, in this case the power of science and technology. At the level of discourse, the power is open to challenge.

Clearly, the underlying discourse in *Jurassic Park* is connected with a distrust of technology. But to call this technophobia would be too crude. 'Technophobia' is an irrational fear, literally of art, although, because the Greek origin has died, it now relates to the modern usage of technology. The proponents of the concept describe it as innately conservative.[16] This may come as a surprise to those who have seen the first and probably most haunting vision of the evils of technology in sf film, Fritz Lang's *Metropolis*. Adapted from the novel by Thea von Harbou, the film was faithful to her simplistic socialist vision. The argument that technophobia is aligned with conservatism appears to be that opposition to technology is equitable with a longing for the natural and the old values of pre-industrial society.[17] Such a naive polarization between nature-with-liberty and industry-with-society ignores the political realities of the second half of the twentieth century. While it may have been valid in the 1890's, it is somewhat less than adequate in the 1990's   Indeed, the British Conservative Party and the conservative administrations of the USA have, for over a decade, shown scant regard for either nature or liberty, in the face of industrial and military demand for unfettered use of such things as chemical contaminants and nuclear reprocessing plants.   They have been consistently opposed by environmental pressure groups of all kinds, none of whom would take kindly to being misrepresented as conservative. *Jurassic Park* addresses issues in its discourse which are much wider than the simple 'technophobic' label encompasses.   The fundamental ideology which dominates the plot is that of environmentalism. The story-line is little short of a morality tale, a Greek Myth or an Aesop's Fable which cries out for the one-line summary *'and the moral of the story is...'* at the end.

In this case, the lesson to be drawn is surely that human interference with nature will lead to humanity's come-uppance. Abridged in verse, the narrative would not be out of place in *Struwelpeter* or as a Stanley Holloway monologue. The discourse of *Jurassic Park* exposes the myths about science which we hold in our society, and it does so in the form of a contemporary parable. It exposes the economic equation at the outset, with hero and heroine tempted away from their painstaking scientific duties as palaeontologists by a more lucrative offer they can hardly refuse. At the same time, they retain their credibility as stereotype scientists by maintaining their scientific duty of independence, even though they are paid by John Hammond. Although this is the stereotype of the Good Scientist as Wonderworker, it might be noticed that others lack the integrity of Grant and Sattler. The fat computer wizard, Nedry, is quite prepared to sell out to the highest bidder - and gets his just reward by being eaten by dilophosaurs. The physics buff, Ian Malcolm, whose main role seems to be to justify any vagaries in the plot by calling upon the sacred god Chaos Theory as a universal explanation, is a stereotype of the laconic, disinterested scientist, indifferent to morality, but capable of doing the right thing at a push. Perhaps John Hammond's island is an analogy for the rain forests. The lesson to be drawn is not just *don't tamper with nature*, but equally to admire the glory of the natural world. There are scenes in *Jurassic Park* which have all the qualities of a David Attenborough nature series. So persuasive are the effects and so skilful the cinematography that we almost forget that the herd of gallimimuses, stampeding from the horizon through the middle distance into close-up, are actually models, and likewise the closing shots of pteradons winging across the water, lit by a setting sun, is as beautifully filmed as any 1950's Disney wildlife footage. No wonder one British celebrity was so impressed by the special effects, as to reportedly

declare that she couldn't tell the difference between the mechanical models and
the real dinosaurs. This exquisite detail has a function in the narrative, as we
have seen. The verisimilitude is vital if the fantasy's bluff is to be maintained.
But it also has the function of carrying a sense of wonder and excitement which
only the best nature films convey.

Instead of the negativity of 'technophobia', we could use the more
positive term of *ecocentric* to describe the discourse of films like *Jurassic
Park*. It is surely missing the point to try to squeeze the scientific ideology of
such films into an archaic and irrelevant political container. We have
established that there is a paradox which is the product of innate aspects of the
genre of sf and the requirements of film. It is a paradox between the reliance
on science necessary for scientific plausibility, which we have now seen goes
beyond the mere requirements of verisimilitude, and an apparently anti-science
discourse which some have termed 'technophobic'. This, we have seen, is
initiated by the requirements of the narrative, but has deeper implications. It is
possible to explain the paradox in three ways. The first is simply the
descriptive way that we have been considering so far. It is clear that the
essential ingredients of sf as a discursive genre involve generic imperatives
which are especially important in the medium of film. These in turn govern the
parameters of discourse and result in an apparent contradiction between the
values underpinning the narrative and the values to which the narrative leads.
A second way of looking at this is the ideological perspective of the
proponents of technophobia. As we have seen, this involves adherence to an
ideological assertion which requires re-examination. The third way is to
recognise that there have been quite sweeping changes in the ideology of
science during the second half of the twentieth century, and that science fiction
interacts with such change.

The dominant discourse of sf film is revealed not by the paradox itself
but by the resolution of the paradox. Within the limitations of the narrational
constraints which we have been examining, it is possible to construct stories
which do not have the negative view of technology which *Jurassic Park*
suggests. The *Star Wars* and *Star Trek* series both exemplify resolutions to
crises which glorify the technological fix. In both those cases, the discourse is
technophiliac rather than technophobic, and is clearly ideologically
conservative in every sense. The old order is happily restored, and the
capitalist values of progress and modernism are reasserted. These discourses
come from the same stable as Flash Gordon and Buck Rogers. Technology is
allied to ontology in a scientific conquest of the universe. No-one ever stops to

ask why, or whether the methods used are appropriate. If the starship runs out of dilithium crystals or whatever it supposedly runs on, there is always a ready supply on some other planet, even if access to them may involve a bit of a skirmish with Klingons or other latter-day substitutes for 'savages'. *Jurassic Park* is a much more thoughtful story, in which Science includes epistemology and axiology. The respect for nature is not an eighteenth century Romantic view, nor is it juxtaposed in contrast with industry. The technology has, after all, released the latent powers of nature. We can leave the cinema after watching *Jurassic Park* and reflect on ideas about the purpose of science and technology, unlike films in the Star Wars mould. *Jurassic Park* is not post-modernist, but it is anti-modernist. The main discourse of *Jurassic Park* encompasses a negative view of science as technology, but it is not technophobic. It maintains the epistemological and ontological dimensions of the myth of science, but at the axiological level it replaces assumed technological values by ecological ones.

Having spent so long attempting to articulate and explain it, I now want to argue that the paradox is illusory. It presupposes that science must be what de Solla Price called 'big science', and that the discourse is indeed focused on issues of science as technology, even if it is not one of technophobia.[18] When the government uses the term 'science' it is indeed in this technocentric way. Consequently we are currently going through a phase in which scientists and educators are donning hair shirts in vain attempts to explain the unpopularity of science among the young.[19] But science is not unpopular. What may be unpopular is the type of science which facilitates machines of intentional or incidental destruction, the type of science which is wanted for virtually non-existent scientific jobs in industry, the type of science which is allied to market forces and subordinated to capitalism. But the spirit of scientific inquiry and the interest in scientific questions has not disappeared. Rather, it has turned to the non-technological sciences, to ecology, cosmology and complementary therapies, paralleling the successful popular participatory sciences of the nineteenth century: natural history, astronomy and quack medicines.[20] The discourse of *Jurassic Park* is very much in keeping with this interest in science. Just as it is not unscientific to conduct scientific inquiry into the effects of pollution and radiation, so it is not technophobic to argue against interference with the ecology of the planet. Whereas Crichton's own theme-park film, , may be reasonably described as technophobic, *Jurassic Park*, which resembles it in many aspects of the plot, is ecocentric in its discourse. As such it is conveying an impression of science in a positive light, fully in keeping with the view of science as awesome which the initial scenes of the park create.

But its rejection of an inadequate and arrogant technology is far from a conservative view of science, and in this respect it encapsulates the current ambivalence toward science in contemporary culture.

Dave Hinton

NOTES

1. Probably the best explanation of the technophobia theme is Michael Ryan and Douglas Kellner, 'Technophobia' in Annette Kuhn (ed.), *Alien Zone*, London: Verso, 1990.

2. See, for instance, discussion by Jane Feuer, 'Genre Study and Television' in R.C. Allen (ed), *Channels of Discourse Reassembled*, London: Routledge, 1992.

3. This is a currently fashionable position among poststructuralists, long since foreshadowed in definitions such as those by Leon Stover and Harry Harrison (Science fiction is what I am pointing at when I say 'science fiction') in their introduction to *Apeman Spaceman*, Harmondsworth: Penguin, 1972, George Hay (SF is what appears on the library shelves under that category) or Brian Aldiss (Science Fiction doesn't exist), according to S.J. Lundwall, *Science Fiction: What it's All About*, London: Sphere, 1971, p1.   The extent of confusion among the public may be inferred from different audience responses to television genre classification in Tulloch and Jenkins, *Science Fiction Audiences*, London: Routledge, 1995, pp.218-219; 244.

4. A review of the range of complex examples is given in Darko Suvin, 'The State of the Art in Determining and Delimiting SF' in Colin Lester, *The International Science Fiction Yearbook*, 1978, reprinted from *Science Fiction Studies*, no.16, Nov. 1978.

5. Perceptive readers may recognise that the following discussion parallels and simplifies the classic but convoluted definition by Sam Moskowitz in *Explorers of the Infinite*, New York: Hyperion, 1963, viz:
'Science Fiction is a branch of fantasy identifiable by the fact that it eases the "willing suspension of disbelief" on the part of its readers by utilising an atmosphere of scientific credibility for its imaginative speculations in physical science, space, time, social science and philosophy.'

6. Erich von Daniken, *Chariots of the Gods*, London: Corgi, 1968.

7. Orson Welles's 1938 radio adaptation of H.G. Wells's *War of the Worlds* has recently been made available on tape by Hodder Headline Audiobooks, 1995; Streiber's *Communion*, both as film and as novel, has been presented as autobiography; Daniel Keyes's *Flowers for Algernon*, 1960, is written in diary form.

8. See, for example, the discussion of technological consistency in Jerry Pournelle, 'Building Future Worlds: Logic and Consistency in the Craft of Science Fiction' in C.L. Grant (ed.), *Writing and Selling Science Fiction*, London: Writer's Digest, 1976, pp.94-97; or Mark Andrew Golding's 'Shortcuts Through Space in Star Trek' in Walter Irwin and G.B. Love (eds.), *The Best of Trek*, London: Signet, 1978.

9. Following its world-wide success, of course, the film has itself been the reference-point for reporting current developments in genetic engineering. In response to press articles, Mark Mueller quoted the assistant curator of the American Museum of Natural History, in an article entitled 'Bollocks!' in *Empire* magazine, August 1993. The article vindicates my differentiation between plausibility and current paradigmatic science.

10. For examples, see Don Shay and Jody Duncan, *The Making of* Jurassic Park, London: Boxtree, 1993

i1. For example, Barbara Creed, Judith Newton, Vivian Sobchak, Anne Cranny-Francis and others' contributions to Kuhn (ed) *op. cit.* (see note 1 above). See also Anne Cranny-Francis, *Feminist Fiction: Feminist Uses of Generic Fiction*, Cambridge: Cambridge University Press, 1990

12. This is a simplification of a complex story which has yet to be satisfactorily covered. The best attempt so far is Brian Aldiss, *Billion Year Spree*, London: Corgi, 1973. The term 'science fiction' is generally attributed to the magazine editor Hugo Gernsback in 1929 - see, for instance, Franz Rottensteiner, *The Science Fiction Book*, London: Thames & Hudson, 1975.

13 . Some critics at the time of the film's launch would not agree, though. Derek Malcolm in *The Guardian*, 17/7/1993, thought 'acting and screenplay are only adequate' in a 'best-selling film that's fun while it lasts - sheer if not memorable entertainment.'

14. Some of the best examples may be found in S. Whitfield and G. Roddenberry, *The Making of Star Trek*, 1968, rep. 1994.

15. In Britain, the alleged association of the 'Chucky' doll in the horror movie Child's Play 3 with two separate murders gave rise to headlines such as 'Burn Your Video Nasty' (*The Sun*, 26/11/93) and 'Tortured to Death by Chucky' (*Daily Star*, 18/12/93). See John Martin, *The Seduction of the Gullible*, London: Procrustes Press, 1993, and Martin Barker (ed), *The Video Nasties*, London: Pluto Press, 1984, for necessary perspective on such folk devil crusades.

16. See Ryan and Kellner, *op. cit.*, pp.58-9.

17. *Ibid.*, p.65; the authors recognise the antinomy inherent in their position, but do not let it affect their judgement.

18. D.J. de Solla Price, *Little Science: Big Science*, New York: Columbia University Press, 1963.

19. This is a regular feature of science broadcasting in Britain, and has given rise to the establishment of the Committee for the Public Understanding of Science (COPUS), a collaborative venture with participation by representatives of the London Science Museum and the Royal Society.

20. D.A. Hinton, *Popular Science in England, 1830-1870*, Ph.D thesis, University of Bath, 1980.

13.

UNEASY READINGS / UNSPEAKABLE DIALOGICS

There was a red-haired man who had no eyes or ears. Neither did he have
any hair, so he was called red-haired theoretically. He couldn't speak,
since he didn't have a mouth. Neither did he have a nose. He didn't even
have any arms or legs. He had no stomach and he had no back and he had
no spine and he had no innards whatsoever. He had nothing at all!
Therefore there's no knowing whom we are even talking about. In fact
it's better that we don't say any more about him.[1]

The quality of the *terrifying sublime*, if it is quite unnatural, is
adventurous. Unnatural things, so far as the sublime is supposed in them,
although little or none at all may actually be found, are *grotesque*.
Whoever loves and believes the fantastic is a *visionary*; the inclination
toward whims is a *crank*.[2]

The fantastic is increasingly being viewed as a reading effect, at the same time
some scholars have begun to explore the potential of Mikhail Bakhtin's work
in relation to reader theory.[3] This paper on the dialogics of the fantastic will
attempt to combine both elements in theorising the fantastic as a reading effect
from a broadly Bakhtinian perspective. 'Dialogics' is a shorthand way of
describing Bakhtin's philosophy of language in which each word is produced
in response to an answering word. The genre of the novel becomes the site
where diverse voices drawn from innumerable centres of culture blend and
clash. Heteroglossia, this struggle of contending voices, is both a descriptive
category and a source of value, since it becomes a utopian expression of the
voices of the people against the authority of monologism which seeks to have
the final authorised word. While would-be Bakhtinian concepts and
vocabulary are currently wide-spread in Anglo-American critical writing, I
share the concern voiced in Hirschkop & Shepherd that the political aspects of

Bakhtin's texts are becoming submerged in uncritical adulation from a wide variety of perspectives. The apparent ease of many of Bakhtin's texts masks their engagement with formative philosophies of modernity: neo-Kantianism, Hegelianism and, most problematically, Marxism. A proper understanding of dialogism would need to engage both with the dialectic and with Martin Buber. This is not the place to embark on such contentious matters, for the present I would direct readers of Bakhtin to the readings in Hirschkop & Shepherd. I shall outline Bakhtin's disagreements with Wolfgang Kayser over reading the Grotesque. I shall then introduce Bakhtin's concept of chronotope (literally 'space-time') and explore some Kantian aspects, then relate Bakhtin's ideas to a central concept in Reception Aesthetics, that of 'Concretization'. Finally I shall attempt a Bakhtinian reading of three texts as examples of chronotope; *The Golden Ass*, Mikhail Bulgakov's *The Master and Margarita* and Angela Carter's *Nights the Circus*.

A useful starting point would be Bakhtin's critique, in the introduction to *Rabelais and His World* of Wolfgang Kayser's discussion of the grotesque.[4] Kayser's book *The Grotesque in Art and Literature* had been published in German in 1957, enabling Bakhtin to take notice of it when his Rabelais book was finally published in 1965.[5]

Kayser's work is extremely wide-ranging, embarking upon a philological exploration of the word 'grotesque' (from Italian *grotta* 'cave', then moving from Bruegal, *Commedia dell'Arte* and *Sturm und Drang* drama to 'romantic grotesque', then finally nineteenth and twentieth century manifestations. Kayser's work is by no means a celebration of his subject:

> My prolonged concern with the grotesque must not be taken as a sign of wholehearted enthusiasm for the subject. I gladly admit that I, too, experienced the negative reaction likely to be provoked in the reader by certain chapters of my book or by a glance at its illustrations.[6]

This sort of comment is characteristic of analysis of the grotesque, the fantastic and horror genres as too is the negative affect which Kayser rushes to embrace least his audience brand the author himself as grotesque or crank. Kayser's final chapter 'An attempt to define the nature of the grotesque' is interesting in that the grotesque is proposed as a basic aesthetic category - it is seen to apply to three different realms - 'the creative process, the work of art itself, and its reception.... Nevertheless, it remains true that the grotesque is experienced only in the act of reception.'[7] Kayser then goes on to propose three structural properties, which are capitalised in the English text: THE GROTESQUE IS THE ESTRANGED WORLD, THE GROTESQUE IS A PLAY WITH THE ABSURD, THE GROTESQUE IS AN ATTEMPT TO INVOKE AND SUBDUE THE DEMONIC ASPECTS OF THE WORLD[8] Estranged, because suddenness and surprise are essential elements in an encounter with madness, showing that our world has ceased to be reliable, so in Kayser's words 'The grotesque instils fear of life rather than of death.' Structurally, the grotesque 'presupposes that the categories which apply to our world view become inapplicable.'[9]

> We have observed the progressive dissolution which occurred since the ornamental art of the Renaissance; the fusion of realms which we know to be separated, the abolition of the law of statics, the loss of identity, the distortion of 'natural' size and shape, the suspension of the category of objects, the destruction of personality, and the fragmentation of the historical order.[10]

This is a covert theory of modernity, which may appear old-fashioned. However, both Lukács and Bakhtin shared similar views so one shouldn't leap to use Kayser as a whipping-boy. Similar sentiments are often voiced about post-modernism by our contemporaries. Kayser's reference to absurdity situates his text in relation to the popularisation by Beckett and Sartre of existential ideas in the immediate post-war period . Absurdity for Kayser is meaningless, 'It is primarily the expression of our failure to orient ourselves in the physical universe.'[11] In Greek Tragedy, on the other hand, absurd actions are finally revealed to be meaningful, by understanding them in relation to divinely ordained fate and the suffering of the tragic hero. By contrast, the grotesque is impersonal and meaningless. But in spite of his negative view of the grotesque, Kayser concludes that 'the truly artistic portrayal effects a secret liberation'.[12] Enlightenment finally triumphs over the powers of darkness in language redolent of *Lord of the Rings*:

> The darkness has been sighted, the ominous powers discovered, the incomprehensible forces challenged. And thus we arrive at a final interpretation of the grotesque: AN ATTEMPT TO INVOKE AND SUBDUE THE DEMONIC ASPECTS OF THE WORLD.[13]

Modernity is seen to question the validity of the anthropological and the synthesis of nineteenth century science. Indeed, 'the various forms of the grotesque are the most obvious and pronounced contradictions of any kind of rationalism and any systematic use of thought.'[14] By 'anthropological' I take Kayser to refer to nineteenth century comparative studies such as Frazer's

Golden Bough which ostensibly rationalised superstition.   Kayser's own rational discourse and rational project of writing about the grotesque is in contradiction to its object, the unsystematic, meaningless terror of the grotesque itself. Kayser's view of laughter is directly contrary to Bakhtin's:

> Laughter originates on the comic and caricatural fringe of the grotesque. Filled with bitterness, it takes on characteristics of the mocking, cynical, and ultimately satanic laughter while turning into the grotesque.[15]

Christoph Wieland even felt the urge to laugh even in the presence of Brugel's portrait of hell, and Kayser speculates that such laughter is an involuntary response to situations which cannot be handled any other way.   Such involuntary and abysmal laughter forms part of classic fantastic texts, the narrator of Bonaventure's *Nightwatch* who laughed uncontrollably in church, E. T. A. Hoffmann's characters who shake with laughter, when there is nothing at all to laugh about.

Turning to Bakhtin's critique of Kayser in *Rabelais and His World*, one should note that Bakhtin acknowledges Kayser's book as 'the first and at the present writing the only serious work on the theory of the grotesque. It contains many valuable observations and subtle analysis.'[16] Nevertheless, Bakhtin criticises Kayser for speaking only of modernist forms of the grotesque, for Kayser sees the Romantic age through the prism of his own time. According to Bakhtin, 'a new and powerful revival of the grotesque took place in the twentieth century.'[17]   There are two main lines of development, *modernist form*, Bakhtin's example is Alfred Jerry, connected with romanticism and influenced by existentialism and the second, *grotesque realism* (Thomas Mann, Brecht, Pablo Neruda) is seen as related to the tradition of realism and folk culture, reflecting at times the direct influence of carnival forms. Clearly the second is in keeping with Bakhtin's own aesthetic tastes as we might initially reconstruct them from his published work. A critic in Bakhtin's situation would need to tread carefully in writing about modern literature, while it used to surprise me that it was Roman Jakobson who celebrated Mayakovsky, while Bakhtin seems to have published nothing on modern writing, it does so no longer. Bakhtin encountered enough problems, without writing about Joyce or Bulgakov or Kharms. This does not vitiate the potential of Bakhtin's texts as a resource for exploration of the most extreme twentieth-century fantastic texts.

According to Bakhtin, 'the true nature of the grotesque... cannot be separated from the culture of folk humour and the carnival spirit' and remains unexplained by Kayser.[18] It is true that in the Romantic period the link was loosened and reduced, but 'even at that stage all the basic elements, which clearly have a carnival origin, retain a certain memory of that mighty whole to which they belonged in the distant past.'[19] For Bakhtin artistic forms have a cultural memory, hence the novel 'remembers' Mennipian satire which is the origins of the genre. But the 'modernist grotesque' which inspires Kayser has 'almost entirely lost its past memories. It formalizes the heritage of carnival themes and symbols.'[20] Coming from a writer in the Soviet Union in 1968, a charge of formalism, was no light matter.

Bakhtin argues that 'the best works of Romantic grotesque' as exemplified in different ways by Sterne and Hoffmann awaken the memory of the carnival spirit   They 'are more powerful, deep, and joyful than the objectively philosophical idea which they express.'[21] In opposition to Kayser's limited view, Bakhtin offers his own historical survey, characteristically written in terms of great time:

Kayser's theory cannot be applied to the thousand-year-long development of the pre-Romantic era: that is, the archaic and antique grotesque (for instance, the satyric drama or the comedy of Attica) and the medieval and Renaissance grotesque, linked to the culture of folk humour.... Kayser's definitions ... strike us by the gloomy, terrifying tone of the grotesque world that alone the author sees. In reality gloom is completely alien to the entire development of this world up to the romantic period. We have already shown that the medieval and Renaissance grotesque, filled with the spirit of carnival, liberates the world from all that is dark and terrifying; it takes away all fears and is therefore completely gay and bright. All that was frightening in ordinary life is turned into amusing or ludicrous monstrosities. Fear is the extreme expression of narrow-minded and stupid seriousness, which is defeated by laughter.[22]

Bakhtin's view is characteristically utopian, and may justly be compared to the 'warm stream' of theologically inclined marxism expressed by Ernst Bloch.[23] The utopia of 'the golden age' was disclosed in the pre-Romantic period not for the sake of abstract thought or inner experience, but lived by humans in thought and body.   'This bodily participation in the potentiality of another world, the bodily awareness of another world has immense importance for the grotesque.'[24]

It is well known that Bakhtin celebrated the material existence of the body, such views imbue his lyrical appreciation of grotesque realism.

It is usually pointed out that in Rabelais' work the material bodily principle, that is, images of the human body with its food, drink, defecation, and sexual life, plays a predominant role. Images of the body are offered, moreover, in an extremely exaggerated form.... In grotesque realism, therefore, the bodily element is deeply positive. It is presented not in a private, egotistic form, severed from the other spheres of life, but as something universal, representing all the people.... The material bodily principle is contained not in the biological individual, not in the bourgeois ego, but in the people, a people who are continually growing and renewed. This is why all that is bodily becomes grandiose, exaggerated, immeasurable. [25]

This stress on the positive materiality of the grotesque body has seldom been read in conjunction with Bakhtin's own bodily state. From the age of sixteen, Bakhtin suffered from osteomyelitis, a degenerative bone disease, which spread to his left shin, thigh, hip joint and right hand. After contracting typhoid in 1921, Bakhtin required an operation on his right leg, and subsequently the hip joint became inflamed. He suffered periodic fevers and the condition is extremely painful. Bakhtin's right leg was amputated in 1938 and for the rest of his life he used crutches or a stick. [26] This gives particular irony to Bakhtin's celebration of bodily excess in Rabelais. Rather as Foucault urged that the voices of the mad should be listen to, one could develop a philosophical anthropology of disablement from Bakhtin. Space is differently dimensioned on crutches. Several of William Gibson's stories in the *Burning Crome* collection may be seen as explorations of this space. In 'Red Star, Winter Orbit', by Bruce Sterling and William Gibson, Colonel Korolev the 'last man in space' on board his obsolete space station has a crushed hip following an accident, but is able to move in zero gravity, in a way that would be quite impossible on earth. In 'The Winter Market', Lise is able to transcend her worn out body, propped up by its polycarbon exoskeleton and designer drugs to achieve a kind of immortality by buying her place on a corporate mainframe. Her personality and imagination will continue to function in this new artificial space after her death. [27] However, such positive readings need to be balanced with the realisation that Korolev would never have be allowed in space in the first place if his accident had happened on earth, Lise's existence, if indeed she can be said to exist, has to be paid for beyond her death and in 'Dogfight' the wheelchair-bound war veteran Tiny Montgomery is broken after he is defeated in a virtual reality dogfight. Gibson's futuristic extrapolations are dystopian even in their technical potential for liberation.

Bakhtin is a prolix, repetitive, deliberately unsystematic writer. Grotesque images 'remain ambivalent and contradictory; they are ugly, monstrous, hideous from the point of view of "classic" aesthetics, that is the aesthetics of the ready-made and completed.' [28] Bakhtin's own open texts which flout the conventions of the classically shaped essay (compare Lukács's beautifully poised *The Theory of the Novel*) would seem deliberately unclassical themselves.

Ken Hirschkop has pointed to a little quoted passage, in 'Epic and Novel' in which Bakhtin remarks on the 'simultaneous birth of scientific cognition and the modern artistic-prosaic novel form.'

> A comparison made more specific when he [Bakhtin] claims they are linked by the notion of an 'experimental' approach to reality: the secularisation of knowledge through laughter 'delivers the object, so to speak, into the fearless hands of investigative experiment- both scientific and artistic - and of a free experimental fantasy serving the aims of this experimentation.[29]

Hirschkop argues that the passage[30] is doubly significant, for it alerts us to an inevitably scientific moment in the pursuit of self-knowledge through discourse and the comparison with science indicates, in Hirschkop's words 'the more exact sense in which we can describe a historical narrative as relativised.'[31] For my purposes the passage points to a way of thinking with Bakhtin, or using Bakhtin to think with, in relation to texts undreamed of by him. As I have said, Bakhtin's attitude to much modern writing is conjectural, and can be only estimated from the gaps and hints in his work.

So far this article has stuck deliberately to textual exposition, in the second part I intend to extrapolate Bakhtin's ideas in relation to my own perspective and the texts I've read through him. While carnival and dialogics have been avidly taken up by the contemporary scholarly community, the same is not true of Bakhtin's ideas of chronotope. Bakhtin uses this term, literally 'space-time' to talk about 'the intrinsic connectedness of temporal and spatial relationships that are artistically expressed in literature.'[32] 'The chronotope is the place where the knots of narrative are tied and untied.[33] Bakhtin uses the concept of chronotope notably in 'Forms of Time and of the Chronotope in the Novel'[34] and in the fragment 'The *Bildungsroman* and Its Significance in the History of Realism' which consists mainly of a reading of Goethe.[35] Very unusually for Bakhtin, we are told when and where the chronotope was first encountered; in the summer of 1925 Bakhtin attended a lecture on the chronotope in biology. While acknowedging that space-time is used by Einstein as part of his Theory of Relativity, Bakhtin denies that the special meaning there is important because 'we are borrowing it for literary criticism almost as a metaphor (almost but not entirely).[36] But a footnote on the following page is revealing:

> In his 'Transcendental Aesthetics'(one of the main sections of his *Critique of Pure Reason*) Kant defines space and time as indispensable forms of any cognition, beginning with elementary perceptions and representations. Here we employ the Kantian evaluation of the importance of these forms in the cognitive process, but differ from Kant in taking them not as 'transcendental' but as forms of the most immediate reality. We shall attempt to show the role these forms play in the process of concrete artistic cognition (artistic visualisation) under conditions obtaining in the novel.[37]

It is in his neo-Kantianism that one can relate Bakhtin to the aesthetics of reception. 'Concrete' here does not have the meaning of 'sensuously immediate', but is a philosophical term meaning roughly 'something made manifest'. 'Concretization' is a term used by Roman Ingarden building upon the phenomenology of Edmund Husserl. The reader concretises indeterminacies to build the world of the text. I am not suggesting any influence of Ingarden on Bakhtin, but rather that both shared a heritage of neo-Kantian and Husserlian philosophy. Concretization features in the work of the German aesthetics of reception, the work of Wolfgang Iser, which postulates a reader forever trying to close gaps and resolve indetermanicies and the more historically orientated work of Hans Robert Jauss.[38] Jauss's work is much closer to Bakhtin's in its historical concerns. In reading Daniil Kharms's 'Incidence' at the start of this article, the place Russia, and the date 1937 concretise a chilling Stalinist disappearance as the Red-Haired Man' becomes a non-person; the absurd story takes on a sinister significance. Concretization would appear to be crucial to fantastic texts as a process through which the reader is made to experience the abject, sublime or uncanny through reading. But in the texts I shall be considering, the effect is not one of looming ghosts, but an shift in perspective, often a spatial view that induces vertigo. The flying figure experiences a shiver of consciousness and sees the world below drop away from her.

'What a long way down the floor looked! It was only a few feet below you understand, no great distance in itself - yet it yawned before me like a chasm, and indeed, you might say that this gulf now before me represented the grand abyss, the poignant divide, that would henceforth separate me form common humanity.' [39]

Fevvers's experience in Carter's *Nights at the Circus* will exemplify this identity in difference. The circus is a significant place and night a significant time here, Together they make what Foucault called a heterotopia, a counter-site which he linked to utopia exemplifying both in the mirror:

> The mirror is, after all, a utopia, since it is a placeless place. In the mirror, I see myself there where I am not, in an unreal, virtual space that opens up behind the surface; I am over there, there where I am not, a sort of shadow that gives my own visibility to my self, that enables me to see myself there where I am absent: such is the utopia of the mirror. But it is also a heterotopia in so far as the mirror does exist in reality, where it exerts a sort of counter action on the position that I occupy. From the standpoint of the mirror I discover my absence from the place where I am since I see myself over there. Starting from this gaze that is, as it were, directed toward me, from the ground of this virtual space that is on the other side of the glass, I come back toward myself; I begin again to direct my eyes toward myself and to reconstitute myself there where I am. The mirror functions as a heterotopia in this respect: it makes this place that I occupy at the moment when I look at myself in the glass at once absolutely real, connected with all the space that surrounds it., and absolutely unreal, since in order to be perceived it has to pass through this virtual point which is over there.[40]

The space of the mirror, the circus, the gothic vault, hyperspace, functions typically in the fantastic texts as heterotopia, their presence concentrates in post-enlightenment fantasies. Frequently peculiarly disturbing modern fantastic will charge their power by reflecting older chronotopes.

A crucial text for Bakhtin's was *The Golden Ass* otherwise known as *The Transformations of Lucius* by Lucius Apuleius, which was one of the earliest surviving Latin prose texts dating from the second century AD. The chronotope of this text extends to contemporary fantastic texts such as Angela Carter's *Nights at the Circus* (1984) and Salman Rushdie's *The Satanic Verses* (1988), but the transformation is complicated by Mikhail Bulgakov's *The Master and Margarita* which was written in the 1930s, but only published in 1966-67. *The Master and Margarita* remembers Lucius and in turn transmits the chronotope to Rushdie and Carter. The posthumous fame and carnival theme of Bulgakov echos that of Bakhtin's theoretical texts. Indeed it is impossible to speak of sources and influence here, since Carter doubtless read and transformed both Bulgakov and Bakhtin in her *Nights at the Circus*.

The Golden Ass describes the picaresque adventures of Lucius, except that the picaresque had not been named yet. It is a satire, of the sort called Mennipian satire by Bakhtin and seen by him as the birth of the novel genre. Lucius is transformed into an ass, by mistake, he passes from master to master

observing the vices and follies of humans.   Finally, he is turned back into
human shape by the goddess Isis and in return he is initiated into her cult.   The
transformation scene becomes a chronotope which is reproduced and
remembered in later texts.   The human Lucius receives hospitality from Milo,
whose wife, Pamphile is revealed to be a witch.   Lucius makes love to
Pamphile's maid, Fotis who allows him to see her mistress transform herself
into an owl.   She does this by undressing then smearing a magic ointment all
over her body:

> After this she muttered a long charm to her lamp, and shook herself; her
> limbs vibrated gently and became gradually fledged with feathers, her arms
> changed into sturdy wings, her nose grew crooked and horny, her nails
> turned into talons, and Pamphile had become an owl.   She gave a
> querulous hoot and made a few little hopping flights until she was sure
> enough of her wings to glide off, away over the roof-tops.[41]

But things go disastrously wrong when Lucius tries it and he is transformed
instead into an ass.   Fotis assures him that all can be reversed if only he eats
some roses, but alas there are no roses to be had and Lucius embarks on his life
as an ass.   Like Kafka's Gregor, Lucius is both human and inhuman.   He has a
dual perspective being neither fully donkey nor fully human.   He cannot speak,
only bray and he retains the human mind and memories of the human Lucius.
There is a bawdy tone to many of Lucius's adventures, his shock at his sudden
transformation into an ass is tempered by the possession of a donkey-sized
member.   Lucius is saved from a fate worse than death of being publicly
exhibited in a cage engaged in sexual congress with a criminal woman, by the
timely intervention of the goddess Isis.   It is not the trans-species sex which
horrifies Lucius, since he has already had his donkey's body sold to a rich and
powerful lady, but the fact that the woman is a criminal and the act will take
place as a public exhibition.   The tone of the text changes dramatically when
Isis appears and it seems that Apuleius incorporated genuine cultic rituals here.

Mikhail Bulgakov's *The Master and Margarita* is a complex multi-layered
novel which layers narrative strands inside each other like so many Chinese
boxes finally the layers are merged together, but the outcome is deceptive and
it is never clear what happened.   In chapter 20 Margarita anoints herself with
with a special ointment given her by the magician's assistant.   Immediately it
has a rejuvenating effect, she looks ten years younger when she looks in the
mirror.   Her headache is cured, her complexion turns a healthy pink, the
muscles of her arms and legs grow firmer and she even loses weight.   She can

defy gravity: 'She jumped and stayed suspended in the air just above the carpet, then slowly and gently dropped back to the ground.' [42]

The anointing had not only changed her appearance. Joy surged through every part of her body, she felt as if bubbles were shooting along every limb. Margarita felt free, free of everything, realising with absolute clarity that what was happening was the fulfilment of her presentiment of that morning, that she was going to leave her house and her past life for ever. [43]

Margarita had longed to leave her boring husband and join her lover, the Master, who is the Master of the title. But as she pencils a farewell note to her husband, she is interrupted by her maid, Natasha, who she rewards by giving her all her clothes. Margarita then opens the window and flies away on her broomstick, shouting 'I'm invisible! Invisible!' as she had been instructed. And so she is. [44] But while Margarita is invisible and can fly, she has to take care not to crash into lamp-posts. The magic ointment, the figure of the flying woman who 'becomes a witch' the presence of the maid all indicate the *Golden Ass* chronotope. Bulgakov introduces a note of erotic comedy by having Margarita fly off naked after blinding her boring neighbour Nikolai Ivanovich by dropping her final item of underclothing over his head. He falls off his bench onto the flagged path with a crash. Margarita is enabled by her invisibility and flying prowess to take revenge on the literary establishment who she blames for ruining her lover, the Master's life. She smashes a grand piano, overflows the bath and breaks all the windows in the chairman's flat. Having exacted revenge, Margarita takes off on her broom again, she then notices that she is being followed by a dark curious object. This proves to be her maid, Natasha:

> Completely naked too, her hair streaming behind her, she was flying along mounted on a fat pig, clutching a briefcase in its front legs and furiously pounding the air with its hind trotters. A pince-nez, which occasionally flashed in the moonlight, had fallen off its nose and was dangling on a ribbon, whilst the pig's hat kept falling forward over its eyes. After a careful look Margarita recognised the pig as Nikolai Ivanovich and her laughter rang out , mingled with Natasha's, over the forest below. [45]

Like Margarita, Natasha had made a satisfactory transformation, but is admiring her magical beauty in front of the mirror when she is propositioned by Nikolai Ivanovich. After they romp about in the bedroom, Natasha smears some of the cream on his bald head.

The face of her respectable neighbour shrank and grew a snout, whilst his arms and legs sprouted trotters. Looking at himself in the mirror Nikolai Ivanovich gave a wild, desparing squeal but it was too late. A few seconds later, with The face of her respectable neighbour shrank and grew a snout, whilst his arms Natasha astride him, he was flying through the air away from Moscow, sobbing with chagrin. [46]

Like Lucius in *The Golden Ass* he is transformed into a beast, but this time into a pig not a donkey. Circe's transformation of men into swine in *The Odyssey* is remembered by the chronotope.

Angela Carter has attested to the importance of *The Golden Ass* in her early reading[47] In *Nights at the Circus*, she deploys elements of the scene. Fevvers, her cockney heroine, is a winged aerialiste, who claims, like Helen of Troy, to be hatched from an egg. Her slogan 'Is she fact or is she fiction'[48] is the central ambiguity of the text. It never is clear whether Fevvers can really fly or if she is an illusionist. Jack Walser, the American journalist reasons that the wings of birds are nothing but the equivalent of human arms, so if Fevvers really was a bird she should possess no arms at all 'for it's her arms that ought to be her wings.'[49] On the other hand, Fevvers flies very slowly, much slower than human arialistes. There is the paradox of the simulacrum: 'For, in order to earn a living, might not a genuine bird-woman ... have to pretend she was an artificial one?'[50] While the novel is set in Russia, Fevvers needs no magic ointment but according to her own story, grew her wings and flew naturally. Her maid / dresser Lizzie takes a sisterly / motherly part, but is not transformed herself. Walser is transformed by his ordeals. Fevvers on her first flying lesson goes naked [51] and in the manner of Bulgakov her underwear is strewn around during her first interview with Walser. Like Bulgakov's Margarita, Fevvers circles the house and encounters a cherry tree,[52] she also has to avoid telegraph wires.[53] Cold cream makes a minor appearance,[54] as does a pig. These are the incidentals of the Bulgakov scenes which are transformed.

The symbolism of the flying woman is indicate by the text itself: '... I think you must be the pure child of the century that just now is waiting in the wings, the New Age in which no women will be bound down to the ground.'[55] The picaresque narrative moves through space and time, Fevvers is an image of the future, of time not yet come into being. The larger than life figure of Fevvers is surely heroic, yet for all the bravura this novel contains much tragedy, the story of Mignon being perhaps the most poignant. Mignon is a character in Goethe's *Wilhelm Meister's Apprenticeship* (1777 -1829), she is a fairy-like waif rescued by Wilhelm from a troupe of rope-dancers. She dies of unrequited love for Wilhelm. Carter's Mignon has a happier fate, but she functions as an image of the abused female orphan child. Fevvers's primal

scene is a picture of Leda and the Swan, 'my own conception, the heavenly
bird in a white majesty of feathers descending with imperious desire upon the
half-stunned and yet herself impassioned girl.'[56] Fevvers might be seen as a
tragic, rather than heroic figure. At one level, she is a freak, an exhibit in
Madame Schreck's museum of women monsters, in company with the
hermaphrodite Albert/ Albertina, the Sleeping Beauty, the midget Wiltshire
Wonder and Fanny Four-Eyes who has another pair of eyes instead of nipples.
When clothed to hide her wings, Fevvers appears hunchbacked,[57] her
disablement is emphasised when she breaks a wing in the train crash in Book
Three. But the accident makes her more ordinary too:

> Since she had stopped bothering to hide her wings, the others had grown
> accustomed to the sight it no longer seemed remarkable. Besides, one
> wing had lost all its glamorous colours and the other was bandaged and
> useless. How long would it be before she flew again? where was that
> silent demand to be *looked* at that had once made her stand out?
> Vanished; and under the circumstances, it was a good thing she's lost it -
> these days, she would do better to plead to be ignored. She was so shabby
> that she looked like a fraud.... [58]

Fevvers will not fly in the novel again; however she does display her feathers at
Lizzie's bidding when encountering Walser transformed into a Shaman who
has taken on the totemic identity of a bear.

> Fevvers felt the hairs on her nape rise when she saw that he was looking at
> her as if, horror of horrors, she was perfectly natural - natural, but
> abominable. He fixed her with his phosphorescent eye and, after a
> moment, his voice rose in song;
>   'Only a bird in a gilded cage-'
> 'Oh, my *Gawd!* ' said Fevvers. For he had translated the familiar tune
> into some kind of chant, some kind of dirge, some kind of Siberian
> invocation of the spectral inhabitants of the other world which coexists
> with this one, and Fevvers knew in her bones his song was meant to do her
> harm....
> Fevvers felt that shivering sensation which always visited her when mages,
> wizards, impresarios came to take away her singularity as though it was
> their own invention, as though they believed she depended on their
> imaginations in order to be herself. She felt herself turning, willy-nilly,
> from a woman into an idea....
>   For one moment, just one moment, Fevvers suffered the worst crisis of
> her life: 'Am I fact? Or am I fiction? Am I what I know I am? Or am I
> what he thinks I am?'
>   'Show 'em your feathers, quick!' urged Lizzie.
>   Fevvers, with a strange sense of desperation, a miserable awareness of
> her broken wing and her discoloured plumage, could think of nothing else

> to do but to obey. She shrugged off her furs and, though she could not
> spread two wings, she spread one -lopsided angel, partial and shabby
> splendour! No Venus, or Helen, of Angel of the Apocalypse, not Izrael of
> Isfahel... only a poor freak down on her luck, and an object of the most
> dubious kind of reality to her beholders, since both the men in the god-hut
> were accustomed to hallucination and she who looks like a hallucination
> but is not had no place in their view of things.[59]

Walser in his trance as a Shaman sees her as a grotesque in Kayser's
sense, 'horror of horrors... perfectly natural, but abominable.' But this abject
vision and the music-hall song 'Only a bird in a gilded cage' which has echoed
through out the text and which positions Fevvers as entrapped victim is not
sustained. If there is an image of abjection in the text, it is surely that of
Madame Schreck, who is earlier reduced by Fevvers to an empty bundle of old
clothes, 'a sort of scarecrow of desire.'[60] In his totemic identity of the bear,
Walser's hostile song assails Fevvers: she felt herself turning, willy-nilly, from
a woman into an idea.'[61] But this patriarchal vision is defeated, Fevvers is not
mere idea, mere symbol. She refuses the mythological identities forced upon
her: 'No Venus, or Helen or Angel of the Apocalypse... only a poor freak down
on her luck.[62]

Fevvers was surely born out of the matrix of Tod Browning's *Freaks*, the
photography of Diane Arbus, Bulgakov's Margarita, 'Leda and the Swan', but
also certainly Paul Klee's *Angelus Novus*, that image of an angel flying before
the storm of modernity that Walter Benjamin so tellingly commented on. The
epigraph from Gerhard Scholem which prefixed Benjamin's comments also
bears a relation to the trick with the stopped clock which Fevvers and Lizzie
play on Walser:

> Mein Flügel is zum Schwung beteit,
> ich keherte gern zurück,
> denn bleib ich auch lebendige Zeit,
> ich hätte wenig Glück.
>
> (My wing is ready for flight/ I would like to turn back/ If I stayed timeless
> time/ I would have little luck.)
>
> ... This is how one pictures the angel of history. His face is turned toward
> the past. Where we perceive a chain of events, he sees one single
> catastrophe which keeps piling wreckage upon wreckage and hurls it in
> front of his feet. The angel would like to stay, awaken the dead, and make
> whole what has been smashed. But a storm in blowing from Paradise, it
> has got caught in his wings with such violence that the angel can no longer

close them. This storm propels him into the future to which his back is turned, while the pile of debris before him grows skyward. This storm is what we call progress.[63]

Carter has transformed the image and the sex of the flying figure, but the storm of progress is consistent. Lizzie had interpolated 'It's going to be more complicated that that.' when Fevvers had given her utopian vision of the future. 'This old witch sees storms ahead, my girl. When I look to the future, I see through a glass darkly. You improve your analysis, girl, and *then* we'll discuss it.'[64] Beauty's troubled dreams are divined by Fevvers and Lizzie as portents of the coming century,[65] but Fevvers is certainly no angel and Carter insists that she be seen neither as allegory nor freak. It seems to me important politically to resist a grotesque reading of Fevvers as abject freak, or victim, but instead to affirm her flying figure as a utopian potentiality. The novel ends with the spiralling tornado of Fevvers's laughter, laughter at Walser's question '...why did you go to such lengths... to convince me you were the "only fully-feathered intacta in the history of the world"?'[66] Fevvers's laughter is deeply Bakhtinian.

Derek Littlewood

NOTES

1. Daniil Kharms, *Incidences*, trans. Neil Cornwell, London: Serpent's Tail, 1993, p. 49.
2. Immanuel Kant, *Observations on the Feeling of the Beautiful and Sublime*, trans. John T. Goldthwait, Berkeley & Oxford: University of California, 1960, p. 55 [first published in German, 1764].
3. See David Shepherd, 'Bakhtin and the Reader' in, *Bakhtin and Cultural Theory*, edited by Ken Hirschkop and David Shepherd, Manchester: Manchester University Press, 1989, pp. 91-108 for Bakhtin in relation to reader theory.
4. For another account of Kayser and Bakhtin see Geoffrey Harpham, *On the Grotesque: Strategies of Contradiction in Art and Literature*, New Jersey: Princeton University Press, 1982 and Rene Wellek, *A History Of Modern Criticism: 1750-1950*, vol. 7, New Haven and London: Yale University Press who usefully describes Kayser's earlier work.
5. Wolfgang Kayser, *The Grotesque in Art and Literature*, trans. Ulrich Weisstein, Gloucester, Mass.: Peter Smith, 1968, [first published in German, 1957].
6. *Ibid.*, pp. 10 - 11.
7. *Ibid.*, pp. 180 -181.
8. *Ibid.*, pp. 184 -188.
9. *Ibid.*, p. 185.
10. *Ibid.*
11. *Ibid.*

12. *Ibid.*, p. 188.
13. *Ibid.*
14. *Ibid.*
15. *Ibid.*, p. 187.
16. Mikhail Bakhtin, *Rabelais and His World*, trans. Helene Iswolsky, Cambridge Mass. & London: MIT Press, 1968, [first published in Russian, 1965], p.46.
17. *Ibid.*
18. *Ibid.*, p. 47.
19. *Ibid.*
20. *Ibid.*
21. *Ibid.*
22. *Ibid.*, pp. 46 - 47.
23. See Michael Gardiner, *The Dialogics of Critique: M.M.Bakhtin and the Theory of Ideology*, London: Routledge, 1992.
24. Bakhtin, *op. cit.*, p. 48.
25. *Ibid.*, pp. 46 - 47.
26. Katerina Clark and Michael Holquist, *Mikhail Bakhtin*, Cambridge Mass. & London: Harvard Belknap, 1984, pp 27, 51, 261.
27. William Gibson, *Burning Chrome*, London: Grafton, 1988.
28. Bakhtin, *op. cit.*, p. 25.
29. Hirschkop & Shepherd, *op. cit.*, p. 27.
30. Mikhail Bakhtin, *The Dialogic Imagination*, trans. Caryl Emerson and Michael Holquist, ed. Michael Holquist, Austin: University of Texas, 1981, p. 23.
31. Hirschkop and Shepherd, *op. cit.*, p. 27.
32. Bakhtin (1981), *op. cit.*, p. 84.
33. *Ibid.*, p. 250.
34. *Ibid.*, pp. 84-258.
35. Mikhail Bakhtin, *Speech Genres and Other Late Essays*, trans. Vern McGee, ed. Caryl Emerson and Michael.Holquist, Austin: University of Texas. pp. 10 -59.
36. Bakhtin (1981), *op. cit.*, p. 84.
37. *Ibid.*, p. 85.
38. Hans Robert Jauss, *Toward an Aesthetic of Reception*, trans. Timothy Bahti, Minneapolis: University of Minnesota Press, 1982, pp. 72-74.
39. Angela Carter, *Nights at the Circus*, London: Picador, 1985, p. 29.
40. Michel Foucault, 'Of Other Spaces', *Diacritics*, vol 16, pp. 22-27. This text is a translation of lecture notes from a lecture delivered by Foucault in 1967.
41. Lucius Apuleius, *The Golden Ass*, trans. Robert Graves, revised Michael Grant, Harmondsworth: Penguin , 1990,[written c AD 158], p. 48.
42. Mikhail Bulgakov, *The Master and Margarita*, trans. Michael Glenny, London: Collins Harvill, 1988, p. 264.
43. *ibid.*
44. *ibid.*, p. 268.
45. *ibid.*, pp. 277-278.
46. *ibid.*, p. 278.
47. Angela Carter, *Expletives Deleted: Selected Writings*, London: Vintage, 1992, p. 1
48. Carter (1985), *op. cit.*, p. 7.
49. *ibid.*, p. 15.
50. *ibid.*, p. 17.

51. *ibid.*, p. 34.
52. *ibid.*, p. 36.
53. *ibid.*, p. 84.
54. *ibid.*, p. 13.
55. *ibid.*, p. 25.
56. *ibid.*, p. 28.
57. *ibid.*, p. 127.
58. *ibid.*, p. 277.
59. *ibid.*, pp. 289-290.
60. *ibid.*, p. 84.
61. *ibid.*, p. 289.
62. *ibid.*, p. 290.
63. Walter Benjamin, *Illuminations*, trans. Harry Zohn, ed. Hannah Arendt, London: Fontana, 1970, pp. 259-260.
64. Carter (1965), *op. cit.*, p. 286.
65. *ibid.*, p. 86.
66. *ibid.*, p. 294.

Index

Adorno, Theodor, 76
Aldiss, Brian, 136, 145, 151, 162, 172, 188, 189
Allen, Woody, 24, 36, 131, 180, 188
Althusser, Louis, 111, 124
Amis, Kingsley, 108, 124
Angenot, Marc, 129, 144
Apuleius, Lucius, 199-201, 206
Arbus, Diane, 204
Arnold, Thurman, 16, 17, 23, 25, 32, 124, 184
Asimov, Isaac, 63, 127
Attenborough, David, 185

Bakhtin, Mikhail, 122, 125, 162, 191-207
Ballard, J. G., 54, 127-146
Banks, Iain M., 58, 60, 73,
Barker, Martin, 162, 189
Barrell, John, 31
Barthes, Roland, 78, 141-142, 146
Baudrillard, Jean, 46, 55
Bax, Arnold, 25, 32- 37
Beckett, Samuel, 75, 193
Beddoes, Thomas Lovell, 167
Benford, Gregory, 151
Benjamin, Walter, 102, 205, 208
Bloch, Ernst, 196
Bontemps, Arna, 88
Borowski, Tadeusz, 76
Boughton, Rutland, 32
Brecht, Berthold, 194
Briggs, Raymond, 81
Brown, Frederic, 90
Browning, Todd, 205
Buber, Martin, 49, 52, 56, 192
Bulgakov, Mikhail, 192, 195, 200 - 204
Bulwer Lytton, Edward, 28
Burke, Edmund, 173
Burnham, James, 13, 22-24
Burroughs, Edgar Rice, 88, 102
Butler, Octavia, 87, 101-102
Byron, George Gordon, 164-166, 168, 172, 175

Campbell, John W., 180

Campbell, Thomas, 165- 168, 175-176, 180
Camus, Albert, 81
Carnell, John, 127
Carter, Angela, 41, 192, 199-200, 204
Carver, George Washington, 96
Changeux, Jean-Pierre, 143, 146
Chatman, Seymour, 142, 146
Cherryh, C. J., 154-157
Chesney, George T., 88
Chesnutt, Charles W, 95
Chopin, Kate, 95
Cixous, Hélène, 42, 44
Clareson, Thomas D., 89, 103-104
Clarke, Arthur C., 109, 113, 163
Clement, Catherine, 42, 44
Conrad, Joseph, 132
Cousin de Grainville, J-B., 163
Crichton, Michael, 179, 187
Cruso, Solomon, 89

Dali, Salvador, 142
Daniken, Erich von, 179, 188
Dante Alighieri, 165
Delaney, Samuel R., 57-64, 73,
Derrida, Jacques, 47-48, 53, 55-56, 85
Dick, Philip K., 45- 47, 50- 56, 175
Disraeli, Benjamin, 88
Dowling, David, 81, 85
DuBois, W.E.B., 93, 95, 96
DuPlessis, Rachel Blau, 38, 43
Durham, Scott, 54, 56

Eddison, E.R., 25
Einstein, Albert, 99, 101, 198
Elgar, Edward, 32
Equiano, Olaudah, 91

Flores, Angel, 120, 125
Foreman, Lewis, 35, 37
Foucault, Michel, 41, 44, 57-58, 196, 199, 206
Franklin, H. Bruce, 23, 85, 87, 102
Frazer, James, 194
Freeman, Michael, 81, 85
Freud, Sigmund, 116, 131, 139, 145

Galbreath, Robert, 52, 56
Garvey, Marcus, 92, 95-96, 105

Gerrard, Nicci, 41, 44
Gibson, William, 148-149, 153-154, 158-
161, 163, 197, 206
Gilman, Charlotte Perkins, 91
Godwin, William, 104, 174
Goethe, Johann Wolfgang von, 198, 203
Greene, Graham, 132, 139
Greenlee, Sam, 101
Gunn, Thom, 167

Hachiya, Michihiko, 81, 85
Haraway, Donna J., 58, 63, 71, 73- 74
Harbou, Thea von, 184
Harryhousen, Ray, 181
Hay, William Delisle, 88
Heidegger, Martin, 48
Heinlein, Robert, 63, 129
Herbert, Frank, 93, 157
Hillegas, Mark R., 90, 104
Himmler, Heinrich, 75
Hirschkop, Ken, 191, 197, 205- 206
Hobsbawm, E.J., 27, 36
Hodge, T. Shirby, 89
Hoffmann, E. T. A., 131, 194- 195
Hollinger, Veronica, 46, 55
Holloway, Stanley, 185
Hood, Thomas, 167, 168, 171, 175- 176
Howe, Irving, 18, 19, 23
Hughes, David Y., 12, 23, 36, 37, 104
Husserl, Edmund, 48, 55, 199
Huxley, Aldous, 24, 81, 84, 109, 124

Ibuse, Masuji, 82
Ingarden, Roman, 199
Irigaray, Luce, 39, 43, 47, 54-55
Iser, Wolfgang, 114, 125, 162, 198

Jackson, Rosemary, 24, 26, 36, 93, 147- 152,
161
Jakobson, Roman, 195
Jameson, Fredric, 45, 55
Jauss, Hans Robert, 198, 206
Jarry, Alfred, 189, 194
Johnson, James Weldon, 93, 95
Joyce, James, 195
Jung, Carl Gustav, 133-134, 145

Kafka, Franz, 109, 119, 120, 124-125, 128,
201
Kayser, Wolfgang, 192- 195, 205-206
Keller, David H., 94
Kellman, Martin, 30, 36
Kennedy, John Fitzgerald, 143
Kermode, Frank, 114, 124, 169, 176
Keyes, Daniel, 179, 189
Kharms, Daniil, 194, 198, 205
King, Katie, 63
Kingsley, Charles, 28, 108, 124
Klee, Paul, 204
Klein, Richard, 82

Lacan, Jacques, 57-58, 73, 116, 119, 125
Lang, Fritz, 130, 184
Larsen, Nella, 95, 131
Larson, Charles R., 95, 104
Le Carré, John, 66
Le Guin, Ursula, 108, 114, 124, 155- 156,
163
Lefanu, Sarah, 37, 43
Lem, Stanislaw, 151
Levi, Carlo, 77
Levi, Primo, 77, 84
Levinas, Emmanuel, 47- 57
Lewis, C. S., 25, 29, 35
Lifton, Robert J., 82, 85
Lucas, George, 180
Lukács, Georg, 193, 197
Lyotard, Jean-François, 47, 54-55, 67

Malmgren,Carl, 147-152, 161-162
Malory, Thomas, 30, 31
Mann, Thomas, 194
Martin, John, 30, 48-49, 52, 56, 153, 161-
162, 167, 189, 192
Matheson, Richard, 128
Mayakovsky, Vladimir, 194
McCaffery, Larry, 45
McCarty, Mari, 40, 43
McHale, Brian, 46, 55, 62- 63, 72-74, 143,
146
Miller, Warren, 101
Morrissey, Thomas, 81, 84
Mullen, R. D., 54, 96, 104-105

Neruda, Pablo, 194

O'Byrne, Dermot, 32- 33, 34
Ornstein, Robert, 47
Orwell, George, 22, 24, 109, 124
Ouseley, Thomas John, 167

Palmer, Christopher, 51, 53-56
Parker, Patricia, 42
Parrinder, Patrick, 112, 114, 124-125, 144
Philmus, Robert M., 91, 104
Piaget, Jean, 116
Plath, Sylvia, 79
Poe, Edgar Allen, 131
Pohl, Frederik, 12, 22
Powys, John Cowper, 29
Pratchett, Terry, 25
Price, D. J. de Solla, 187, 190
Priestley, J. B., 127
Pringle, David, 143, 145-146
Pynchon, Thomas, 21, 24

Rabkin, Eric S., 46, 52, 55-56, 102, 103
Ransmayr, Christoph, 72
Reade, Charles, 167
Redfield, Robert, 20, 24
Rey, Lester del, 90
Reynolds, Mark, 90
Rose, Mark, 63, 73, 63, 73, 85, 116, 119,
    125, 161
Rosenfeld, Alvin, 76, 78, 84
Roshwald, Mordecai, 14
Ross, Andrew, 56, 160, 163
Roussel, Raymond, 142, 143
Rushdie, Salman, 54, 72, 200
Russ, Joanna, 41, 43-44, 63, 108, 124

Sanders, S., 124, 138
Sartre, Jean Paul, 48, 150, 193
Schachner, Nat, 90
Schatt, Stanley, 18, 23
Scholem, Gerhard, 204
Schuyler, George, 88, 91-92, 94-97, 99-100,
    103-105
Scott, Walter, 28, 32, 51, 56, 163, 176
Shaked, Gershom, 77, 84
Shelley, Mary, 41, 59, 72, 116, 147, 164,
    166, 168-170, 172-176
Shelley, Percy Bysshe, 172-173

Shepherd, David, 191, 206-207
Sibelius, Jean, 34-35
Slotkin, J. S., 20
Spencer, Kathleen, 87
Spengler, Oswald, 89
Spielberg, Steven, 109, 118, 177, 183
Steiner, George, 75, 76, 80, 84
Sterling, Bruce, 54, 197
Sterne, Lawrence, 195
Stevens, Wallace, 90
Strauss, Richard, 32, 33
Streiber, Whitley, 179, 189
Suvin, Darko, 54, 103, 117, 125, 188

Taylor, Frederick Winslow, 11, 56
Tennyson, Alfred, 29, 81
Thiong'o, Ngugi wa, 91
Todorov, Tzvetan, 125, 128, 129, 144
Tolkien, J. R. R., 25-26, 29, 32, 34-36
Trotsky, Leon, 61
Twain, Mark, 95

Vonnegut, Kurt, 11, 13-16, 18-24

Wagner, Richard, 28, 30, 32-33, 35
Wallace, King, 88
Walsh, Chad, 20, 24
Warner, Sylvia Townsend, 30, 36
Washington, Booker T., 84, 96
Weber, Eugen, 18, 23, 28, 109
Weber, Max, 18, 23, 28, 109
Weinbaum, Stanley G., 90
Weinsheimer, Joel, 142, 146
Welles, Orson, 179, 189
Wells, H. G., 96, 109, 113, 189
White, T.H., 25, 30, 31, 33- 36, 89, 92, 95
White, Walter, 92, 95
Whyte, William H., 17, 19, 24
Wieland, Christoph, 194
Wiener, Norbert, 14, 23
Wilde, Oscar, 61
Williams, Charles, 25, 29, 32, 34, 101, 105
Williams, John A., 101
Williams, Ralph Vaughan, 32, 34
Wittgenstein, Ludwig, 75
Wollstonecraft, Mary, 173, 176
Wolmark, Jenny, 38-41, 43-44
Woolf, Virginia, 107-108, 114

Index 211

Wyndham, John, 82, 85, 132
Yeats, William Butler, 33
Yerby, Frank, 88

Young, James, 76, 78, 84
Zagat, Arthur Leo, 89
Zamiatin, Evgeny, 14, 24, 109, 124

ROLAND A. CHAMPAGNE

The Ethics of Reading According to Emmanuel Levinas

Amsterdam/Atlanta, GA 1996. 118 pp.
(Collection Monographique Rodopi en Littérature Française
Contemporaine 27)
ISBN: 90-5183-919-7   Hfl. 35,-/US-$ 23.50

Reading a text is an ethical activity for Emmanuel Levinas. His moral philosophy considers written texts to be natural places to discover relations of responsibility in Western philosophical systems which are marked by extreme violence and totalizing hatred. While ethics is understood to mean a relationship with the other and reading is the appropriation of the other to the self, readings according to Levinas naturally entail relationships with. the other. Levinas's own writings are often frought with the struggle between his own maleness, the concerns of feminism, and the Judaism that marks his contributions to the debates of the Talmud. This book uses male feminism as its perspective in presenting the applications of Levinas's ethical vision to texts whose readings have presented moral dilemmas for women readers. Levinas's philosophical theories can provide keys to unlock the difficulties of these texts whose readings will provide models of reading as ethical acts beginning with the ethical contract in *Song of Songs* where the assumption of a woman writer begins the elaboration of issues that sets a male reader as her other. From the reader's vantage point of seeing the self as other, other issues of male feminism become increasingly poignant, ranging from the solicitude of listening to Céline (Chapter 2), the responsibility for noise in Nizan (Chapter 3), the asymmetrical pattern of face-to-face relationships in Maupassant (Chapter 4), the sovereignty of laughter in Bataille and Zola (Chapter 5), the call of the other in Italo Svevo (Chapter 6), the Woman as Other in Breton (Chapter 7), the ethical self in Drieu la Rochelle (Chapter 8), the response to Hannah Arendt (Chapter 9), and the vulnerability of Bernard-Henri Lévy (Chapter 10). The male feminist reader is thus the incarnation of the struggle at the core of the issues outlined by Levinas for the act of reading as an ethical endeavor.

USA/Canada: Editions Rodopi B.V., 2015 South Park Place, Atlanta, GA 30339, Tel. (770) 933-0027, *Call toll-free* (U.S. only) 1-800-225- 3998, Fax (770) 933-9644, *E-mail:* F.van.der.Zee@rodopi.nl
All Other Countries: Editions Rodopi B.V., Keizersgracht 302-304, 1016 EX Amsterdam, The Netherlands. Tel. + + 31 (0)20-622-75-07, Fax + + 31 (0)20-638-09-48, *E-mail:* F.van.der.Zee@rodopi.nl

JEERING DREAMERS
Villiers de l'Isle-Adam's
L'Eve Future at our Fin de Siècle

A Collection of Essays edited by John Anzalone
Preface by Alain Raitt

Amsterdam/Atlanta, GA 1996. 210 pp.
(Faux Titre 111)
ISBN: 90-5183-939-1   Hfl. 60,-/US-$ 40.-

Contents: ALAN RAITT: Preface. JOHN ANZALONE: Introduction: On the Eve of Tomorrow. MARILYN GADDIS ROSE: Do Authors Control Translators? Second Thoughts by a Translator of *L'Eve future*. ASTI HUSTVEDT: The Pathology of Eve. Villiers de l'Isle-Adam and Fin de Siècle Medical Discourse. MARIE LATHERS: The Decadent Goddess: *L'Eve future* and the *Vénus de Milo*. ANNE GREENFELD: The Shield of Perseus and the Absent Woman. GWENHAEL PONNAU: Désaccords et dissonances: le corps et la voix dans *L'Eve future*. PASCAL ROLLET: «Inflexions d'une féminéité surnaturelle»: la voix résistante de *L'Eve future* de Villiers de l'Isle-Adam. ALAIN NÉRY: Hadaly et Schéhérazade. JOHN ANZALONE: Danse macabre: le pas de deux Villiers-Baudelaire. CAROL DE DOBAY RIFELJ: Minds, Computers and Hadaly. FELICIA MILLER-FRANK: Edison's Recorded Angel. WARREN JOHNSON: Edison's Comic Dualism. BERTRAND VIBERT: *L'Eve future* ou l'ambiguïté. Contribution à une poétique du satanisme moderne. CATHERINE BORDEAU: The Gendering of the Creator.

USA/Canada: Editions Rodopi B.V., 2015 South Park Place, Atlanta, GA 30339, Tel. (770) 933-0027, *Call toll-free* (U.S. only) 1-800-225- 3998, Fax (770) 933-9644, *E-mail:* F.van.der.Zee@rodopi.nl
All Other Countries: Editions Rodopi B.V., Keizersgracht 302-304, 1016 EX Amsterdam, The Netherlands. Tel. + + 31 (0)20-622-75-07, Fax + + 31 (0)20-638-09-48, *E-mail:* F.van.der.Zee@rodopi.nl

LAURENCE STERNE
IN MODERNISM
AND POSTMODERNISM

Ed. by David Pierce and Peter de Voogd

Amsterdam/Atlanta, GA 1996. 210 pp.
(Postmodern Studies 15)
ISBN: 90-420-0011-2   Bound Hfl. 110,-/US-$ 73.-
ISBN: 90-420-0002-3   Paper Hfl. 30,-/US-$ 20.-

Laurence Sterne's *Tristram Shandy* is the most wayward — and in some respects the most powerful — critique of Locke's theory of knowledge, while his interest in the gulf between biological and clock time makes him a contemporary of Proust and Bergson. In obscuring the fine line between autobiography and fiction, Sterne belongs to the generation of modern writers that includes Joyce and Nabokov. In his deliberate refusal to construct a 'goahead plot' Sterne commends himself to contemporary narratologists. In his concern with personal identity, he anticipates the Derridean stress on 'trace'. In his promiscuous borrowings from past authors, he offers himself as a suitably perverse model for the school of postmodern theory. In his attention to matters of typography and to a visual language, he provides a running commentary on almost every aspect of the relationship between word and image. Himself influenced by Rabelais, Montaigne, Cervantes and Burton, Sterne has influenced writers as diverse as Cabrera Infante, Kundera, Márquez, Rushdie and Beckett. And James Joyce. These influences are traced here by sixteen scholars from Europe and the USA, proof if any were needed that Laurence Sterne today is as rewardingly puzzling as he was in his own century.

USA/Canada: Editions Rodopi B.V., 2015 South Park Place, Atlanta, GA 30339, Tel. (770) 933-0027, *Call toll-free* (U.S. only) 1-800-225- 3998, Fax (770) 933-9644, *E-mail:* F.van.der.Zee@rodopi.nl
All Other Countries: Editions Rodopi B.V., Keizersgracht 302-304, 1016 EX Amsterdam, The Netherlands. Tel. + + 31 (0)20-622-75-07, Fax + + 31 (0)20-638-09-48, *E-mail:* F.van.der.Zee@rodopi.nl